To: Mam,

With all my love
and Thanks for
all you do and
are.

Pat

A Thorn in the Side

For my mother, Jo

A Thorn

in the

SIDE

FR PAT BUCKLEY

THE O'BRIEN PRESS
DUBLIN

First published 1994 by The O'Brien Press Ltd.,
20 Victoria Road, Rathgar, Dublin 6, Ireland.

British Library Cataloguing-in-publication Data
Buckley. Pat
Thorn in the Side
I. Title
282.092

ISBN 0-86278-364-X

Typesetting, layout, design: The O'Brien Press Ltd.
Cover separations: Lithoset Ltd., Dublin
Printing: The Guernsey Press Co. Ltd.

CONTENTS

1 – My Own Story *page 7*

2 – Beginning Parish Work *34*

3 – My Current Ministry *63*

4 – My Spirituality *77*

5 – The Catholic Church – *An Inside Perspective* *108*

6 – Women and the Church *129*

7 – Sex – *the Gateway to Hell* *144*

8 – Marriage, Annulment, Divorce
and Remarriage *180*

9 – Northern Ireland – *Religion, Politics, Bigotry* *198*

10 – The Republic – *a Catholic State* *220*

11 – Is Our Catholic Church
Losing Credibility? *230*

CHAPTER 1

My Own Story

'There are three partners in every man – God,
his father and his mother'

Jewish proverb

WHEN I WAS ONLY THREE YEARS old and still learning to speak, I used to say to my mother: 'Mammy, I'm gonna be a priest.' I have always wanted to be a priest. I don't know what first put the idea into my head. I have often asked myself why. Was it because my father brought me to early morning Mass every day of my childhood? Was it because my granny, of whom I was very extremely fond, was very religious? Was it because a saintly Jesuit priest, Father John Hyde, used to visit my childhood home and became a sort of hero to me, partly because he always gave me the tops of his two boiled eggs? Or did I want to become a priest because God called me to be one? I like to think God did call me. But, unlike Saul on the road to Damascus, I had no direct message from heaven and I always suspect those who claim one. If God called me, he did it through other people, including those I have mentioned already. I know that God occasionally works miracles. But he always uses ordinary people, the everyday circumstances and happenings of our lives, to accomplish his work. As the poet said: 'The greatest part of a good man's life are those little unremembered acts of kindness and of love.' And the words at the beginning of the Book of Jeremiah in the Old Testament have always had a deep significance for me. God addresses Jeremiah: 'Before I formed you in the womb I knew you; before you were born I consecrated you.' (Jer.1:5)

The older I got the more my desire to be a priest grew. As a child I used to play at being a priest. I used to 'steal' candles from the parish church and set up a table in my bedroom as an altar. A cup served as my chalice. Water from the kitchen tap was my wine. A slice of bread cut into a circle was my wafer. A large white sheet was my priestly robe. I celebrated those early childhood 'Masses' with great and fervent love. I heard 'confessions' too. Dressed in my white sheet, I would make my younger brothers and sisters kneel and tell me their sins. With pride I would pronounce the words of absolution.

My parents were not always very religious. My Dad was a very questioning kind of Catholic. He fought with God in the way he would have fought with managing directors in his role as a trade unionist. He often stopped going to Mass for years at a time. For instance, when my last little sister, Sandra, was born mentally handicapped, my father confronted God. His case was very logical. He claimed that he had done everything God's way and the Catholic Church's way. He had accepted all the children God had sent him. He had never used contraception and now God was letting him down by allowing his last little girl to be born brain-damaged. He was very angry with God and showed it by staying away from church.

But when I was four or five years of age and living in Carlow my father was in a religious phase of his life. He would call me very early and together we would attend dawn Mass in the cathedral in that town. I was delighted to be heading off on these early morning expeditions with my Dad. But I was also deeply moved and almost hypnotised by what happened in the cathedral. I marvelled at the dim lighting, the early morning sun slanting through the stained-glass windows, the antique stone and wood of the cathedral, the burning candles, the robed altar boys, not much older than I, and the robed priest whispering the Latin liturgy. All of this seemed to touch something very deep within me. I thrilled at the snow-white host being placed on my father's tongue by the priest's ivory fingers. I longed for the day when it would be placed in my mouth too. From that time I have hardly ever missed daily Mass.

My paternal grandmother, Catherine (Kate) Buckley, had also, I think, a great spiritual influence on me. She was a very devout Catholic and when she could she was a daily Mass-goer. I can remember as a very young child going to stay with her in her home in the middle of the bog in Co. Offaly. We would have marvellous days working at cutting and 'footing' the turf. My granny could work as hard as any man. Lunch break on the bog was special. Some of the women carried up big tins of boiling hot tea, made with water from a bog spring. The water was brown to begin with, and the tea it made was really strong and smoky. With the tea came sandwiches, griddle bread and buttered currant bread. What a feast! And what an appetite was on us from the work and the fresh bog air. In the evening, turf-cutting, wheeling and 'footing' finished, we returned home. Everybody had a great feed of bacon and cabbage and a huge bowl of floury boiled spuds was set in the centre of the table. At that stage, my biggest sin was gluttony. When the visitors were gone, my granny would light the oil lamps – we had no electricity – and she would take me on her knee and read to me from *The Blessed Martin Magazine*, a publication in honour of the saintly Dominican monk, Martin de Porres, of Lima, Peru. On Sundays in my granny's we had to walk to Mass. The walk was quite a few miles from Turraun, where she lived, to Pullough. Mass was, I think, at 8 a.m. Then we had the long walk back. But again what a welcome awaited us. As we approached my granny's tin-roofed cottage we could smell the frying bacon, sausages, black and white pudding and eggs. There was also potato bread and fried soda bread. Looking back, it all seems to have been so happy and perfect then.

As I say, my grandmother was very religious and, like many Irish Catholics, had great faith in 'relics' – pieces of cloth, etc. that had been touched to the body of some long-dead saint. On one occasion she had a very badly ulcerated leg. My Dad, who was a bit of a prankster, brought her a special new relic. 'It is most powerful', he told her. My granny kept the relic on her leg for two weeks and it was completely cured. When my father next visited, my grandmother waxed eloquent on the powerfulness of this new relic. My Dad, with a twinkle in his eye, asked her to open the relic. Reluctantly she did so. After she had unwrapped several pieces of paper she came to a small piece of red string. With the string was a description of the relic. It read: 'This is a piece of the rope that hanged Tom Dooley.' My granny was furious but my Dad fell around the floor laughing. Obviously it was my granny's deep personal faith that had worked the 'cure'.

But my granny was not a 'blind' believer. Like my father, she occasionally wrestled and fought with God. My granny's other child, a daughter, Mary, had been seriously ill and had had a lung removed. She seemed to be doing well after the surgery. My granny had a statue of the Blessed Virgin Mary. Several times a day she lit a candle in front of it and knelt on the stone floor to pray to Our Lady for her only daughter's survival and recovery. This went on for months and years. One night the local Gardaí in Tullamore came to my grandmother's door to tell her that she had to rush to the hospital where her daughter was dying. My granny was shocked and angry. She felt let down by God and the Virgin Mary. All her prayers, fastings and sacrifices seemed to have gone unheeded. She put on her coat and at the door of her poor home she looked back. Her eyes fell on the statue of the Virgin in the corner. She picked up something hard and heavy and flung it, smashing the statue to pieces. 'Fuck ye,' was her prayer to Mary as she left her home to attend her daughter's death-bed. As it turned out, her daughter recovered and lived. Who knows? Perhaps the Lord respects and loves those who have such a personal and real faith in him as to be able to express their anger to him.

My mother, Jo, was not particularly religious in the traditional sense of always going to church. For two decades she was nearly always expecting a baby, having one or recovering from having one. So she didn't always have the opportunity to get to Sunday church. However she had a deep and simple faith and always prayed. She was a Mass-goer when she could. But my mother's religion was of a more practical and rare kind. She had and has tremendous love and depth of feeling, especially for her children. There was no sacrifice she wouldn't have made for us. I can remember times when we were not so well-off. We would have mashed potatoes and an egg for dinner. She would have mashed potato only, there not being enough eggs. My mother's huge reservoir of warmth and affection gave all her children great security. We could talk to her in a way we could not talk to my Dad. She would listen and understand. She was always ready to help, forgive and protect. We could always bring any friend home. I can remember one time, after I had been ordained, taking my mother to a Dublin convent where a party was being held for some of Dublin's poor prostitutes. One of the prostitutes was locked out of the hostel where she lived. My mother and I brought her home to our house for tea. My mother looked after her as if she were her own daughter. But my father was furious. When the girl left he made my mother go upstairs and clean the toilet seat with a very strong disinfectant. But my mother's religion was the kind that welcomed 'broken' people like that into our home.

In my teenage years I loved going on retreats. This kept me reasonably calm and patient in my desire to be a priest. I went on special week-end retreats for those thinking of the priesthood to places like the Dominican Friary at Tallaght, Dublin, to the White Fathers of

Africa seminary at Blacklion in Co. Cavan and to the Dublin seminary, Clonliffe College. I also enjoyed the yearly parish missions. I used to attend the women's week as well as the men's, so fond of these occasions was I. But I was really in pain desiring to be a priest. I can remember going to confession on several occasions when I was 14 and 15 years old and telling the priest that I wanted so badly to be a priest that I couldn't possibly wait. Some priests gave me a right telling-off for being so presumptuous. However the parish priest of Tullamore, Co. Offaly, a Monsignor Clarke, consoled me a bit by telling me that my impatience to be a priest was a good sign. 'A good dog', he said, 'is one which is always straining at the leash.'

Two priests of my home parish in Ballygall, Dublin, also helped and inspired me. Our curate, Fr. Joe Collins, a Kerryman, was kind and friendly and a great preacher. I was inspired by attending the Masses he celebrated. Our parish priest, Canon John Pierce, who later became the parish priest of Rathmines, Dublin, was also a tremendous help and inspiration. I visited him often. He brought me to films and meals regularly. Occasionally we had to leave a film if he did not approve of the language or if steamy love scenes occurred. On such occasions he always embarrassed me by sending for the cinema manager on the way out to complain and demand his money back. Canon Pierce, although conservative, was a deeply compassionate man. He had a huge ministry to the street girls and homosexuals in Dublin long before these types of ministry became respectable. He worked in a hostel for the street-girls into the early hours of each morning. From Canon Pierce I got a great example of how a priest should be open, approachable and loving to people struggling with very difficult problems. Incidentally, it was Canon Pierce, a great friend, too, of Archbishop McQuaid, who arranged for me to enter the Dublin diocesan seminary, Holy Cross College, Clonliffe.

Before this, when we had lived in Tullamore, Fr. John Hyde, the Jesuit priest I have mentioned earlier, used to call regularly at our house. Fr. Hyde was a lecturer in Philosophy and Theology to the Jesuit seminarians. He was at once a clever and a simple man. He was very 'other-worldly'. He had a reputation among the ordinary people for having the gift of healing. He was shy and maybe even a bit odd. But he was special. So convinced of his utter holiness was my grandmother that, when he was not looking, she would put his hat on her head and, after he had left the house, she would drink the tea he had left in the bottom of his cup.

Fr. Hyde was such a simple man that he communicated best of all with children. I was quite transfixed by his jet-black clerical suit and his huge, white round clerical collar. I would sit and talk to him while he had a simple meal. He was of an extremely slight build but I have never seen anyone put away a feed of boiled eggs, brown bread, apple-tart and tea the way he did. I loved watching him and talking to him, although the talk was scant. In my own childish way, I wanted to be a priest, a priest like Fr. Hyde.

Fr. Hyde was so odd and 'humble' that some of his fellow Irish Jesuits referred to him as 'Hyde and seek'. He was a man of very few words, even to his theology students. He would simply sit for ages in silence. While this did not seem to bother him it made others feel most uncomfortable. One time in the Jesuit House of Studies in Milltown, Dublin, the students decided to challenge Fr. Hyde. One of them was appointed to go to his study and sit him out! The student knocked at the study door. Fr. Hyde whispered: 'Come in.' He pointed the student to a chair by the fire. Fr. Hyde sat on the other side. For an hour the student said nothing and Fr. Hyde said nothing back. After an hour there was another knock on the study door. Fr. Hyde raised his eyes from the fire and said: 'I think we're going to be disturbed.'

Fr. Hyde continued to visit my home throughout my childhood and teen years. I occasionally visited him in his religious house. When eventually I myself became a theology student, I once asked Fr. Hyde, a conservative, how he regarded the radical Catholic Swiss theologian, Fr. Hans Küng. John Hyde stared hard at the floor. After several minutes' silence and still staring at the floor, he whispered: 'Hans Küng? When I hear the name Hans Küng I get a terrible pain in me belly. He's almost a Protestant.'

If any priest was responsible for inspiring and encouraging me towards the priesthood it was Fr. Hyde. He has since died and I concelebrated his funeral Mass in the Jesuit church in Gardiner Street, Dublin. Above all else, John Hyde was a priest who identified with ordinary people and spent most of his time sharing their lives and troubles. That made him a great priest in my eyes. I'm sure that Fr. Hyde, a stickler for religious obedience and a man who prayed in Latin until the day he died, would be quite shocked at the way my life as a priest has worked out. He was a man of his own time. However, from where he is now, I'm certain that he sees things far differently from what might be thought.

* * *

But let me start at the beginning. I was born in Tullamore, Co. Offaly on 2 May, 1952. Tullamore is famous for its 'Tullamore Dew' whiskey and that favourite liqueur of Irish-Americans, 'Irish Mist'. All over Tullamore and, indeed, all over Ireland, the billboards read: 'Give every man his Dew'. Many of my forbears had worked in the distillery. My maternal grandfather, in whose home I was born, was chauffeur to the Williams family who owned the distillery. That grandfather, Johnnie Geoghegan, married twice. He had nine children the first time round and five in round two. When he was marrying for the second time, someone asked him if children were possible. He replied: 'There's nothing as bad as the sting of a dying wasp.'

At the time of my birth, my father, Jim, worked as a supervisor in the Salts textile factory in Tullamore. I have very pleasant memories of being carried on his bikes and motor-bikes when I was only two years old. My mother's sisters were very good to me while we lived in Tullamore. They brought me gifts and often took me for walks or for rides on their bicycles. One aunt, Nan, now dead, God rest her!, brought me on many excursions. She was an extremely nervous woman. Once, when I was about two, she took me with her to visit a friend who had a small farm in the country. While we were there, my aunt wanted to visit the toilet which was out in the farmyard. As she opened the door to come out, she was surrounded by about twenty greyhounds which all started barking together. She panicked and tried to beat them off by picking me up and swinging me at them. This only excited the dogs further. Finally, my aunt threw me into the middle of the pack and ran off. The farmer rescued me but the experience gave me a vivid insight into how the early Christians must have felt when they were thrown to the lions in Rome!

My father had been involved as a voluntary trade union official in the Irish Transport and General Workers' Union and this whetted his appetite to apply for a full-time union job. He was appointed branch secretary of the Union's Carlow branch and we moved from Tullamore to there. While in Carlow, my father led a dispute in the town's sugar beet factory, which was run by an ex-Irish Army general, Michael Joe

Costello. I don't know what transpired between my dad, the sugar company and Costello. I do know, however, that my father ended up being transferred from Carlow to Dublin. My father never forgave General Costello and his trade union bosses. To his dying day, Costello's name always evoked a string of swear words from my Dad!

My father, as I have indicated, was a socialist and a bit of a champion for justice. I suppose that's why he became involved in trade unionism. I think he 'infected' me with his insistence on justice. Some of my earliest memories are of being on picket lines with him or waiting for him outside factories while he was at meetings slogging it out with management on behalf of the workers. One such experience haunts me still. It was among the most embarrassing moments of my life.

I was 12 or 13 at the time and experiencing puberty, that time when one feels self-conscious, awkward in groups and painfully sensitive to anything of a sexual nature. My Dad had a long meeting with the manager of a Dublin electronics factory. Four hundred female workers were on strike. It was a bad day and the women were sheltering in the large shed at the front of the factory. I was put in there with them to wait for my Dad. The women were bored and decided to have some fun with me. They locked the shed, pushed me out into the middle and danced around me, sometimes touching me. They shouted and screamed obscene remarks. They kept singing a blue song, part of the chorus of which went: 'Show me your yo-yo tonight.' I died a thousand deaths that afternoon.

*   *   *

Looking back over the years, I can see that I had no real childhood. I am the eldest of seventeen children, eleven of whom have survived into adulthood. I spent most of my younger days acting as a 'third parent' to the younger members of the family as it grew in numbers. It fell to me to take my brothers and sisters to doctors, nurses, dentists, school, etc. My Dad was too busy earning money to keep us all going. When we came to live in Dublin, sometimes he had two jobs, a full-time day job in the trade union and an evening job as a telephone operator. My mother was busy at home. Every Sunday afternoon, it was my job to bring all the younger members of the family for a three-hour walk while my parents went to bed for a 'rest'. So the Buckley 'caravan' would set off for such exotic places as the Botanic Gardens, Tolka Park and Glasnevin Cemetery on the north side of the city. In later years, I began to wonder if some of my siblings had not been conceived on those restful Sunday afternoons!

As I was growing up, we were relatively poor. My parents had a lot of mouths to feed, a lot of bodies to dress and a lot of feet to be shod. Our food was basic but we were well-fed. Our clothing was hardly ever new. One of the things for which Dublin is famous is the market area known as Moore Street. Here you could buy meat and vegetables. However, there was also a huge array of second-hand clothing and footwear stalls. It was from these that I got most of my childhood clothes and shoes. This did not bother me in the least. I was proud of the items that my parents bought me. I appreciated both their financial difficulties and their efforts to care for us. The younger members of the family had it much better later on. But I think that they were more spoiled and therefore more selfish.

One of the jobs I had to do as a kid was to go around the family creditors every Saturday, paying a few shillings here and there off the bills. I had to tell many lies and make many excuses. Often I had to go to the Dublin Sheriff's office to pay something off fines my father would have had for his failures to meet his financial commitments. I found this very unpleasant. Knowing so much about the poor state of the family finances, I worried greatly. I used to think about this in bed at night and it would make me cry. Like all children, I would also sometimes think in bed about the prospect of losing my parents. This made me weep too. I loved my parents deeply.

Another of my jobs was to shop for the week's groceries. I would buy these in Dublin city centre and then get the number 13 bus home to Ballymun laden with bags of groceries. I was always regarded as the sensible one of the family. Having so much responsibility perhaps gave me a seriousness and a maturity beyond my years. On one of my weekly shopping expeditions I was waiting at the bus-stop. A middle-aged lady came along with her groceries too. We started to talk. She forgot herself and told me her whole life story, including all her personal and marriage problems. As she finished she suddenly looked shocked and turned to me and asked: 'What age are ye, son?' 'Fourteen,' I answered. 'Jaysus, Mary and Joseph', she exclaimed, 'and me after telling ye everything about myself.'

My shopping expeditions were not confined to groceries. As I mentioned, my mother was often expecting a baby or recovering from a birth. That meant that she did not go out that much during those years. Obviously she needed clothing. And I was often the one to do the shopping for her. I bought her dresses, skirts, cardigans. I even was sent for her underwear. I came to know all about ladies' underwear and about cup sizes for bras, etc. When I got to a certain age I got embarrassed about this particular aspect of the shopping. The problem was solved by my taking a note with me written by my mother.

But my childhood was not all hard. My parents were always demonstrative of their affection in front of us. My father never left the house without giving my mother a hug and a kiss. We developed the same habit. We always had enough to eat and adequate clothing and footwear. My father always tried to get us a family holiday, usually in a caravan at Courtown in Co. Wexford. My Dad generally had a car from his union job. So indeed we were a great deal better off than many. But being the oldest of such a large family was not easy.

I have always been very sensitive and self-conscious anyway. When I was fourteen I found it hard to cope with my peer group in school. I started 'mitching', as they call it in Dublin – leaving home for school but not actually going. Eventually I was found out. Various things were tried but I just would not – in fact, could not – go to school. School filled me with fear and with real psychological panic. I was dragged to the family doctor. He recommended me to the Child Guidance Clinic at the Mater Hospital in Dublin. There I met a very nice and kind man, Dr. Paul McQuaid, nephew of the then Archbishop of Dublin. He tried everything with me to get me to open up. He hospitalised me for six weeks. But even then I didn't co-operate. When Paul McQuaid got too near my sensitivities I used the oldest put-off trick of all. I cried. I never confided in Dr. McQuaid. I regret that now. But I was too afraid and vulnerable then.

Eventually my father reluctantly accepted that I was not cut out for school. But he was not prepared to let me sit around the house. So I was sent to work. My first job was as a lift-boy in a Dublin drapery store. It was a boring, badly-paid job. But I was relatively happy. Anything was better than school. Every second person who got into the lift would come up with the old wisecrack: 'I'd say this job has its ups and downs.'

From the drapery store I progressed to Ireland's national transport company – Córas Iompair Éireann – as a messenger boy. At 15 years my wages were £4.6s.2d (£4.31p) per week. When I became 16 my wages went down to £3.19s.6d. (£3.97p) as I had to pay tax and insurance. My job was to bring company documents between all the company's offices and depots throughout Dublin. I had a bus pass which gave me free travel. I enjoyed that. I used to flash my pass like a Los Angeles detective does his police badge. But my boss preferred me to use a messenger bike – one of those great heavy black bikes with a square message compartment at the front. It was a crucifixion pushing that bike up Dublin's hilly streets. So I devised a plan. Beside the Liffey River in the centre of Dublin was a notorious neighbourhood called Oliver Bond Flats. I had heard stories of how everything that went in there was stolen and disappeared. One morning I cycled from the CIE offices at Broadstone to the Liffey. I wheeled my messenger's bike into the heart of Oliver Bond Flats and left it invitingly against a wall. I returned to my boss and told him a lie. I said that my bike had been stolen in the city centre. I was quite certain that some resident of Oliver Bond Flats, with no conscience, would see to that. I was wrong. The very next day a big policeman wheeled the bike into our office complex. A civic-minded resident of Oliver Bond Flats had brought it to the Gardaí. Obviously someone in Oliver Bond Flats had more principle than I.

But CIE was good to me. After a while they sent me back to school during working hours a day or two a week. They sent me, not to a church school, but to a state-sponsored 'Technical College', the College of Commerce, Rathmines. Unlike the previous schools I had attended, there were no priests, nuns or monks. And there was no corporal punishment. If you worked they encouraged you. If you didn't they simply let you be. I liked this freedom. I thrived in the informality. I eventually returned full-time to school there and completed my secondary education at the normal age of 18 years in spite of two years away at work. Those two years were good for me. They gave me the space to resolve some of my internal struggles. When I returned to school at 16 I was a little more mature and confident. And, more importantly, I was happy to be there.

My father had a real hang-up about education. He had been deprived of education himself, even though he had intelligence and aptitude. But he was handicapped by family poverty and by having a father who had both a drink problem and no regard for academic pursuits. My Dad, therefore, was taken out of school at the age of 12 and sent to work to bring in a 'half-crown' a week, which I imagine was squandered by his father on Guinness and Tullamore Dew. My Dad would have done anything to educate us. However his concentration on the importance of education had an off-putting effect on my brothers and sisters and most of them left school early. When I returned to school my father was overjoyed. By this time he had taken up his own education again. He had started English correspondence courses and he was studying part-time in University College, Dublin, for his B.A. After school in Rathmines I would walk to the city centre to Liberty Hall, the headquarters of the Irish Transport and General Workers' Union. We would have our tea and sandwiches and then walk together to the National Library where we would study side-by-side for four hours a night, five nights a week. In this way I managed to gain my school Leaving Certificate. My Dad did better and went from strength to strength academically, eventually gaining his B.A. degree in philosophy, archaeology and economics. Not satisfied with that he studied for many more years and, in his middle fifties, he received his B.L. degree and was called to the Bar in Dublin. He had certainly made up for lost time and lost opportunity. What a pity, though, that he had not been given the opportunity to continue his education when he was younger. It would have made his life a lot different and much easier. But perhaps there's a providence in these things?

* * *

All my long waiting to begin my priestly training ended on 28 September 1970. On that day I was received into the seminary for the Archdiocese of Dublin, Holy Cross College, Clonliffe. My entrance had been arranged by our parish priest, Canon Pierce, who had been one of the main influences on my call to the priesthood. My father was coming home from work to take myself and my mother to the seminary. There was to be a meal for the new students and their parents. I was very nervous and excited as I waited on my father. I decided to walk over to the parish church to say a short prayer for the success of the new life on which I was embarking. On my way back, I saw a small card lying in a pool of water on the ground. I picked it up. It was a picture of a vineyard and printed on the bottom were the words: 'Go you also into my vineyard' (Matthew 20:7). Rightly or wrongly, I felt that the card was meant for me and providential. I still have it.

I was very proud and happy that day leaving home for the seminary. I was dressed in black from head to toe like a priest, save for the clerical collar. My 'official' dress required a white shirt and a black tie. Looking back, I realise that I was dressed like an undertaker! I had received a list from the Dean of the seminary telling me what I had to bring with me. The list included a black suit, white shirts, a black tie, grey or black socks, etc. I was also provided with a laundry number which was to be put on all my clothing so that it would not be mixed up with the clothing of other students when the college laundry was collected and delivered. My number was A23. I asked my Aunt Mary to sew this number on my things. She regarded it as my new 'church number'. Whenever she wrote to me afterwards, she embarrassed me greatly by addressing me as Mr. P. Buckley, A23, Holy Cross College, Clonliffe, Dublin 3. I felt as a prisoner in a jail feels when his mail arrives with his prison number on the envelope. To this day, when writing to prisoners, I prefer not to write their numbers on the envelope. There's something terribly dehumanising in allotting a number to human beings.

Being in the seminary thrilled me. Inside the college we wore the long black cassock and the clerical collar. I felt that at last I was nearly a priest. The college rules were rigid. We were up at the crack of dawn. We had half-an-hour to wash and dress. We had prayers and meditation for another half-an-hour. We then had Mass for a further half-hour. And then breakfast. The rest of the day was ruled by both the clock and the bell. Everything – meals, study, lectures and even recreation time – was regulated by those two enemies of youth, the clock and the bell. We were all, one hundred and twenty of us, aged between eighteen and thirty. We were normal young men with normal feelings and desires. But we were locked away in a monastic and male world. Particular friendships were frowned upon. The authorities were afraid of homosexuality. And, indeed, homosexuality was about. How could it not be in such a repressed and deprived world? Every morning for ten minutes before the daily Mass the Spiritual Director of the seminary sat in a little room at the back of the chapel to hear the confessions of those who had 'sinned' during the night. Confession was necessary before one could go to communion. The 'sin' in question was masturbation. Going into that little room before the daily Mass was the equivalent of a public confession. Anybody foolish enough to do so was jeered over breakfast for his naughty nocturnal misdemeanours. Some of us simply took the risk of making an 'unworthy' communion!

Sex was a big preoccupation in that celibate empire. Very soon after entering Holy Cross each of us new students was interviewed individually by the then Archbishop of Dublin, the famous John Charles McQuaid. We were sent over to him one by one. We were ushered into his presence by a priest secretary. We genuflected and kissed his huge episcopal ring. His Grace would put us sitting down at his desk. He would offer tea and cake. And then came the first question: 'My son, do you know about the facts of life?' We had previously been warned to say: 'No, Your Grace.' A 'Yes, Your Grace' would have got you into very serious trouble because you would have then been asked: 'Tell me about them, my son.' Imagine the predicament you would be in then having to explain the facts of life to His Grace the Archbishop of Dublin. I was a 'No, Your Grace' man.

John Charles then spent ages with you explaining the facts of life. It was a bit of a shock hearing the words 'penis' and 'vagina' from such a holy mouth. But John Charles brought us through the whole of the 'facts of life', occasionally drawing diagrams and using his fingers to explain what he meant. Each time he made an important point he would press hard on your foot with his foot. Between the hot tea, the roaring fire in His Grace's grate and the embarrassment of a two-hour chat about sex with the Archbishop, one was inclined to leave Archbishop's House somewhat hot under the collar. If the interview had gone well, John Charles had a gift for you of a wooden and silver crucifix. He pressed it firmly into your hands saying: 'My son, when temptation strikes, grasp this crucifix.' Apparently the crucifix was the antidote for the masturbation poison. It was generally felt by the student body to be a rather ineffective and unattractive option!

The College President was Bishop Joseph A. Carroll, now deceased, one of the most pompous men I have ever met. In spite of that I hope he is in Heaven. He was auxiliary to the Archbishop of Dublin and walked about the college wearing every bit of purple he could get his hands on. He had purple socks, purple shirts and a little purple skull-cap on his head. We students used to speculate as to whether he also wore purple long-johns! When we met him we had to take our hands out of our pockets, walk very respectfully and say 'Good morning, My Lord.' He once made me walk past him three times intoning 'Good morning, My Lord' because, unwittingly, I had passed him the first time with a hand in one pocket.

The students had to take turns serving his private Mass at 9 each morning in the college oratory. It was a dreaded experience. Everybody else had to leave the oratory. One had to bow and scrape to His Lordship. We had to help him remove his Batman-like cloak. We had to have a drink of cool water awaiting him. We had to help him vest for Mass and then attend to answer the prayers for him. He said Mass for the empty seats and the stained-glass windows every morning. Serving his Mass was a horrific ordeal as even the slightest mistake earned a rough ticking-off. Once he refused to begin Mass until I had vacuum-cleaned and straightened the carpet. So much for the Eucharist being a celebration of love!

I fell foul of Bishop Carroll a few times. Our college dining-room seated the 120 students at tables of eight. The top table was set for the priests, with Bishop Carroll in the centre. Bishop Carroll rang a little brass bell for grace before and after meals and, at lunch-time, for the Scripture reading to commence. One day I was sitting at a table within earshot of the Bishop. He took up the bell to ring for dinner to finish. The bell's tongue had fallen out and, failing to make it sound, the Bishop was disappointed and embarrassed. I said to one of my fellow students, quietly I thought, that Bishop Carroll should get the 'No-bell' prize. The table burst out laughing. The Bishop had heard. I was later summoned to an audience and severely reprimanded for making a joke of a Bishop, who was Christ's representative and a successor of the Twelve Apostles.

Another time a student was reading the Scriptures during lunch-time and, with Bishop Carroll's eye on him, was so nervous that he fluffed his lines. Instead of saying 'Jesus went into Peter's house and found Peter's mother-in-law in bed with a fever', he read: 'Jesus went into Peter's house and found Peter's mother-in-law in bed with Peter.' The student body fell about the place laughing and Bishop Carroll had a hard job using his little brass bell to restore silence.

'Pride cometh before a fall' goes the old saying. Joe Carroll had his fall one day and we were all there to witness and, God forgive us, to relish it. At around 11 many mornings, Joe Carroll's black chauffeur-driven Mercedes called to the college to take His Lordship away to administer the sacrament of Confirmation in one of the parishes of the

Archdiocese. Joe would waltz down the college steps, dressed from head to toe in episcopal purple. His appearance always reminded me of the novel *Glenanaar* by the famous Canon Sheehan: 'He suddenly appeared in our village street, caparisoned from head to foot in all kinds of sartorial splendour.' As he came down the steps Bishop Carroll would wave to us students as if he were the Pope. We would be out for a stroll in between lectures. 'The ould bastard' we used to mutter to ourselves.

One day a new chauffeur arrived, very nervous to be driving a bishop. As he left the college gates he did not spot another vehicle coming. There was a loud crash and Bishop Carroll was involved in an accident. I don't know if he was thrown from the car, but he staggered back up the college driveway looking like an aged actress who had accidentally fallen off the stage and into the orchestra pit. His purple was everywhere. He went straight to his suite of rooms and didn't appear for months. His pride, I think, was more wounded than his body. Later, I discovered a little gold-edged card that he had sent down to the college porter and telephonist. It read: 'His Lordship is indisposed. He is not taking telephone calls, with the exception of His Grace the Archbishop, His Excellency the Papal Nuncio and His Excellency the President of Ireland.' Bishop Carroll, in his hour of grief, was prepared to communicate only with the 'great'. He had been chaplain to the President of Ireland, Eamon de Valera. Later, during my studentship at Clonliffe, I came across a file of correspondence between Bishop Carroll and the rest of the Catholic Bishops of Ireland. The correspondence referred to Bishop Carroll's consecration as bishop. I was amazed to find the correspondence so petty. There were references to gossip about Protestant bishops and clergy and to matching what bishops would wear for the consecration. I thought: 'What's all this talk about ordaining women? Some of our present clergy are ould women anyway.'

Our Dean was Father Séamus Conway, a young and very serious Kildare man from Ballymore-Eustace. He had been chaplain to Mountjoy Prison in Dublin and was so strict with us that we felt he may not have realised he had been transferred from the prison to the seminary! Torch in hand, he patrolled the seminary corridors after 'lights out' at 11 p.m. when what was called a 'grand silence' was in force until morning. It was not uncommon for Father Conway to open your door and shine his torch around your room to see if you were in bed and, as we interpreted it, in bed alone! He would then go about the grounds, prayer-book in hands, to see if your light was on. We used to joke that he could read his prayer-book in the dark.

The tighter Father Conway turned the disciplinary screws, the more we protested and tricked him. We would cover our windows with blankets and secretly make tea until the small hours. We would sneak out of college and go to a city centre restaurant at 2 a.m. Or we would telephone him at 3 a.m. on the house intercom and treat him to a bit of heavy breathing. One April Fool's Day we posted him a pair of women's white tights with 'Séamus, we love you' printed on the bum with a heavy blue marker. That night he assembled us in the college and gave us a lecture on cynicism and how a cynic was unsuitable for the priesthood. He regularly interviewed students, especially those known for not being the best rule-keepers. I had fortnightly interviews with him. Going to his study, I felt like a suspect being interrogated by the intelligence services.

The rules prescribed that individuality was to be avoided. We all had to dress the same way, eat the same food. All rooms should be furnished the same – wooden bed, a desk, a wooden locker and a built-in wardrobe. It was forbidden to have any electrical equipment. At the beginning of my third year in College, I had begun to rebel against this thwarting of my sense of individuality and had furnished my room according to my own ideas. One evening in September 1972, I was entertaining some fellow-students to tea and coffee. The Dean arrived on the scene. Cheekily, I invited him to have coffee. Somewhat embarrassed, he accepted. I saw his eyes wandering around at the signs of my flouting of the rules – my colourful curtains, my electric kettle, my coal-glow electric fire, my hi-fi system. It was all noted and later was the cause of an interview on rule-breaking. I also broke the rules by having lay visitors to my room, including females!

Despite all the restrictions, I liked the seminary, especially the religious atmosphere and the companionship of my fellow-students. I was also doing something I had wanted to do for a very long time and that pleased me. But something always made me push against the prison-like regime. The most notorious stunt I was involved in at Clonliffe was the 'Flying Chamber-Pot Affair.' Against the rules, four of us were gathered after 'lights out' in my room three or four floors up.

We were bored stiff. Many students had a ceramic chamber-pot under their beds for use during the night when we were not supposed to leave our rooms. One of my four companions, looking at the pot, said to me: 'Throw that fucking thing out the window.' Without thinking I lifted the potty and let it fly. It crashed on the tarmacadam somewhere below my window. In the dead stillness of the seminary night the crash was like a bomb going off. We could hear blinds and windows going up everywhere. My companions quickly departed my room. I closed my window, undressed quickly, switched off my light and hopped into bed. Within a very short space of time there was a thud on my door. The Dean's voice demanded: 'Mr. Buckley, out on the corridor.' When I arrived out on the corridor the Dean had the whole landing lined up along the wall. In our striped pyjamas we were like prisoners out of Auschwitz. The Dean demanded to know who had thrown what he called 'the vessel'. No-one spoke. Very few knew who was responsible and those who did said nothing. After half-an-hour of lecturing the Dean allowed us to return to bed. He continued his investigation in the days and weeks that followed. But no-one pleaded guilty. This angered the Dean greatly and I was, in fact, his number one suspect. But he was without proof. The incident greatly tickled the imagination of the student body. The day after the potty had been thrown we had Benediction in the college chapel. Part of the Benediction service involves the recitation of the Litany of the Blessed Virgin Mary. The Dean was reciting the invocations. When he came to the part 'Vessel of Honour, Singular Vessel of Devotion', the whole college chapel fell apart laughing. We could all only think of one 'vessel'.

Each year the students at Clonliffe had a student concert which was not attended by the college staff or lecturers. This was our chance to slag, jeer and take off staff members. After the incident of the 'Flying Vessel', there was always a special presentation at the student concert to the student who had contributed most to humour and fun in the previous year in the college. The trophy was a decorated ceramic potty which was called: 'The Ballymore-Eustace Perpetual Trophy' in remembrance of the Dean's native place.

However difficult my dealings with my college superiors, I must recount an important relationship I had developed. The Archbishop of Dublin, John Charles McQuaid, resigned his episcopacy in 1972. He was then 75 years old, the mandatory age for a bishop to submit his resignation. Dr. McQuaid, who was in excellent mental and physical health, was reputed to be certain that his resignation would not be accepted and that he would be given an extension by the Pope. He merely sent in his resignation to comply with the rules. However, apparently he had some enemies in Rome. As soon as his resignation arrived, it was seized upon and activated. So John Charles found his resignation accepted and a successor appointed. I had visited Dr. McQuaid a few times in Archbishop's House after the famous 'facts of life' interview. I liked him and he seemed to like me. I went to see him a week or two before his resignation was to take effect. He told me that he was sorry to be going. He further said: 'Will you come and visit me in my retirement? Now that I have power I have many friends. But as soon as I lose my power I will lose many friends too.' I assured him that I would not forget him and that I would visit him at his home in Killiney.

I kept my promise. Many Friday afternoons I got the bus from Clonliffe to Killiney and spent several hours with him. We would chat in his upstairs study. Sometimes we would be silent for a long time and stare into the fire or out through the window into his beautiful and spacious gardens. I used him as a spiritual director and confessor. I found him old-fashioned and strict. But I wanted to use him as a confessor as much for his sake as for mine. I wanted him to feel that he was needed and trusted. He always had afternoon tea with me and he never failed to give me my bus fare. He did not want my visits to cost me. Occasionally he would have his chauffeur drive me some of the way back to Clonliffe and he always came along for the drive. John Charles was a strange mixture of a man. On questions of faith and theology he was very much of the 'old school', and God help you if you dared to suggest anything that was even slightly against the 'true faith'. But when it came to people and their problems and struggles he was deeply compassionate and helpful. There are many stories of priests who got into trouble with drink or women or money during his time as Archbishop and John Charles left no stone unturned to help them. He was famous for his hospital visitations and for the stream of poor people who came daily to Archbishop's House in Dublin for help. He never turned them away.

McQuaid had a good sense of humour too. On one of my visits to him I noticed that he had a bandaged wrist. I asked him what had happened to him. He pointed through the window to a little puppy that was playing happily in his garden. A friend had given it to him as a retirement present and he had tripped over it and fallen. 'What's the dog's name, Your Grace?' I asked. 'I haven't named him yet,' he replied, 'but I'm seriously thinking of calling him Lucifer, as he has tripped up an Archbishop.' McQuaid was a strange mixture, but a very kind man and a much misunderstood one. I feel the richer for having known him.

During my stay in Clonliffe we had a 'state' visit from Cardinal Pio and some of his flock from Samoa. There was a banquet in the college dining-room. We were tickled pink to be eating with Samoans in grass skirts. After the meal Bishop Carroll ordered the tables to be moved back so that our guests might entertain us with dance and song. It was like a scene from a royal court and Joe Carroll was the presiding monarch. We were all thrilled and had pains in our sides from laughing when the Samoans started one tune. It began with three bangs on a drum, followed by words which sounded like 'Fucky Ucky'. Bishop Carroll was not amused with our laughter. Next day the Cardinal celebrated Mass in the college chapel. His flock provided the liturgical music. We were all full of expectancy when once again we heard the three bangs on the drum. We were waiting for 'Fucky Ucky' but were disappointed.

I had been warned a few times by the Dean that I was in trouble. I was occasionally late for morning prayers. Sometimes I skipped the boring philosophy lectures. I was number one suspect over the 'Flying Vessel'. The fact that I had denied my involvement led the Dean to suspect that I was 'cynical' and 'deceitful'. I had been hauled once before the disciplinary council and had received what they called 'a solemn warning'. When I was leaving for my summer holidays in early June 1973 the Dean assured me that I had 'improved' and that there should be no problem. However within a few days I received a letter from Bishop Carroll summoning me into his presence. I went, thinking that it was a review interview. I rang the bell just outside his suite of rooms. He had 'traffic lights' outside his door. If the red light came on you were to go away; if the orange you were to wait. If it shone green you could enter. I got the green light so I entered.

The prelate sat behind his huge desk, the walls of his study lined with books and college files. He was dressed in his deepest purple. A purple lamp was lit on his desk. I stood in front of him like a condemned man about to receive his sentence. 'Mr. Buckley', he announced in a cold and pompous tone, 'I must ask you to resign from the college.' I immediately went into some kind of shock. My nose started bleeding and I was weak all over. His Lordship put me lying down and got me a glass of water. When the bleeding stopped he put me out of his room. I collected a few pieces of my A23 laundry that were still in the college and walked back down the long drive to where my Dad was waiting in the car. When he saw my blood-stained face he presumed that someone had hit me and he immediately jumped from the car ready to deal with the attacker. I was expelled and shattered. It looked as if my dream of being a priest was finished for ever. I spent the next six weeks in total mental despair. I tried to pray. I begged God to help me solve the problem. I couldn't sleep or eat. I told my parents that if I could not be a priest I would end up in a mental hospital. Perhaps my reaction was extreme. But that's how I felt then. I wrote a poem at the time:

A Time Of Crisis

I had a fear, an abiding fear
That for years grew in my heart;
And then one day that fear was real,
My world was sad and my future dark.
I could not see the point in life,
Nor could I see the reason why
I felt my sentence was far too harsh,
And that the punishment did not fit the crime.
So having failed by the use of reason,
I turned to Him who had wrongly died;
I told Him that I had been misjudged,
He answered: 'I know, was I not crucified?'
And all at once I knew the reason why
And that no more could I complain.
For once again had I been taught
A lesson hard, but well worth knowing.
There is a mystery basic to life,
And man must know it to live in peace;
God is the potter knowing all that is good,
A moulded vessel may never doubt the Eternal design.

What do they do to people in seminaries? Looking back on the time I spent there, I don't approve of the way they set out to train priests. I think it is a mistake to remove young men from the community for years to train them for service back in that community. It would be better for them to live in parish presbyteries during their training and go out for their philosophy and theology lectures from there. Obviously, there is benefit to be had from, perhaps, one year of spiritual formation in a monastic setting. This would give students the opportunity to grow internally and make the journey into 'inner space' which would make them deep-thinking and spiritual men. But monastic-type training for six or seven years is no real preparation for the active and complicated life of a pastoral priest in a parish. Saint Thomas Aquinas, asked whether the active or the contemplative life was better for a priest, is credited with answering that the best life was a mixture of both.

However, those of us who have 'done our time' do not regret the seminary years. There are many positive aspects to the training and it would be unjust not to give it due credit. Most would have to agree that a priest should be spiritual and prayerful. Surely it is his job to be in touch with God in order to help others to do the same. If one does not have a personal relationship with God, it is difficult to lead others to such a relationship. So a priest has to be a pray-er. And prayer needs some training and practice.

Here the seminary plays an important role. It gives young men the opportunity to develop their prayer-lives. As a growing boy, I prayed a lot. The seminary helped me to deepen my prayer-life. In Clonliffe, the half-hour morning meditation helped me to make progress in my spiritual life. I thank Clonliffe for that. We also had weekly sessions with the spiritual director, Father Tom O'Flynn, one of the leading lights of the Legion of Mary. 'Tommo', as we called him, was very traditional and conservative. But he was very human. His weekly lectures were a little heavy and dry but permeated with a deep sincerity. Some of his spirituality rubbed off on us. In later years, when I was beginning to have problems with the authoritarian nature of the Church, I would meet Tommo as we frequented the same church for prayer and confession. He was always kind and non-judgmental. He has now gone to his very well-deserved reward.

Yearly retreats were an important feature of Clonliffe life and I must say I enjoyed them greatly, especially when the retreat master was interesting or witty. At the beginning of my second year, I undertook the 30-day retreat according to the principles of Saint Ignatius of Loyola. I found it very helpful although a few of my companions found it too intense and discontinued it.

The seminary training is very important from the human point of view. It forces people into very close contact with one another over a period of years and bonds are forged which often last a lifetime. I found the companionship and friendship of my fellow-students a vital support during the time I was developing from youth to adulthood. Unfortunately, because of the direction my life has taken, I have lost contact with most of them. The group I used to be part of is still intact and supportive of each other. It seems, though, that I no longer fit in.

Academic life in the seminary can sometimes be interesting and pleasant and sometimes dull and boring. I think there is a great deal to be said for the grounding seminarians get in philosophy, psychology, theology and Scripture. Such knowledge always stands to one. When I meet people who left the seminary before ordination, they invariably say they do not regret the time spent learning what they did.

The philosophy we were taught in the seminary was, of course, Thomistic and Scholastic. The course had been laid down by the Popes in the last part of the 19th century and by the 1917 Code of Canon Law. It was heavy and uninteresting. Fortunately, our principal lecturer, Monsignor Horgan of University College, Dublin, was somewhat eccentric and this gave some relief to his lectures. One minute he would be lecturing on angels and the next giving a very accurate imitation of a spider in his bath or a robin hopping around the yard of his house in north Dublin. I got on well with him, partly perhaps because he was fascinated by the fact that he was also teaching philosophy at night in the university to my father.

Archbishop McQuaid had seen to it that the changes of the Second Vatican Council had not had a great deal of effect in Dublin. The Church we were introduced to as seminarians was definitely the pre-Conciliar one, patriarchal and hierarchical. The Church was seen as a pyramid, with God on top, the Pope next, then the bishops, followed in further tiers by the priests, the religious and, finally, the laity. We were taught to see the priest as special, 'another Christ' on a pedestal as far as lay people were concerned. We were trained to become part of a priestly elite that was to receive the respect, the admiration and – dare I say it? – the adoration of the laity.

I found Clonliffe to be too strict and too restrictive. As the oldest of seventeen children, I was used to being, as it were, a leader, out in front and free. From the beginning in Clonliffe I resisted the attempt to take away my individuality. Jesus said that he came to set his disciples free. He came to remind us all that we are all special and unique in the eyes of God. And yet in these seminaries the Catholic Church tries to destroy and eradicate the student-priest's individuality. In other words, the Church desired robots, future priests who would merely be mouth-pieces and operatives for the organisation but who would not think for themselves. The nearest thing that I ever saw to the seminary was while I was a curate in the parish of Kilkeel, Co. Down. Here a parishioner had a fish-processing plant. The herrings came in on the assembly line. Firstly they were beheaded. Then they had their guts removed. Finally they had their backbones taken away. This is what, far too often, happens in Catholic seminaries. Student-priests are 'beheaded', forbidden to think for themselves. They have their 'guts' and backbones removed. They are frightened into total submission to an authoritarian Church and afterwards never have the courage to stand up and resist the abuse of authority that is so prevalent in the Catholic Church. There are, of course, many good and coura-geous priests in the world who show tremendous integrity. But they are in a minority and they often end up either leaving the priesthood or being ejected from it. In the past 30 years since the Second Vatican Council some 120,000 priests have left the priesthood worldwide, 1,000 of those in Ireland. Many of those had been the best of priests but could no longer put up with the oppressiveness of the present-day Church structures. All I think we can do is to pray for the Catholic Church hierarchy and authorities in the words that Christ himself prayed on the Cross: 'Father, forgive them for they know not what they do.' And any of them who do know what they are doing will have to answer for it some day somewhere.

As for me, Clonliffe tried to break me and failed. And so they felt they had to ask me to leave. After six weeks of prayer, mental hell and a lot of crying I noticed one Sunday an advertisement in a Dublin newspaper announcing that the Archdiocese of Cardiff in Wales was short of priests and invited applicants from Ireland. I had been assured that no other Irish bishop would touch me after my expulsion from an Irish seminary. By nature I am a 'home bird' and never really have wanted to live outside Ireland. Bishop Carroll had agreed that perhaps I deserved a second chance and had suggested Australia! So I still wanted to be a priest and Wales was the nearest place to Ireland and certainly a more agreeable option than Joe Carroll's Australia. I wrote to the Vocations Director for the Archdiocese of Cardiff. The Vocations Director was a Fr. Michael Martin, a Donegal man and a late vocation who had worked for the famous Magee store in Donegal town. Within a few days I met Fr. Martin in Dublin. He was kind and understanding. He communicated with his Archbishop, John A. Murphy. They decided to accept me as a priesthood student for Cardiff and nominated a new seminary for me – St. John's College, Waterford, Fr. Martin's old college. I was to report there the following September. So, as far as the priesthood was concerned, I was on the road again.

* * *

I was much happier in Waterford than I had been in Clonliffe. There were only 60 students, half the number in Clonliffe. The environment was much more relaxed and normal. We had more free time. The student body was very friendly. We were treated as trusted adults, and could enter each other's rooms without coming under suspicion. There were far fewer rules and they were applied with humanity and flexibility. On the other side, the food was not as good as in Clonliffe, the rooms were more poorly furnished and there was not the same emphasis on personal hygiene and table manners. Academic standards were not as high. The Waterford students ranged in age from 18 to the sixties and were destined for Great Britain, the United States, Australia and other 'missionary' countries whose bishops were short of priests and could not pick and choose the 'cream'.

At the start, I was very nervous. I was still smarting from my Clonliffe experience. The President of St. John's at the time was a kind man called Canon Fitzgerald. On my first day there he spoke to me: 'Now, Mr. Buckley, you're coming here with your cards stamped. We don't know if you'll do. But we're giving you a chance.' For the next two or three years I lived in fear lest I be expelled again. I coped by praying a good deal and by asking the Lord to see me through. I was greatly helped by the college Vice President, Father John Shine. I had regular chats with him and he soon became President himself. He helped me through a tough three years. Fr. Shine is now Monsignor Shine, Vicar-General of the Diocese of Waterford and Lismore and the parish priest of Tramore, Co. Waterford. He would, I imagine, be a reasonably traditional man and is a canon lawyer. I still exchange Christmas cards with him. A year or two ago I sent him a card and I wrote after the greeting: 'I'm sure you don't understand what I'm at these days.' He sent a card back returning my Christmas greetings with a P.S. – 'You're right, I don't understand. Be careful. You have a long way to go.'

Some of us were chosen to study for the Diploma in Theology which was granted by Maynooth. I completed my diploma in 1975. Our theology professors encouraged us to think and to question. Our text-books included the writings of some of the more go-ahead and liberal authors. In our Dogmatic Theology class, we were encouraged by our professor, Dr. Tom Marsh, now at Maynooth, to look critically at such concepts as the 'real presence' in the Eucharist. Strangely enough, at that time I might, in my immaturity and simple faith, have been more conservative on the subject than Dr. Marsh.

The Waterford seminary placed a great deal of emphasis on students doing pastoral work as a preparation for their work in the real world. Every week I visited the city's psychiatric hospital and saw at close range the sufferings of the patients. To this day, I have a great interest in and compassion for the mentally ill. We also attended local schools to teach religion and were involved in various ministries to the elderly.

Waterford is a beautiful city and I have happy memories of walks and drives round the country roads. The Ursuline nuns who ran a school near the college befriended us and the culinary treats they provided made up for the rather basic fare in the college dining-room. I did not get up to the same degree of joking and 'prankstering' as I had done at Clonliffe. I didn't have to. I was free. When I look back at my time in Waterford I feel warmed. Looking back at Clonliffe is like seeing dark clouds in the sky. The standard of living was higher at Clonliffe. But the standard of love in Waterford was far superior.

At last the great day came. I was ordained a priest on 6 June, 1976 – Pentecost Sunday – by the Bishop of Waterford, Dr. Michael Russell. Bishop Russell was from Cashel diocese and a favourite of the then Archbishop Morris. Morris was apparently responsible for Russell's elevation to Waterford, so Russell inevitably ended up with the nickname: 'Morris Minor'. Bishop Russell was very kind to us as students. His house was in our college grounds and he often gave us a lift in his car as he passed. He was the first human bishop I ever met. My family and friends gathered from the four corners to see me ordained. During the ceremony, I looked back and saw my father cry for the first time. We had two days of celebration. We had a reception and meal after the ordination in the Árd Rí hotel in Waterford. The following day I celebrated my first Mass at Ballygall in Dublin and we had another party in the Clarence hotel on the quays. All of us were on a high. I was so happy I was floating. I spent the following summer travelling to various places visiting family and convents. I was as proud as punch. At last I was a priest and no-one – and I mean no-one – could ever take it from me. I didn't know then that some would try. I was, of course, immature and inexperienced then. I embarrassed my mother in front of a Protestant neighbour by counting all the money I had received as ordination gifts in the car on the way from Waterford to Dublin. But I wasn't really worried about money. I did not want my parents to be out of pocket over my ordination and I was simply checking if I had enough to pay for our two days of celebration. As it turned out I had. An hour before the ordination ceremony the college president, Canon Shine, made two big concessions. Firstly he invited us ordinands into the priests' diningroom in the college for morning coffee. Secondly he told us: 'Now you can call me John.' Yes, indeed, I had arrived!

St. John Bosco is the Catholic Patron Saint of youth. On the morning of his first Mass in an Italian village church his ageing mother told him: 'Now that you have said your first Mass your suffering will begin in earnest.' Her words were prophetic. He suffered greatly at the hands of the Church and his fellow-clergy. While not sharing in his saintliness, I feel that I can identify with his difficulties and his mother's prophecy. The Catholic Church has a way of hurting her priests, especially any of her priests who are in anyway 'different' or 'dissident'. I'm glad that I did not know then what I know now. I don't know if I could have faced it.

CHAPTER 2

Beginning Parish Work

'You think it a miracle when God does what your
priest asks; we deem it a miracle when the priest does
what God asks'!

Jewish saying

DURING THE SUMMER OF 1976, while I was enjoying my post-ordination
holiday, I received a letter from Archbishop Murphy of Cardiff telling
me that he was appointing me as assistant priest to the parish priest
of Bridgend, Wales, Fr. Bernard Driscoll. I immediately wrote to Fr.
Driscoll and told him that I was looking forward to joining him in
Bridgend and would help him all I could. I received a very curt answer
from him telling me that all he could promise me was hard work and
that if I let him know when and where I was arriving he would have
me picked up. I was a little hurt by the tone of his letter, hardly
encouraging to a newly-ordained, but replied giving him my date and
time of arrival.

I arrived at Cardiff airport with a few cases containing my belongings
and felt quite lost. I could see no-one waiting for me. After a while I
noticed a gangster-like figure, dressed in black, with a black hat, sitting
against a red car. He appeared to be a clergyman. I approached him.
'Are you Father O'Driscoll?' I queried. 'Drop the "O", sonny,' he replied.
'You're not in Ireland now.' I was embarrassed and blushed. I was
dressed in my black suit and clerical collar. I held out my hand. 'I'm
Pat Buckley.' 'You're no use to me if that's who you are,' he responded.
'I was waiting on a FATHER Buckley.' 'That's who I am,' I said, more
embarrassed than before. 'If that's who you are, would you please
fucking say that's who you are.' He continued: 'I have no time for these
trendy young priests who try to impress parishioners and others by
telling people to refer to them by their first name.' My cases were put
into Fr. Driscoll's boot. We had a 45-minute journey to the presbytery
in Bridgend. Not a word was spoken. 'A nice day', I tried. 'Is it?' he

replied. I realised that perhaps the less I said the better.

When we arrived at the priest's house in Bridgend, Fr. Driscoll simply got out of the car and left me sitting there not knowing what to do. After a while I got out and ventured in. The curate I was replacing was bringing his belongings down the stairs. He greeted me with some warmth. We talked a bit and I got the impression that I was in for a hard time. I brought my belongings in. It was a large house with several empty rooms. The parish priest had a sitting-room and a bedroom. Miss Hope (an inappropriate and unfortunate name) had her two rooms also. I was given one room at the top of the house which was to serve as my living quarters. I was simply an unwelcome lodger in the household. Among priests the yarn is common that the pecking order in the priest's house is as follows: the parish priest, the housekeeper, the dog, the budgie and then the curate.

I went down to the dining-room for my first meal with Fr. Driscoll. He sat at one end of a linen-covered table and I at the other. A large radio was in the middle of the table, separating us. The ugly back of the contraption faced me. At meals Fr. Driscoll had the radio switched on. If not, his newspaper was propped up in front of it. He spoke at me from above his spectacles and through both radio and newspaper. Sometimes he spoke to me in Latin, which I didn't understand. The meat and vegetables were brought in by Miss Hope and left in front of him. He decided how much food I was to receive, placed that ration on a plate and passed it over the radio to me. During my first meal with him he gave me a lecture on the rules of the house. 'You will drink coffee at dinner like the rest of us, not tea. You will be on time for all meals. You will not bring visitors to this house. You will keep letters and incoming telephone calls to a minimum. You will not make outgoing telephone calls.' There were many other rules. He then informed me that I would be the chaplain to the local general hospital but that I was not allowed to visit the maternity wards. He explained why, without my even requesting an explanation. 'You Irishmen have a passion for swollen bellies and pregnant women. You will not indulge in that fantasy while with me.' He further informed me that 'Irishmen's brains dangle between their legs.' I was not allowed to enter Miss Hope's kitchen either and therefore I was forbidden to make myself a cup of tea either day or night.

They have a saying in South Wales: 'If you're not careful you'll end up in Bridgend.' Bridgend had several very large mental hospitals in it. And I had ended up in Bridgend. I was supposed to be in my room each evening at around 9 p.m. I was not allowed out after that time. And I was 24 years old at this time. After Fr. Driscoll had gone to bed, I used to climb out of my bedroom window, onto the church roof, onto a garage roof and from there onto the ground and go off to visit some families in the parish in an attempt to keep myself sane and human. I could not have gone down the stairs as he would have heard me passing his bedroom. Once or twice he caught me on the way back in and he was very angry. He met me at the top of the stairs, holding the fly of his pyjamas closed with one hand, the other hand swinging in the air with anger. 'And where do we think we are going?' he would shout. One morning the ceiling in Fr. Driscoll's bedroom fell into the bed on top of him. His door was locked and he was trapped in the bed. Miss Hope and I were both at his bedroom door. She was praying loudly that he wasn't dead. I was praying quietly, God forgive me, that he was!

Every Sunday I had to travel to celebrate Mass in a community hall in an outstation of the parish. At the time my curate's salary was £60 per year. Eacht Monday morning Fr. Driscoll left a brown envelope at the bottom of the stairs with my £1.20 in it and £3.50 for seven Mass stipends. I was expected to live on £4.70 per week. At the outstation we had a church collection in a basket. I used to take some of this money to supplement my wage. Driscoll eventually cottoned on to this and had a carpenter friend of his make a locked wooden collection-box which he gave me to use instead of the basket. This, he thought, was Buckley-proof. I was supposed to pass around this box and then the contents were safe from me. But I beat him on that one. I used still to pass around the old basket and then after the Mass and before I came home to the presbytery I would take my 'supplementary' benefit and put the rest into his locked box. He never discovered the fraud!

*　　　*　　　*

I became increasingly unhappy in Bridgend. The constant pressure from him and the coldness of the presbytery really got to me. I had been used to a warm family home while I was growing up. Even in the seminary, with all its difficulties, I had the warmth and companionship of very close friends. But in Bridgend I was alone. An ocean separated me from my family and friends. I knew very few people in the town. One lady, a Miss Mary Hoddinott from Pontypool, had been very good to me. I had no car. She gave me £1,000 which was a lot of money in 1976. I bought a second-hand car for £860 and spent the other £140 on my first year's tax and insurance. In Bridgend, I became very depressed and anxious. I spoke to the auxiliary bishop, Daniel Mullins, himself an Irishman from Limerick. He took the view that there was something wrong with me. 'Will you see a psychiatrist?' he asked. I agreed. I'd have done anything to get out of Bridgend. I had a nice Sunday afternoon visit to a Catholic psychiatrist who wrote to the bishop telling him that there was nothing wrong with me but that I was living in a very unacceptable environment. The bishop refused to move me. 'It is your cross,' he said. 'Go back and offer it up.' I tried that and it didn't work. I then rang the Archbishop. He refused to meet me to discuss the matter. I rang his secretary and told him that I had had enough and that if His Grace did not telephone me by 4 p.m. that day I would buy a ferry ticket and leave for Ireland with my few belongings. The Archbishop never rang and I went at 4 p.m. and bought my ticket. I packed my things in the car and left a note under Fr. Driscoll's dining-room plate. As I drove out of Bridgend, heading for the ferry to Ireland, a great weight lifted off me. I felt free and normal again. My first posting as a priest had been a very disturbing one.

After some weeks, during which I had Christmas at home with my family, the Archbishop corresponded with me. He offered me a move to a new parish. I accepted and was back in Wales within 24 hours. This time I was sent to the parish of Briton Ferry, near the town of Neath on the outskirts of Swansea. My parish priest here was the auxiliary bishop's brother, Edmund Mullins, a Limerick man too. He was also the Archdiocesan treasurer and a keen golfer. In fact, he golfed with the Archbishop. He was away a great deal and that left me more or less to run the parish. I enjoyed the autonomy. I worked hard. I had a good relationship with Fr. Mullins which was spoiled only by a disagreement with his long-time housekeeper. I had a long time in this parish, the best part of a year. After that all three of us, Fr. Mullins, his housekeeper and I were moved.

I ended up in Whitchurch, Cardiff, with a Tipperary man, a Canon Creed. This appointment was a disaster. It was nearly as bad as Bridgend. Canon Creed and I did not get on. As I saw it, he imposed far too many restrictions on me. I knew that there was no future in this situation. I had told Archbishop Murphy about my misgivings in being sent to Canon Creed. I said: 'Your Grace, it is only sheer obedience that would take me there.' 'A priest never went anywhere for a better reason, Father,' he replied. So I went to Creed.

After six weeks I knew it wouldn't work. I returned to Archbishop Murphy. 'I told you, Your Grace, that Whitchurch wouldn't work and it hasn't.' Murphy was angry. 'Trying to find you a parish priest would be like going on a witch hunt,' he said. He demanded that I return to Canon Creed and stay there. I refused. I told him I would return to Ireland. 'If you do,' he threatened, 'I'll see to it that you never work again as a priest. I'll designate you a *fugitivus*, a church criminal.' I replied that I would prefer to be a *fugitivus* than a nut-case. I left Archbishop Murphy's palace and the Archdiocese of Cardiff, never to return again. My exile was over. Archbishop Murphy had preached in Cardiff Cathedral: 'Some people in the world accuse us of preaching "old hat". We do not preach "old hat". We preach "eternal hat".' I had had enough of Archbishop Murphy's eternal hat as I boarded the Irish ferry for the last time. I must say, however, that the vast majority of the people I met in Wales were nice people and were very good to me. I enjoyed much of my work among them. I especially enjoyed my work with the young people in Briton Ferry. When I left Wales I was genuinely sad to be leaving so many friends behind. If it wasn't for some of the churchmen I had met in Wales I might very well be there still working as a priest.

In all I was in four parishes in Wales, one as a deacon and three as a curate or assistant priest. I spent the Summer of 1975 as a deacon in the parish of Llanrumney, a housing estate on the outskirts of Cardiff. My three parishes in Wales as a curate were Bridgend, Briton Ferry and Whitchurch in Cardiff city. In two of the four parishes my relationship with my parish priest was excellent. In the other two the relationship left a lot to be desired.

But wherever I've been as a priest my relationship with the laity has always been warm and good. In fact, I could say without fear of contradiction that the laity took me to their hearts. I wasn't very long in Bridgend before I grew close to the people there by visiting them extensively in their homes, by being an attentive hospital visitor and by socialising with them (which the parish priest did not do and did not approve of) in the parish social club behind the church building.

The people of Bridgend also liked my lively liturgies and my sermons and were loud in their praise. I also developed a good relationship with the teachers and young people in the Catholic schools where I spent a lot of time each day. The Bridgend parishioners liked to come to confession to me and almost immediately after I arrived they used me as a counsellor and adviser, trusting me with their most delicate problems. Unfortunately, because of things at the presbytery, I was gone from there in a few months. I still get Christmas cards from Bridgend parishioners.

I spent a year as a curate in Briton Ferry and that gave me ample time to work very closely with the laity there and to draw very close to them. As mentioned, I served as barman to Catholics, Protestants and atheists in the parish club. I was deeply involved in the schools there too and had an excellent relationship with the teachers and young people. I took the young ones on regular trips in a large minibus. We visited such places as Gloucester, Stratford-upon-Avon, and Cork and Kerry in Ireland. I was good at the liturgy and at sermons, and the parish priest, Father Mullins, was excellent at singing and music – we were a powerful pair at Sunday Masses. I was chaplain to Neath General Hospital and worked well with the patients, the nurses and other medical staff. I ran a weekly prayer group which was attended by people of mixed religions. And it was at Briton Ferry that I played my one and only game of cricket – disgracing myself and others! I would imagine that during my time in Briton Ferry the people felt they had a priest who was warm, cared about them, was close to them and involved in all their issues.

Whitchurch was a disaster. The presbytery relationships were not good and I didn't last long there. But even during my short stay there I had a good rapport with the laity and was appreciated, I think, for my sermons and liturgies. Archbishop Murphy was a 'parishioner', but he would not have been one of my fans!

Some priests have a problem in their relationship with the laity. I have never had that problem. I have merely fallen foul of parish priests.

And so, I returned to my family home in Dublin as a canonical or church criminal. I spent eight or nine months at home doing voluntary work in the Legion of Mary hostels in Dublin that cared for the street-girls and the down-and-outs. I drew the dole (unemployment benefit) for a few weeks. The dole office did not know what section to assign me to. They had never had an 'unemployed' priest before. All I was entitled to was £4 per week as I was living at home. Eventually I didn't bother collecting it. It was not worth the weekly waiting, signing and humiliation. I went each morning to the Regina Coeli Hostel and said Mass for the Legion of Mary staff and the residents of the hostel. I then had some breakfast and spent the day doing some washing and cleaning in the hostel and working with and talking to Dublin's down-and-out fraternity. I prayed for a few hours each evening at a convent in Dublin. I didn't know where my future lay. But I was happy to be a priest and happy to be back in Ireland. I approached the Archdiocese of Dublin to look for priestly work. The auxiliary bishop of Dublin, Dermot O'Mahony, interviewed me. He couldn't offer me work, he said, but he would pray for me. I felt rejected. I also met the Bishop of Meath in a Dublin hotel during this period. I had been born in the Diocese of Meath and I had heard that he was short of priests. I asked him for priestly work. He got a bit red around the face and told me that he would let me know. I never heard from him since.

Eventually after some correspondence Archbishop Murphy of Cardiff released me from his diocese. He gave me a document which was to be very important to me later, a letter of 'absolute discharge'. In that letter John A. Murphy said: 'Fr. Patrick Buckley worked for one year in this diocese and then at his own wishes he returned to Ireland. I now grant him an absolute discharge with permission to seek an *episcopus benevolens*.' I was free – free to seek a benevolent bishop. I wondered if one of them would be hard to find!

*　　*　　*

Later, through a family contact, I went for a week-end to Saint Agnes's parish in Andersonstown, Belfast, to stay with and assist the curate, Father James Doyle, a Wexford priest on loan to the Diocese of Down and Connor. He introduced me to the Vicar-General of Down and Connor diocese, Monsignor Patrick Mullally, who really ran the diocese. The bishop, William Philbin, was a shy and intellectual recluse, with the nickname 'Bo-Peep' in clerical circles – 'Little Bo-Beep has lost her sheep.' Some of the Down and Connor clergy resented Monsignor Mullally's power.

For some reason, Monsignor Mullally took a liking to me. Within three days he was in touch to tell me that he was appointing me a curate in Saint Peter's, the cathedral for the diocese, located in the centre of the by then infamous Divis Flats in Belfast. I arrived there in the Summer of 1978.

Driving into Divis Flats on the Falls Road, Belfast, for the first time was, for me, like walking on the Moon! I had only been to Belfast for the first time in my life a week earlier. Divis (the flats have since been knocked down) was generally accepted as being one of the worst housing complexes in Western Europe. The unemployment rate for the men was somewhere around 80 per cent. You found every possible social problem there – alcoholism, tranquilliser dependency, marital breakdown, one-parent families, incest, car-stealing ('juvenile joy-riding') and every other problem and crime that you can think of. Added to this, there was a general environment of lawlessness. Divis was a staunchly Republican area and very dangerous for the British Army and the police force, the Royal Ulster Constabulary. When the security forces did come to Divis they came in convoy! Nearly every family in Divis had been touched by tragedy – someone injured, killed or imprisoned. At the time I went to Divis the strongest paramilitary group in the area was the INLA – the Irish National Liberation Army. The INLA's political wing was the IRSP – the Irish Republican Socialist Party. Divis was locally known as: 'The Planet of the Erps' (IRPS). Immediately upon arriving in Divis I was accepted because I was a priest. Immediately also, I fell in love with the accent. On my very first afternoon in Divis, I took a stroll through the flats. As I walked along, a young voice shouted from three storeys up: 'Bout ye, Far', meaning 'What about you, Father?'

I was horrified at the conditions in which these thousands of people were being forced to live. Each flat was merely a plaster-board box. There were up to 70 flats per balcony. Nobody had any space or privacy and therefore nobody cared for the balconies, which were littered with rubbish and dog droppings. The walls between each flat were paper-thin and everybody heard everybody else's business. At night as you lay in bed, people walking on the balconies above your bedroom made a noise like thunder. The waste disposal chutes on each balcony were inadequate. Household rubbish littered the stairways beside the chutes. The balcony lighting was nearly always missing, having been broken by either the paramilitaries or the British Army so that they could work under cover of darkness. Many of the lifts were regularly out of order. The lifts were small and when someone died the coffin had to be stood upright in the lift by the undertaker to get the remains down to the hearse. This caused grieving relatives great distress. The electricity supply to flats broke down regularly. Burst pipes in empty flats often flooded the flats below. There were rats everywhere. I often had to walk through groups of 50 and 100 of them. The Belfast City Council pest control people told me that they did not have enough poison in the city to kill all the rats in Divis. They therefore kept the rodent population at an 'acceptable level'. Rats often appeared in flats seven storeys up or on people's window-cills. The public areas surrounding the flats were littered with rubbish and burnt-out cars. A general feeling of hopelessness hung heavily in the Divis air. People were simply weary, having been worn down over the years by the violence, the social deprivation, the unemployment and poverty. Was it any wonder some of the residents referred to them not as the Divis Flats but as the 'Devil's Flats?'

In stark contrast to all of this stood, right in the middle of the flats, the 120-years-old St. Peter's Pro-Cathedral with its mansion-like presbytery behind it. In the presbytery life was absolutely different. Five priests lived there. Each had his own suite of rooms. There were several housekeepers who cooked, cleaned and pampered the clergy in every way. The priests' meals were served on a dumb waiter that ran from the basement kitchen to the clergy dining-room where only clergy could enter. In the flats the people survived most often on junk food. In the priests' dining-room we ate the best – cooked breakfasts, steak, meat joints, fish, etc. Lunch was at 1 p.m. each day and every day there was sherry before lunch, claret with lunch and brandy in the coffee. At special times like Confirmations and other big occasions in the Pro-Cathedral, a feast of food, drink and cigars was produced at which medieval kings would have felt at home. This was the Catholic clerical club at its very best.

Early on in my career in Down and Connor, a priest took me aside. He had advice to offer. 'The people there,' he told me, 'are as thick as bottled pigshit. They're hopeless, absolutely hopeless. There's nothing that can be done for them. Don't hurt your head trying. Just do the basics, say your Masses, hear your confessions, do your funerals and weddings and put your feet up until you get out of St. Peter's to a better parish.' I was horrified at the level of cynicism.

The clerical customs and ways of doing things were very strong and very rigid. One was expected to conform. Conformity was especially required from a young curate like myself and especially one who was being accepted into the diocese for the first time. I found one custom particularly cruel. There was a rule that a wedding Mass and ceremony was to start exactly on time even if the bride had not arrived! This meant that a wedding Mass could be partly or wholly over by the time a bride came and the ceremony itself had to take place afterwards. And the delay might not have been her fault at all. Her wedding-car might have been detained at an army road block. I refused to start a wedding Mass without a bride, even though I was sometimes ticked off about this.

One Sunday, I preached at the Masses and told the parishioners that I was glad to be their priest and that if they needed me I was available to them at any time of the day or the night. This was important, I felt, in a place like Divis where there could be a terrible tragedy at any hour. The people took me at my word. They began to call. This caused a lot of difficulties and confusion. I still have a notice put up on the presbytery door which says: FR. BUCKLEY IS NOT IN. PLEASE DO NOT RING THIS BELL!

The people of Divis came to the presbytery with every kind of problem. On one occasion, at two in the morning, the door-bell rang. Down went the priest on duty. There standing at the door was a middle-aged mother with her very pregnant unmarried daughter who looked as if she would give birth any minute. The mother pushed the daughter into the presbytery hallway. 'She's for having a wean (wee one)', announced the mother. 'For God's sake, not here,' pleaded the priest as he ran to telephone for the ambulance. When he arrived back to the hall the mother was gone and the young girl was jumping up and down with pain on a seat. The mother had gone home to bed convinced that her daughter was now safe in clerical hands. The ambulance eventually came, but passed down the street. Panicking at the thoughts of a presbytery birth, the priest ran down the street after the ambulance. He was dressed only in his pyjamas and dressing-gown. He eventually caught up with the ambulance. 'Are you the father,' inquired the ambulance driver. Thinking he meant 'priest', the priest said 'yes' and directed the driver to the presbytery to pick up the pregnant girl. To this day there are two ambulance men in Belfast who are convinced that one night in the late 1970s or early 1980s they picked up a 'priest's wife' and brought her to the hospital to have her baby. Truth is stranger than fiction.

Another night at 1 a.m. I was on duty. The door bell rang. It was a little boy who pleaded with me to come quickly, that his Daddy was 'dead'. I pulled on a dressing gown, collected what I needed for the 'Last Rites' and headed for the flat in question. There, lying on the carpeted sitting-room floor, was a young man in his late twenties with a bread-knife driven into his chest, right to the very handle. He was blue in the face. I anointed him and the ambulance came and brought him to hospital. Miraculously he survived. There had been a domestic row and his wife had taken the bread-knife to him. Later that day, I went back to the flat to see how the wife was and to comfort her. I was sure that she would be demented with guilt. As I walked in the open door of the flat the television was blaring. The kids were happily playing on the living-room floor where the victim had lain. And there, in the kitchen, was the wife, singing away and cutting the bread for the children's tea with the knife that she had used for the near-fatal stabbing! 'No use wasting a good knife,' she said smiling. Ah dear! The practical Irish.

After about a year, when I had found my feet in the parish I had to make a very painful decision. I had to determine whether I would be friends with my fellow clergy or with the needy people. I opted for the people. All hell broke loose in the presbytery. With the residents I wanted to do something about the housing problems in Divis. We decided that we would start the Divis Residents' Association. I was forbidden to be part of it but I went ahead anyway. I was its first chairman. We couldn't have a public meeting and vote because of paramilitary manipulation and pressure. So we circulated voting papers to flats and collected them ourselves. After acting as a steering committee for some months, this vote authorised us to act on behalf of the people of Divis for a year. We set about our work. Our long-term goal was the total demolition of Divis. But we knew that that would take years. So our short-term aim was to improve the conditions in Divis as much as we could so that, while lobbying for demolition and awaiting it, the community could have the best standard of services and cleaning. We had meetings with senior people in the Northern Ireland Housing Executive and other state agencies to discuss and plan Divis's future.

'What is the biggest immediate problem?' I asked myself. 'The dirt of the place,' I answered. So together we decided to clean up the Divis flats. I contacted the City Council, the Housing Executive and the Department of the Environment. They all promised help and support. We were given free brushes, shovels, paint, overalls and skips to remove the rubbish. I didn't know how the clean-up was going to go. I was nervous. I didn't wish to stage a failure. The Republican paramilitaries accused us of co-operating with the British authorities, the oppressors of our people.

On the first Monday morning of the clean-up, I put on my new overalls and went out on the streets to clean, sweep and paint. Not many joined me initially. Some of the people were shocked at 'God's holy anointed' out sweeping the street. But within days hundreds had joined me and the place began to take on a new cleanliness and a new hope. A lorry-load of brushes and shovels arrived from the City Council. My helpers in the beginning were mainly children and women. But eventually the men followed. We removed burnt-out cars, rotten mattresses and broken furniture, dead rats, used babies' nappies, etc. Skip by skip, loads of rubbish left the area. The roads and pathways were swept and hosed down. Graffiti were painted over, Republican slogans too! People came out and painted the walls and doors of their own flats for the first time. The electricity and water authorities came in and repaired equipment. The lifts were fixed. One man from the gas company drove into Divis and straight back out again. It was so clean that he was convinced he was not in Divis at all! The community spirit was at an all-time high. In the middle of our working day we had cups of tea, and sandwiches and cakes were passed around. There was a carnival atmosphere. The local television and radio stations and newspapers came in to do news items and feature stories. Divis was becoming famous for being clean. We received an award from the Belfast City Council for cleanliness!

The people of Divis were very kind in showing their gratitude to me. On 5 October, 1981, they gathered in the Divis Community Centre and presented me with a set of vestments and a silver tray and goblets. The next morning's *Irish News* carried the headline: THANK YOU GIFTS TO PRIEST WHO CLEANED UP THE FALLS. This was a happy time in the Buckley family also. On 13 November the same year my father was called to the Bar in Dublin.

We always followed our 'clean-ups' with a Divis Festival. From 12 to 22 August, 1982, we had a huge festival in Divis, with an open-air rock concert every day and all kinds of fringe activities for children, adults and the elderly. I was very pleased that our concerts were attended by Protestant people from the Shankill Road. Our festival news was carried extensively in the local media. During our 1982 'clean-up' we were even joined in our work by senior Housing Executive staff. The District Manager of the Executive for the Divis area spent some of her lunch-hours filling rubbish skips with me. During the whole exercise we were joined by the Chief Executive of the Housing Executive, Mr. John Gorman. The *Irish News* of 19 August, 1982, announced: HOUSING CHIEF APPLAUDS DIVIS FLATS 'GREAT HEART'. *Irish News* columnist, Tom Samways, helped us by appealing for funds for us in his column. The well-known personality of the Belfast rock scene, Terri Hooley of *Good Vibrations*, also gave his services free of charge. A Divis clean-up and festival seemed to trigger many imaginations.

Funny things happened in St. Peter's all the time. One Saturday when I was hearing confessions I pulled back the slide in the confession box and a voice said: 'It's Micky, Fa'r. I have two things to say to you. I have 68 convictions for grievous bodily harm. Secondly, can I have the loan of two quid?' I didn't want to be Micky's 69th victim so I hurriedly handed over the £2 ransom fee. After a few minutes I heard singing out in the church. I left the confessional and what a sight I saw. In the Cathedral we had an *Ecce Homo* (Behold The Man) bust of Christ crucified. Micky had removed the crown of thorns from the statue's head and placed it on his old bald head. Little trickles of blood were flowing down Micky's neck and he was going around the Cathedral singing the Catholic Benediction hymn: *Tantum Ergo Sacramentum.* For a long time after the incident I didn't hear anything of poor Micky and then I was told that he had broken into a convent in Co. Down and had stolen six bottles of altar wine. The Reverend Mother caught him drinking the wine and sent for the police. Micky was arrested and brought to trial. He was convicted of 'breaking and entering' and of stealing the wine. The judge enquired if he wished to say anything before sentence was passed. Micky, a devout Catholic, wished to please and impress the judge. He therefore wished His Worship a traditional Catholic blessing: 'May Your Honour have a happy and a holy death.' The judge, a non-Catholic, was not at all impressed with this morbid wish.

I really loved the young people of Divis and my work with them. I spent every night of the week in the parish youth club with Gerry Reynolds, the excellent youth leader. The young people were rough and ready but were as free with their affection as they were with their abuse. Most Sunday afternoons I would take a mini-bus full of youngsters to Bangor or Newcastle, seaside resorts in Co. Down. We would walk and play the amusements and then I would treat them to a basic tea of hamburgers and chips. Occasionally in the bad weather we would go instead to the Castlereagh swimming complex in Protestant East Belfast. The kids would announce to the watching 'Prods' that they were Catholics by blessing themselves with the Sign of the Cross before they hopped off the diving boards.

Every year Gerry Reynolds and myself used to take 150 youngsters to the Salesian College in Pallaskenry in Co. Limerick for a holiday. It was a very difficult mission. Four railway carriages were hired from Northern Ireland Railways to get the kids to Dublin. Those carriages were locked once we got the kids into them. At Dublin we lined the travellers up and marched them across the city to the other train station that brought us from Dublin to Limerick. That train had to be locked too. Buses brought us from Limerick City to Pallaskenry. On one occasion, travelling between Dublin and Limerick, the train suddenly came to a halt. We wondered what was wrong. After a few minutes a very angry-looking guard approached me. 'Fader,' he stuttered, 'wan of your little bastards is up walking along the roof of the train.' One of our nine-year-olds had managed to climb out a window and was walking the carriage roof just like he had seen John Wayne doing in the films. He was lucky he wasn't killed.

For our stay in Limerick we had an action-packed holiday, with sporting events, hiking, day trips, daily Mass and very excellent catering. But the kids were always getting us into trouble. One of the staff at Pallaskenry, which was an agricultural training college, had spent years cultivating a special kind of pheasant. He had just perfected the technique when we arrived one year. We fed the kids and were having our tea. One of the youngsters came running in. 'Come quick, Fa'r,' he screamed, 'Someone has just killed the fuckin' chicken.' I ran out and what a sight awaited me. One of the youngsters had caught the special pheasant and held it down while another dropped a brick on it. The rare bird was as dead as the dodo! I'm sure the man responsible for breeding it cried himself to sleep. On another occasion, two of the older lads came and asked me if they could go out for a jog around the local roads. I said 'yes' and warned them to behave themselves. An hour later they arrived back in a Garda car. They had been out running and spotted an Irish colleen looking from a farmhouse window. They dropped their trunks and gave her a 'flash'. She happened to be the wife of the local police sergeant and I was given an hour to get them out of Limerick. Sadly they had to come home and miss their holidays.

I worked a lot with Divis 'joyriders', the kids who steal cars and go speeding about in them. The youngsters would go downtown in Belfast and steal cars, generally Fords or other British makes. They would then bring them back to Divis Flats and speed around in them, often crashing them. On several occasions they drove right through a flat's bedroom wall and residents woke up from sleep to see a car, with its engine running, at the bottom of their bed! When the cars ran out of petrol they were set on fire. But before that the youngsters would remove valuable car parts and sell them to some 'Fagin'-type god-fathers who lurked in the background. The joyriders were as young as nine. If they were too small, one of them sat and steered the car while the other was down on the floor working the pedals. The older boys used to get the younger ones to lie along the back windows of the cars like human sandbags to take any bullets shot at the car by the police or army. For their trouble they got the princely sum of 50p. And indeed many youngsters were killed, either through crashing the car or, on occasion, by being shot at by the security forces. But the killings did not stop the joyriding. It seemed to be a disease and an obsession with them. The youngsters particularly liked it when the police chased them. In fact the bolder of the joyriders used to go to the police station and beep the horn outside to taunt the police landrovers into coming out to chase them!

The ladies of the Divis Residents' Association and myself used to go out at night chasing the kids and taking the cars from them and bringing them either to the police or to the owners. We rescued literally hundreds of cars in this way. Some converted joyriders decided to work as part of my rescue gang. They gave me special keys stolen from a local locksmith's bin and filed down to be very useful. The kids referred to these keys as 'crackers'. I owned several 'crackers' that could open almost any car and start any ignition. We became famous for our joyriding activities and newspaper headlines read: FR. PAT CREATES DIVIS BOYS' TOWN and HEAVENS, A PRIEST WHO 'STEALS' CARS. I was, of course, stealing the cars from the joyriders and returning them to their owners. It was funny. On many occasions country people would be visiting Belfast for a day's shopping and would lock themselves out of their cars in the Belfast car-parks. I would get a phone call: 'Are you the priest who deals with the stolen cars? You wouldn't come down with your keys and open my car for me, would you?' One night I became a huge hero in the eyes of the Divis Flats joyriders. I was taking a stolen car back to Hastings Street police station. I had a few of my converted joyriders with me. As we approached Hastings Street over some waste ground the kids screamed at me: 'Go on Fa'r, spin the wheels.' To give the kids a thrill I put my foot to the floor to spin the car wheels. I went faster and further than I had planned and didn't stop in time. I smashed straight into a policeman's car as he came off duty. The kids were thrilled silly and for weeks the Divis joyriding fraternity was full of the story of how 'Fa'r Buckley rammed the cops.' As I say, I loved the Divis kids. They loved and respected me too. Every night before going to bed I would do a full tour of the outskirts of the parish on foot just to make sure everything was all right. How do I know that I was accepted by the Divis kids? One night I spotted a very prominent piece of graffiti on a wall on the Falls Road. It was the roll of honour in a particular gang. The legend read: BAP, MONKO, REDSER, MUSCLES, STEVIE, FA'R B. I was deeply moved by this simple and primitive form of group acceptance and I felt that I had made it. I was a member of the gang.

WHERE THE MOUNTAINS OF MOURNE
SWEEP DOWN TO THE SEA

'SHOCK MOVE FOR DIVIS PRIEST' was the heading in the *Belfast Telegraph* on 28 January, 1983. The newspaper reported that my move from Divis had left me 'emotionally shattered'. And so indeed it had. Not only did I love Divis and its people but I was really emotionally attached to the place. At that stage I found it hard to believe that for me there could be life after Divis. But at that time I had confidence in Bishop Daly and felt that he must have an overall plan for the diocese.

I was prepared, hard as it was, to sacrifice Divis for something like the 'good of the whole church'. So I obeyed and went. But the going cost me much heartache, much insecurity and bitter tears.

I had been brought up in a city and had basically always lived in a city. Now, at the beginning of 1983, I found myself living in the mountains of Mourne at the outskirts of the town of Kilkeel, population 4,000. The house I lived in was in the country and, indeed, more or less in a graveyard. I could see the grave-stones from my bedroom window, a sight that spooked me. Two of us curates shared the house. My fellow-curate had been moved from Belfast the same day as I. While I had lived in Divis, he had lived for ten years in another inner-city parish and Catholic enclave, the famous 'Markets' area. We were both lost and suffering from some kind of culture-shock as we sat together on our first night in Kilkeel on our unpacked cases and boxes. All we had between us was a bottle of 7Up. I got two glasses and we divided the mineral between us. We were silent and after about five minutes Fr. Denis Newberry said to me: 'It's so quiet here I can hear the bubbles in my 7Up.' In the days that followed I thought I was going to lose my mind. I remember walking through the graveyard and feeling I was on another planet. For a day or two I felt real panic and had to get tranquillisers from the doctor to keep me calm. I wonder do bishops ever realise the trauma some priests feel by being moved so quickly and with such little notice.

My part of the parish was up in the mountains around the village of Attical, not a stone's throw from the beautiful Spelga dam. I spent my first week in Kilkeel bringing Communion to the sick and elderly in the farm-yards around Attical. I was very lonely for my Divis but the Mourne scenery was so beautiful and the people were so welcoming and friendly. These things comforted me in my homesickness for Divis. Kilkeel at the time had a parish priest called Canon Walter Larkin, who has since gone to his maker. Walter had a name for being a very tough parish priest. He had spent most of his priestly life in teaching and the younger priests of the diocese, who had had him as a teacher and headmaster, were scared stiff of him. When I was 'misbehaving' in Belfast, other priests used to warn me: 'If you're not careful you'll end up in Kilkeel with Walter Larkin.' And indeed I did. In my first days in Kilkeel I had to call on him to report for duty. He took me to his sitting-room. He was a gaunt figure of a man, and he chain-smoked.

He put me sitting down and fixed his steely eyes on me. After a silence he asked me the last question I had expected him to put. 'Well, young Buckley, what do you think of me?' I had decided to call him Walter instead of Canon, to put us on some kind of equal footing. I was also going to start off the way I intended finishing. So I was honest with him. 'Walter,' says I, 'I don't know you, but I've heard that you're very awkward and very conservative.' 'Did you, indeed, now?' he replied. 'Well, I'll have you know that I've heard that you are very difficult and disobedient. Do you realise,' he continued, 'that the whole diocese is waiting for us to fight?' 'No, Walter,' I confessed, 'but I'm not surprised.' 'Well,' smiled Walter, 'let's be friends and fool them all.' And that's what happened. We were very different people and disagreed on many things. But we remained very good friends. Years later when Walter lay dying and I had already been sacked by Bishop Cahal Daly, I went to visit him in St. John of God Hospital in Newry. Before I left, Walter asked me for my blessing. 'Pray for me,' he said, 'you're still as much a priest as any of them in my eyes.' I was very touched by his dying tribute. Walter didn't waste his praise or his compliments.

On one occasion, Walter was worried about all the sins against the sixth and ninth commandments being committed in Kilkeel. He decided that on one particular Sunday we three priests would all preach on the question of 'sins of the flesh'. Canon Walter was in the church in the town. Fr. Newberry was up the mountains in Attical. I was out at the seaside in the church at Greencastle. At midday on that Sunday we reconvened at the curates' house for a chat about how the preaching had gone. The Canon spoke of how he had done in the town. I reported on my day at the sea. And then the Canon turned to Denis Newberry. 'How did you get on in Attical preaching on the sins of the flesh?' he enquired. Denis, who is very large-framed, smiled and blushed. 'I concentrated on sheep-worrying,' he blurted. Even the serious Canon Larkin could not help but laugh.

It took me a long time to get used to country ways. On one of my first Sundays in Attical, I was driving along the country roads going to take a 'Holy Hour' service in the church. I noticed a sheep on the road with what I thought was a piece of string tied around its legs. I stopped the car and got out to release the poor sheep, as I thought. An angry farmer let a roar at me to leave the animal alone. The animal was merely 'langled,' its legs tied to keep it from roving too far. I had never even heard of this sheep-farming technique. On another occasion I went into a farm-yard and saw an amazing sight. Two sows had given birth to thirteen piglets each. I was transfixed by this unusual sight and made great enquiries from the farmer. The farmer eventually asked: 'Which one do you want, Father?' Apparently the people around there had this belief that if a priest threw his eye on something you had to give it to him or you would be cursed with bad luck all your days. I refused a piglet but the farmer insisted. He was convinced that if I had not taken a piglet the other twenty-five would have died of some form of 'mad sow disease'. I didn't know what to do. I had visions of Canon Larkin throwing me out of the priests' house if I arrived home with a pig. So I had an idea. 'I'll take that one there,' I pointed, 'but you keep it for me and rear it for me.' That satisfied the farmer's superstition. I never saw my pig again. Every time I eat bacon and sausage I wonder if I'm eating my pig! Another time, in another farm, I admired an old six-foot wide cartwheel. That night the farmer left it to the priests' house in his tractor. I had to stop admiring things in farm-yards although I've often wondered what a farmer would have done if I had eyed his wife or, better still, his wallet!

I began thoroughly to enjoy my time in Kilkeel. I liked the locality and the people. The folk seemed to take to me very well and they said that they enjoyed my Masses and my sermons. I grew very close to the young people in Kilkeel and in Attical. I spent a lot of time in the schools and I loved that. I used to say a monthly Mass in the primary school in Attical. Listening to the innocent voices of the children singing hymns and at the same time looking out the window over the mountains was like being in heaven. I found those Masses deeply touching. Every Saturday night in the parish hall in Attical I used to help the young people run a disco. It was attended by up to four or five hundred teenagers who were bussed in from all over Co. Down. I stayed at the disco from 8 p.m. until after midnight. I welcomed the kids at the door and walked around all night talking and listening to them. I joked with them and played all kinds of tricks on them. They responded with great warmth. I often discussed their problems with them or heard their confessions in the back rooms, outside in my car or along the country roads. The older people in the parish used to say: 'How do you stick it every Saturday night?' But I loved being there. It was the highlight of my week.

A frightening experience happened to me at one of those Saturday night discos. I had locked the takings away when I heard screaming from outside. There was a loud knock on the door and I opened it to find two gunmen dressed in black with balaclavas over their faces. One had a revolver, the other a sawn-off shotgun. They put a gun to my head and demanded the takings. I refused, ducked back inside, checked that the safe was locked and got out the back to a farm-house to telephone for the police. I returned to the hall to find the young people lined up against the wall and one of the gunmen making a speech. 'We are from the INLA,' he was saying. 'Where's the priest?' No-one knew. 'Well, come to 10 o'clock Mass next Sunday and see him shot if he has gone for the police.' By now the young people were crying and screaming. The gunmen ran from the hall and met me on the road. 'Did you ring the f...g cops?' they asked. 'Yes, I did,' I answered. 'Stay here till they come and we'll see how brave you are then.' The two men ran down the road to a waiting car with me after them shouting 'God help Ireland if you fellas ever get to run it.' I took the number of the car as it drove off. You can imagine my sorrow when they were later arrested and turned out to be two of my own teenage parishioners. One of the families was angry with me. The parents of the other youth were glad he had been stopped before killing someone. I went to prison to visit them. 'Would you have shot me?' I asked. 'We would,' they said. 'We had drink on us.' I later had to give evidence against the two at Belfast Crown Court. I have never supported violence or killing. That is one of the reasons I feel so badly when narrow-minded loyalist types in places like Larne call me the 'Republican priest'. It's easy for them to talk. They have never met a real paramilitary.

After a while Fr. Newberry was moved from Kilkeel and his replacement, who came to live with me, was a famous character in the Diocese of Down and Connor, Fr. George McLaverty. Fr. George had a faithful companion, Cora, a mongrel bitch. One day Fr. George and Cora were out for a walk together. Cora spotted a handsome sheep-dog in a farmer's yard and ran four fields to get to him, leaving Fr. George stranded on the road. The sheep-dog was virile as well as good-looking and started to make serious overtures towards Cora. Fr. George stood watching, helpless and dismayed. A Catholic lady passed by on a bike and asked Fr. George the cause of his sorrow. 'My poor Cora,' groaned

Fr. George, pointing at the love scene being acted out in the farm-yard. 'Arra, Father, what are you worried about?' asked the woman. 'Isn't it only human nature?' Fr. George some weeks later thanked the Lord that no conception had taken place!

Being the curate for the Attical district of Kilkeel parish gave me, for the first time in my priestly life, a little church of my own where, with the people, we could organise things our own way and do as we wished. That made me very happy. I have never been able to work well with someone constantly looking over my shoulder. We had some lovely liturgies in the little church. The highlight of these was at Easter 1984. Two things stand out in my mind. During his ministry Christ himself used parables and told stories from people's everyday lives to get across to them the central message of the Gospel. Kilkeel was very near to the Gospel realities and parables. It was a fishing port and the Lord used fishing parables and examples all the time. It was also a sheep-farming locality and once again the Lord used sheep-farming parables – the Good Shepherd and so on. During Holy Week 1984 I borrowed a lamb from a local farmer and had the local Catholic vet give the lamb a gentle sedative. I laid the sleeping lamb on a purple cushion and put it on the altar. There before our eyes we had a living symbol of the Lamb of God. It was very moving. The only hitch was that near the end of the ceremony the lamb began to regain consciousness. It gave a little jump and a lady in the front seat of the church, who had been deep in meditation, gave a scream. Our Easter Midnight Mass was the highlight that year though. Our little church was beautifully decorated by the ladies with Easter lilies and floral wreaths. At the Attical crossroads we lit a huge Paschal fire that could be seen for miles. We were most fortunate in having visit us for the Midnight Mass an American orchestra and choir who were touring the world. The music and singing was other-worldly. The Americans had played in the previous weeks for Mother Teresa of Calcutta and for the Pope in the Vatican. And here they were now playing for us in Attical! After the Midnight Mass we all retired to the parish hall where there was tea, sandwiches and more music and singing. That Easter I felt that Christ was truly risen. We were all filled with joy and happiness. At four in the morning none of us wanted to go home. That's the way religion should be.

Kilkeel is part of a wider area which comes under the control of

Newry and Mourne District Council. Catholics are, in fact, in the majority in that Council area. The District Council is controlled by the nationalist political party, the SDLP – the Socialist Democratic and Labour Party – of which John Hume, MP and MEP, is leader. However, the town of Kilkeel has a majority Protestant or loyalist population. It's a bit like a saucer. In the middle you have Protestant, loyalist Kilkeel surrounded by a hinterland of Catholics and nationalists. This leads to a reasonably high level of inter-community tension. However, to their great credit, the nationalists on Newry and Mourne District Council had voted for a Paisleyite Councillor, Mr. George Graham, as Council Chairman for a year. Mr. Graham later left the DUP and became an independent. This SDLP generosity has not been matched by the unionist parties anywhere else in Northern Ireland.

Community tensions are always high in July and August each year during the marching season. In July the unionist bands and Orangemen march, much to the disgust of the nationalist community. In August, the nationalist or Catholic bands march and are resented and jeered by the unionists. A large presence of police is required to maintain order. Kilkeel is so utterly divided that there is a 'Protestant' and a 'Catholic' side to its main street! The Protestants walk and shop on the Protestant side and the Catholics walk and shop on the Catholic side. From the day and hour I went to Kilkeel I walked on the Protestant side to make a point to both Catholics and Protestants that such division and prejudice were terribly wrong. I was criticised, mainly by the Protestants, for this symbolic defiance of an old custom.

In Kilkeel was a barracks for the then Ulster Defence Regiment, since amalgamated into the Royal Irish Regiment, of the British Army. The UDR was both a full-time and part-time regiment, consisting mainly of Protestants and folk with unionist sympathies. They were generally resented by the Catholic population in Northern Ireland and were known to have carried out many bigoted actions. The UDR in Kilkeel were particularly difficult and poorly-behaved. They jeered Catholics in the street. They harassed men, women and children. They treated Catholics very differently at their road-blocks than they treated their Protestant friends and neighbours. They set up road-blocks just before Mass-time in Kilkeel and made church-going very difficult for the Catholic population. On several occasions during my stay in Kilkeel, I saw them with a Sunday morning road-block outside our church, their guns trained on the door, which intimidated Catholics going into Mass. I had occasion to telephone their senior officers on these Sunday mornings and have them removed. UDR patrols used to ring our Catholic church bell in the early hours of the morning to anger and disturb Catholic residents. They were particularly hard on Catholic young men and would keep them detained for hours at road-blocks, call them names, swear at them and even physically assault them. I often reported these incidents to the police but I was not satisfied with the results of the investigations. I had much contact with some UDR senior officers, men seconded from the regular British Army. Such officers told me that some UDR men in Kilkeel were 'out of control'! For complaining of the UDR misbehaviour, the local Paisleyite Councillor, George Graham, accused me, as an ex-Falls Road priest, of 'spewing out venom.' My own Catholic authorities queried my challenge to the UDR. In the absence of the Bishop, the Auxiliary Bishop, Paddy Walsh, wrote to me and asked me to explain myself as he had had reports about me. I wrote back to him sending him details and press cuttings. I also reminded him of the words of the famous Cardinal Heenan of Westminster, London, who had said: 'The only priest in my diocese that I would be worried about would be the priest no-one reported to me.' In answer to that, I received a letter from Bishop Walsh saying that he was going on retreat and would keep me in his prayers! On the UDR issue the Catholic residents of Kilkeel supported me with letters to the local newspaper, the *Mourne Observer*.

When leaving the Divis Flats in Belfast in February 1983, and during my interview with the Bishop, Cahal Daly, I had informed the Bishop that we, as a Residents' Association, had two very important projects going in which I was deeply involved – the Divis Residents' Association itself and a late-night club for the joyriders called 'The Joyrider's Rest'. I told the bishop that if these projects were to be kept out of the greedy hands of the paramilitaries then my clerical replacement in Divis would need to become involved in them. In places like Divis there are two powerful groups, the Catholic Church and the Republican paramilitaries. Bishop Daly promised me that these projects would be looked after. I left the keys of both premises with my replacement in Divis, the young Father Gregory Cormican. I was later very greatly distressed to find that, for whatever reason, the Church and the priests had taken no role in either project and that both were now firmly under the control of Sinn Féin and the Provisional IRA! I wrote to the bishop stating my horror and disappointment. He replied that he would take care of the matter. The Bishop, around that time, was incessantly talking about the 'battle for the minds and hearts' of the people between the Church and the IRA. On 9 March, 1984, the *Irish News*, Belfast, published a long letter from me on this issue titled: 'TO SAY THE TRUTH'. In it I recapped my experiences in Divis, the history of the complex and how I felt our housing and joyriding projects had drifted into the hands of the paramilitaries. I believe that this letter was directly related to my move a few months later from the parish of Kilkeel to the parish of Larne in Co. Antrim. The Catholic hierarchy are particularly sensitive to criticism, especially from within. When one does criticise, especially publicly, one can expect episcopal retribution, the famous 'belt of the crozier'. I considered my move from Kilkeel to Larne to be a belt of the crozier. I had concluded my March letter to the *Irish News* with the words of the famous Jesuit priest, Fr. Anthony de Mello: 'To say the truth as one sees it takes a lot of courage when one belongs to an institution. To challenge the institution itself takes even more courage. It was the kind of thing Jesus did.'

In August 1984 Bishop Daly sent for me and told me that he was moving me to Larne. He was unhappy about my controversies in Kilkeel and was moving me to Larne as a 'last chance'. He said I was to 'fade into the woodwork.' He added: 'When I look out on the ocean of priests I don't want to see your head above the waves.' I told him that I was very unhappy about being moved again so soon but that in obedience I would go. I said that I was weary of sharing houses with other priests. He told me that in Larne I would have a house of my own. I went to Larne in September 1984. There I did my ordinary parish work. I got on well with the people there too. I had a good relationship with the parish priest, Father Paddy McVeigh. He was a kind of fellow rebel and was late getting his own parish. Eventually I came to understand that Larne was an 80 per cent Protestant and unionist town where Catholics survived by keeping a low profile. The famous Bernadette Devlin used to say in her heyday: 'Keep your head as low as a Larne Catholic.' There was serious discrimination in employment against Catholics in Larne. I objected to this and publicised my complaints. If a priest is not interested in justice what kind of priest is he? The DUP Mayor of Larne, Jack McKee, rounded on me for complaining.

In October 1985 I had another summons from Bishop Daly asking me to come and see him immediately. I went. He met me, gave me a cup of tea and two biscuits and told me that he was not retaining me in the diocese. He asked me to tell him the date on which I would leave. He promised me a 'resettlement grant'. The figure of £5,000 was floating about and he said that he would help me to get a bishop abroad if I did not wish to return to Cardiff. I told him that I would not be going anywhere. At that stage I had been seven years in Down and Connor, had worked hard and was committed to staying. He insisted that I could not stay. We had a discussion lasting some hours. He asked me if I had read the writings of Saint Ignatius of Antioch. I said I had come across them. He said that he had read them fully, that the voice of the bishop was the voice of God and that when he thought of his position it filled him with utter humility! I came to realise that Cahal Daly really believed this 'the voice of the bishop is the voice of God' theory. I told him that he could not be faithfully representing God. God does not try to get rid of people or send them into exile. God does not do injustices to his children. I further told him that I would not be leaving Larne. 'I'm fifteen years in the Church now,' I said, 'and after all that time I'm morally entitled to a roof over my head.' He said that he would not evict me from the Larne presbytery. 'You will never force me to send the RUC into Protestant Larne to evict you. I know what eviction means in Ireland. I've learned the lessons of history.' We parted that night and have never properly met since. On one occasion a cleric said to me: 'The Bishop is wondering how you are.' 'Tell him,' I replied, 'that I'm dangerously well!' In the Summer of 1986 he wrote to me and asked me to vacate the presbytery. I refused. His secretary, Father Eddie O'Donnell, came to my door with £1,000 in an envelope on condition I surrendered the presbytery. I sent back the money, having first photo-copied the cheque should anyone ever deny he issued it. I included a note with the money saying that this new 'thirty pieces of silver' was not acceptable.

I felt that I had been done a grave injustice by a Church and by a Bishop who was always preaching about justice. I wanted to put the injustice right. I asked Bishop Daly for a Church hearing of my case. At first he refused. Then after intensive publicity he offered me a 'hearing'. The good news was brought to me by the new Vicar General of the Down and Connor diocese, Monsignor Tom Bartley. This was the structure as proposed to me:

1. The panel would consist of five priests, four chosen by the Priests' Council of Down and Connor diocese, a council at whose meetings the three bishops sat, and one priest chosen by me from a list they would give me! They suggested that I use one of the diocesan canon lawyers, Father (later Canon and Chancellor) Raymund Fitzpatrick.

2. The Bishop would meet with the panel. I could only correspond with them.

3. The Bishop would show the panel my private file. I could not see it or any of its contents.

4. I could not hear the charges, witnesses or evidence against me.

5. The panel would be bound by a vow of silence.

6. There would be no right of appeal.

7. The panel would not use the Gospels, charity or justice as a yardstick. They would simply consider the Bishop's decision in the light of Canon Law.

I declined the hearing. I said I would prefer a kangaroo court from the Provos up in the Falls Road. The provisions of this hearing flew in the face of every tenet of natural justice. It was like indicting the devil and holding the court in Hell! I would have done myself greater harm by agreeing. The Bishop could then have said that I had been tried by a jury of my peers and had been found guilty as charged. How could five Irish priests, some of them with a promise of obedience to Bishop Daly, find for me and against him? Since then some clergy have said that I was offered a hearing and refused it! They say this shows that I'm an unreasonable man. I suggested to Bishop Daly that we use the National Conference of Priests of Ireland and their reconciliation document as a way forward. Father Seamus Ryan, the President of NCPI, a Tipperary theologian, offered himself as mediator. I would have been happy to accept him. He is an honourable man. Bishop Daly declined his offer. Through all of this Bishop Daly said that he had no charges to bring against me. When asked about our dispute by the media he replied: 'No comment.' He has no comment because, in my opinion, he has no case.

Having failed to get justice within the Church I went outside it. I've always said that if you can't wash the dirty linen in private you have to go elsewhere. I applied to the Industrial Tribunal for a hearing. The Tribunal, under Judge McKee, heard my case. I was represented by the very able Mr. Oliver Kearney, the Antrim civil rights campaigner and one of the main forces behind the MacBride Principles for combating discrimination in employment in Northern Ireland. Judge McKee found that the Tribunal was not competent to hear my case because I was not an 'employee'. I was a 'sub-contractor'! I withdrew from the Industrial Tribunal and transferred my case to the Belfast High Court. I appointed good Protestant lawyers. I didn't want some 'good' Catholic lawyer who would have a conscience about putting Bishop Daly in the dock. I got legal aid. My case sat for four years on the High Court waiting list. I was happy to let it sit. I was not confident of a victory.

Eventually I had to move. Otherwise my legal aid would run out and be cancelled. My case was put down for hearing. I drew a Protestant judge Mr. Justice Campbell. I was told that he was the best I could have drawn. I liked the way he dealt with matters and I was not without hope. We didn't know if Bishop Daly would turn up for the hearing. He did. He sat at the back of the court room for the full three days smiling and talking, as is his wont, with his eyebrows. I gave evidence. The Bishop's lawyer suggested to me that I was 'imprudent'. I reminded him of Thomas Aquinas's definition of prudence: 'Prudence is that virtue by which bold men make right decisions.' The matter hung on Canon Law. Mr. Justice Campbell did take jurisdiction. The civil law will protect a citizen if a private body or club (which the Catholic Church is in law) breaks its own internal rules in its dealings with a member. Otherwise the state will not intervene. So, in order to achieve the protection of civil law I had to prove that Bishop Daly contravened Canon Law in his dealings with me. Canon Law was written by the hierarchy to protect the interests of the hierarchy. In Canon Law, popes, cardinals and bishops have immense rights. Ordinary priests do not.

In order to prove that Bishop Daly contravened Canon Law I needed a Canon Law expert. Nearly all Canon lawyers are establishment men. Many of the world's bishops have been chosen from their ranks. Canon lawyers are trained by the hierarchy to serve the hierarchy's interests in things like Church marriage annulment cases. Where was I to go to find a Canon lawyer who would support me against a bishop? I searched and found one – Monsignor Dan Shanahan, a parish priest from Essex in England, who was willing to come and give evidence for me. There was one problem. Monsignor Shanahan was ill but he came and he did his best. Bishop Daly had the Professor of Canon Law from Maynooth, Professor John McAreavy, giving evidence for him. He is a youngish man, competent in Canon Law, and Mr. Justice Campbell though kind to Monsignor Shanahan, opted for his opinion. I lost.

The intricacy of Canon Law that lost me my case was the question of 'incardination'. To be incardinated into a diocese is to belong permanently to that diocese. I was incardinated into Cardiff when I was ordained a deacon in 1975. To be later incardinated into Down and Connor I would first have to be excardinated from Cardiff and incardinated into Down and Connor. Archbishop Murphy had given me a 'Letter of Absolute Discharge' from Cardiff, which I contended was an excardination. In order to be incardinated into Down and Connor, I should have written to both Bishop Daly and the Archbishop of Cardiff at the same time, requesting excardination and incardination. If neither objected within four months I would automatically be incardinated into Down and Connor. I had written to Bishop Daly and I have a letter from him which states that he would contact Cardiff. But Bishop Daly's barrister argued in court that because I had not written personally to Cardiff I had failed to fulfil all the requirements of Canon Law and was, therefore, not incardinated. But Bishop Daly had ordered me not to write! That didn't matter. So for obeying my bishop, I was now being punished!

But I achieved two important things in the High Court. I got a civil court to take jurisdiction in a Church matter. That's a beginning. I also established the principle that a Catholic bishop is accountable. Accountability is very important. Before then Cahal Daly told me he answered only to God. Waiting on the Last Day is a long wait. There has to be accountability in this world too. Cahal Daly was a defendant who had to come to court.

A Presbyterian friend of mine, who had sat through the case, approached the Bishop. 'Mr. Daly,' he said, 'I'm a Protestant and watching what's been happening here these last few days I'm very glad the Reformation took place!' We didn't achieve a legal victory.

But without doubt we had won a moral one. And morality and faith are more important than the law to those of us who dare to call ourselves Christian.

CHAPTER 3

My Current Ministry

'I am no saint. I am a sinner, a good sinner.'

Charles Peguy

WHEN, IN THE SUMMER OF 1986, Bishop Daly removed me from my appointment as curate of Larne parish, I began saying Mass in the house where I live. On the first Sunday twenty people turned up. The numbers have gradually grown and as a result I have had to turn two large rooms into one and have created an oratory that seats about 70 worshippers. I have three weekend Masses – a Saturday Vigil Mass and two on Sundays. When it came to deciding the times of the weekend Masses I had a vote. We then had our three Masses at the times the majority found helpful.

People often ask me: 'How many do you have at Mass?' – as if numbers were important. I always reply: 'I don't run bingo. I'm not interested in numbers. I prefer quality to quantity. I prefer 20 people at Mass who really want to be there to 2,000 who might not want to be there.'

When I knocked a wall between two rooms to create space for an oratory, this created an arch. About this I joke: 'The Orangemen in Larne have an arch only during the month of July. I have an arch the whole year around,' In The Oratory I have weekday Masses attended by a small number of people who like daily Mass and communion. At present, I celebrate some 150 to 200 weddings a year – the marriages of ordinary single people, of mixed religion couples and of divorced people. Many couples are referred to me by priests from various parts of Ireland. The priests say to the couples: 'We'd love to help you but we can't. But go up to Father Buckley in Larne. He'll do it for you. But don't tell him I sent you.' I've had couples referred to me by Church marriage tribunals. Recently I had a couple who had been to talk to one of the Irish bishops about their situation. They told the bishop that they were thinking of coming to me in Larne about their problem. The bishop smiled and replied: 'If that is what your conscience tells you to do, then you must follow it.' The couple felt that it was a nod and a wink in my direction. It was nice to hear of an Irish Catholic bishop who believed in the primacy of conscience.

I have baptised over 100 children since I started The Oratory in 1986 – little 'free Catholics' I jokingly call them. Sometimes people ask: 'Are they really baptised?' The Catholic Church has always taught that anyone by pouring water can baptise. So, of course, they are baptised in the eyes of the Church. My baptism certificates are accepted by schools and parishes for entry into school and for children to make their first communion and confirmation. I have also performed a number of confirmations and, thankfully, just a few funerals. My funerals are mainly of non-Catholics, those who have fallen out with the Church or of people who have died of Aids. I am proud to be that final bridge by which marginalised people feel they can celebrate their homecoming to God. I love that Gospel story of the good thief, Dismas, who snatched salvation from Christ at the very eleventh hour. Jesus makes it clear in the Gospel that those called into the vineyard at the eleventh hour will receive the same reward as those who have laboured all day. True Christians will be glad of that instead of resenting it.

I sometimes speak of myself as 'the Red Adair of the Catholic Church in Ireland'. I tackle things that are just too hot for others. Because of my high-profile opposition to the hierarchy I get daily calls from all over Ireland about thorny problems. I'm proud and happy to be the unofficial chaplain to Ireland's liberal or alienated Catholics. Many of the things I now do will be done generally in years to come by the Church in Ireland. In the old cowboy movies the wagon train always had a few scouts – guys who would go ahead to survey the territory for the group that would follow. I'm just a scout, someone that's gone ahead. The scout has a hard and sometimes lonely mission. But it is a most rewarding one. What was it the poet said about there being two paths – the well-trodden one and the one less travelled? I like making trails. And I'm very often comforted by people who write to me in an understanding way and say: 'Stick to your guns, son. Everything will work out all right. You're just ahead of your time.'

MINISTRY TO THE OUTSIDER

I've always been very conscious of my own weakness. I sincerely say without false humility but with honesty, that in all the many thousands of confessions I've heard I've never met a greater sinner than myself

I've always regarded myself as a lame dog – someone who has to struggle to get through life. As a result I am very drawn to other lame dogs. I love the outsider, the outcast, the reject. And that love of the outsider has always been there throughout my life and ministry.

I have mentioned earlier that as a young priest I was very drawn to the work of the Legion of Mary in two hostels in Dublin – the Morning Star Hostel for down-and-out men and the Regina Coeli Hostel for down-and-out women and street girls. I spent a lot of time working in these hostels, saying Mass and helping and counselling the residents. I spent so much time with the street-girls in their hostel rooms that one or two of the more narrow-minded Legion of Mary 'sisters' suspected me of having sex with them!

A number of the prostitutes told me that they had some clerical clients. In many ways they were lovely girls. They had terrible histories of family physical and sexual abuse. And they sometimes had to do weird things. One girl told me of one client she had, a young man whose wife had died in a car accident. He used to collect the girl and bring her to his house in a wealthy Dublin suburb and make her lie in a coffin. Then he would weep for ages, relieve himself sexually and give her a generous fee. How sad a situation for the prostitute. And how sad for the grieving young man who was obviously stuck in time.

When I was in Divis Flats in Belfast I had a whole vast array of outsiders to choose from. I had a lot of contact with the down-and-out men from Belfast's Morning Star Hostel. I listened to these men, offered them tea and food and, sometimes, if they were in a very bad way, gave them a drink or money for a few pints. I also was very drawn to work with the youngsters who got into trouble with the police, and to the adults who got themselves into prison or had other problems. I have always felt drawn to the mentally ill too. And somehow by being just a human friend I have been able to bring help and comfort to some of them. For years I ran a weekly amateur therapy group for people with nervous illnesses. The group helped many of the members in various ways, including helping them to come off drugs. I have always been a regular visitor to psychiatric units. I have never forgotten that it is somebody else's turn to have a nervous breakdown today and maybe mine tomorrow. If I ever break down I hope that there will be somebody compassionate around to minister to me. I feel particularly sad about young people who develop schizophrenia. It is a dreadful illness. And sometimes the people who suffer from it are so untouch-able. They seem to be behind an invisible wall – out of reach. Not being able to reach and help someone in trouble gives me an inner pain that I cannot describe in words. At the same time, my efforts to help them are often successful. There is something about me, my own broken-ness and vulnerability perhaps, that helps me to communicate with other people in life's tight corners.

But I'm not just indulging my own inner dynamic. I have a spiritual motivation as well. Jesus said that he came into the world not for the good people but for the weak and the sinful. As followers of Christ, therefore, I think that we should have a special interest in ministry to the weak and the struggling. And then there is the other line from Scripture that says that the man who helps a brother in trouble makes up for many of his own sins. There is a sense, then, in which I feel that by showing love, mercy and compassion to others I may draw God's love, mercy and compassion on me in my own weakness and misery.

On my ordination card I deliberately had a drawing of Mary of Magdala – the famous sinner of the Gospel. I felt that she was the saint I could most identify with. On the back of the card I had the other verse from Scripture which says: 'We are only the earthenware jars that contain this great treasure.' As a student in the seminary I once committed what I regarded as a very great sin. The next day I went to confession at 7 a.m. and to 8 a.m. Mass. The priest came out and announced: 'Today is the twenty-second of July. It is the Feast of St. Mary of Magdala.' The whole thing struck a deep chord with me that has never left me. When I brought a pilgrimage a few years ago to the Holy Land we had one of our first Masses at Magdala on the shores of the Sea of Galilee. It meant a lot to me to stand and have Mass where Mary, the great gospel outsider, came from. The other saints from the Christian calendar that I like and admire are saints who have had great struggles. In ways I feel that I am involved in a great struggle.

OPPOSITION

As you can imagine I experience opposition. And people have accused me of the most amazing things. A number of years ago a small group of Protestant young people arrived at my door one Saturday at 6 a.m. They were tired, hungry and homeless. I brought them in and gave them breakfast and a temporary home. One of them, a young woman stayed for two years. A nun who had never met me made an amazing – and, of course, totally untrue – telephone call to an English priest one night. 'I know why Bishop Daly sacked Father Buckley,' she announced. 'Apparently he has a Protestant girl staying with him in the house. He is having sex with her and is sending her out to have sex with others.' So not only was I a fornicator in the eyes of that good holy sister. I was also a pimp!

I have experienced opposition from other priests who have gone to amazing extremes to put me down. Occasionally, priests feel it their duty to give sermons condemning my views and my work. Other priests deliberately spread such lies as that I am a 'silenced priest' or that I am 'excommunicated.' One priest I know in Northern Ireland received a phone call from someone who asked how to contact me. The person was told: 'There is no Father Buckley here. There is one in Wales, though, if that's who you mean.' Amazingly, someone rang me looking for the same priest and I had great pleasure in saying that there was no priest of that name in Northern Ireland as far as I knew. I know that the Lord said vengeance was his. But I'm only human. I couldn't resist the temptation.

In this context, I recall two particularly sick incidents. A lady lay dying and the family telephoned for a priest to come and anoint her. No other priest could come immediately so the family telephoned me instead. I went at once, anointed the old lady and gave her Communion. I had just finished when another priest arrived. He excused himself to the dying woman's family, took the half-melted host from her mouth and swallowed it himself. He then leaned over the lady and said to her: 'It's all right, love. You have a REAL priest with you now. I will give you the special indulgence from the Holy Father.' The lady's family was shocked.

The other occasion was this. One of my congregation at The Oratory had a young son who was to be confirmed in Larne by Bishop Cahal Daly. She put my name down as one of the child's sponsors. There was an objection to this even though there was none to other sponsors who were Protestants or so-called 'lapsed' Catholics. The mother insisted that I attend as sponsor anyway. I went up and stood with my hand on the child's shoulder. A priest who was assisting Bishop Daly stepped down, pushed me aside and, without the mother's permission, placed his hand on the child's shoulder and became the sponsor instead. The mother was issued with a certificate of confirmation to that effect.

And, of course, there is always opposition from conservative Catholic lay-people who are obviously brain-washed and who can be very vicious in their attacks – usually by means of anonymous letters and telephone calls. I have had communications from rural Ireland telling me that the Irish Freedom Fighters will be executing me for my opposition to the hierarchy. I get a number of amazing letters from devout Catholics who try to frighten, intimidate or annoy me in various ways. I'll share with you two letters from the early part of 1994.

> The Coven
> West Cork / South Kerry
>
> *Reverend Sir,*
> Accept our compliments on the great work you are doing. By promoting adultery you give us more opportunities of winning followers.
> Our Covens in the USA recruited many nuns who have the courage to defy the pope and bishops. They give a strong lead to timid people. We have to work very secretly in these parts, (I must not give name or accurate address) though we have many non-Irish who came here as 'hippies'.
> You will have read that we can use goats and cats in our work.
> Enjoy the card and keep up the good work.

The card sent shows a beautiful goat staring over a stable door and eight cats all ready to be sacrificed at a black Mass. It wouldn't surprise me to learn that that card was posted in Cork /Kerry by some good daily communicant on their way home from daily Mass in an attempt to insult, horrify or intimidate me.

Another recent letter went:

> *Dear Satan,*
> In every age and in every place Satan has his disciples. His favourite place to put his disciples is within the Church. There they can do the most harm as they are wolves in sheeps' clothing.
> You are one of Satan's biggest disciples in Ireland today. You are encouraging people to sin and go against the teachings of the Church and the Holy Father. You will burn for all eternity with all of Satan's other disciples.

Those of us who follow the True Church and the Holy Father will be in Heaven with the Sacred Heart and His Blessed Mother, The Immaculate Heart of Mary. You can spew out your doctrines from hell all you wish. I will stick to the True Church, to the Holy Father and to my daily Mass and communion. You are lost. I am safe within the true barque of Peter. A curse on you and those who go to you. Hell will not be hot enough for you all.

A True Catholic.

That letter was addressed to 'Father (???) Buckley, Larne, Northern Ireland'.

What can you say to people like that? Nothing I'm sure. Maybe they are mentally or emotionally disturbed. But they've all been through our Catholic schools. And their ability to turn out letters like that is hardly something we should be proud of. What type of spirituality have they been given?

But most of the letters I have received over the years have been of a positive and supportive nature. This one came from a priest:

Dear Pat,

I would like to let you know that I do believe that you have been treated unjustly and I support you fully in your efforts for a reconciliation with your bishop based on the inalienable principles of natural justice and not to mention the radically compassionate ethics of the Gospel.

I think your struggle is a prophetic one. It's about renewing the relationship between people and clergy, priests and bishops along the lines of Gospel witness and the teachings of Vatican II.

The Church as 'Communio' should welcome challenging criticisms such as you have made out of love for the Church. Bishop Daly's 'hearing' would have been a complete 'travesty'. For 6 years on the National Conference of Priests we have sought to secure the Irish bishops' acceptance of the Reconciliation Document. This procedure is certainly not radical but it's opposed by bishops who sadly see themselves as answerable to no one. The closed authoritarian system whereby bishops have been prosecutors, supergrasses, judge and executioner must end.

It's going to be a hard struggle!

Please be assured of my support and prayers that hearts of stone may be turned into hearts of flesh.

A Protestant man wrote:

Dear Father Buckley,

I feel I must write to you on your stand. You impress me with your forthright answers to some very straight questions. I am not of the same religion as yourself but nevertheless I feel that I should put pen to paper to tell you that I feel you are a genuine person who could do a great deal to bring our two factions together. We on the Protestant side tend to be very wary of Catholic priests but I find it the very opposite where you are concerned.

In closing I wish you all the best for your future.

From a Catholic woman I received this letter:

I have listened very carefully to all your interviews and I must say I am very impressed with the fresh air you seem to be blowing through the Church. My husband is a convert but through various circumstances we have both lapsed.

I can't in good faith receive the Sacraments, neither can he feeling the way we do.

We need the Church but not as it is at the moment. We feel that the message of Christ has been drummed out by the other noises coming from the pulpits. The original Church was people, courage and love.

We wish you every success in your struggle – you have lots of courage and love. Let's hope the bishops will have clarity of vision and charity as they deal with you.

How has the hierarchy responded to me? Well, people know how Bishop (now Cardinal) Daly treated me. He sacked me from my parish and suggested an American ministry to me. I haven't had a lot of contact with the rest of the hierarchy. As you can imagine, I'm not invited to their palaces or their conferences or functions.

I had a few meetings with the late Cardinal Tomás O Fiaich. I found him personally to be very kind and hospitable. On one occasion I had a long visit with him in his home in Armagh. He produced a very nice tray of tea and sandwiches and an even nicer bottle of Irish whiskey. But he was uncomfortable discussing controversial issues with me. He had his own private and somewhat liberal views, I think. But he was part of the structure and as a Cardinal was Rome's man in Ireland. He also had to keep an eye on the more conservative members of the hierarchy.

On the few other occasions I met Irish bishops since I became a recognised 'dissident', most of them have just nodded. Others have ignored me or failed to respond to my 'hello'. One or two have been downright rude or ignorant, deliberately slamming heavy doors in my face. Generally they strike me as a very out-of-touch bunch who are threatened by all that's happening around them. They are like ostriches with their heads in the sand. But they've left their rear ends exposed and in the changing Ireland they are, as the Americans say, getting their asses kicked. Instead of setting up structures to examine the situation and plan for change they are standing paralysed.

Recently I had occasion to visit one Irish bishop with a young woman who had just had a baby by one of the curates within his diocese. The bishop saw us for an hour-and-a-quarter. I had a round trip of 400 miles to get to him. It was a dreadful day – rain and driving wind. I was tired and cold. The young woman was nervous and weeping. The bishop never even offered us a cup of tea. I sometimes wonder if these men read the same Bible as I do, the Bible that tells followers of Christ to 'make hospitality your special aim'.

A TYPICAL WEEK

My week begins, as you would expect, on a Sunday. I have three week-end Masses which I must always celebrate myself. As a dissident I find it very difficult to get a priest to fill in for me. Occasionally the other dissident, Father Des Wilson of Belfast, gives me a week-end off. When Father Des is away I celebrate his Sunday night Mass in Ballymurphy in Belfast. One or two other priests will occasionally help but they must do so like Nicodemus in the Gospel, the man who came to see Jesus after dark.

The actual preparation for the week-end begins on a Saturday. I spend a number of hours preparing my sermon and constructing it. I also have to prepare and print my weekly bulletin. This announces the various happenings during the coming week but also has at least one thought-provoking item on it. There are other preparations to be made too – the music and singing for the Masses and the wording of the Prayers of the Faithful. Having said that, the theme of my sermon can be inspired and usually is, at any point of the week. Someone will say something or something will happen. It strikes a chord with me. I say: 'That's my sermon for Sunday.' One recent Sunday afternoon I was visiting a 75-years-old lady in a Co. Down farmhouse. She used an expression which I knew immediately would be the theme of my sermon for the following Sunday. The expression described how proud people are humbled by fate and ran: *The King will come the coggers' (cadgers') road*! It is a marvellous saying – pregnant with wisdom. I thought about it all week and preached about it the following week-end. I have developed the habit of recording my sermons on a dictaphone and a friend types them for me. Often enough I am asked for a copy of my sermon and I like to be able to oblige. Recently a lady in England, who had a dreadful fear of God, was helped by a copy of one of my sermons on the wideness of God's mercy and understanding.

After the Vigil Mass on a Saturday night I generally prefer not to go out. So I have dinner at home, a glass of wine and later a drink or two. At 9 or 10 p.m. I get undressed and watch an hour or two of television in my pyjamas with a dram or two in my fist. My television tastes are quite escapist. I particularly like police stories and court-room dramas. A good shoot-out and a car chase will have me on the edge of my chair. Nero, my Doberman (and, as I say, the only thing Roman about me), lies at my feet and finds it hard to understand my TV preferences. He can't understand why I wake him up from his slumber in front of the fire. He'll only wake up if a dog barks on the TV and he fears that his territory is being invaded.

Sunday is a busy day in my house. I celebrate morning Mass, attended often enough by couples who travel to see me about the possibility of getting married. The interviews with the couples can continue through until mid-afternoon. A sandwich for lunch is grabbed somewhere in between. The rest of Sunday afternoon is used for either study or for answering correspondence. Occasionally on Sundays I have a meeting with some members of the Bethany Revisited Group – the organisation I'm involved in for women who are or have been in relationships with priests.

If I have to celebrate Father Wilson's Mass in Ballymurphy in Belfast I will often couple that with a visit to a Belfast hospital. I must then be back in Larne for my own 8.30 p.m. Mass at The Oratory. After each of the three Masses we offer the congregation tea, coffee and biscuits. So it's often 10 p.m. on a Sunday night when I get my dinner. After that it's upstairs to the sitting-room to the pyjamas, the TV, the police drama, Nero and the night-cap. All of this time, all over the weekend, the telephone, the answering machine and occasionally the fax machine are humming.

Up to a few years ago I took no days off and no holidays. I was highly stressed and eventually my health suffered. I developed a chronic inflammatory bowel disease. It began suddenly by my having intense pain, bleeding from the rectum, serious and sudden weight loss. At first I thought I had cancer of the bowel. I was grateful then to be diagnosed as having Crohn's disease. Over the past few years I have had to have major surgery and have lost several sections of my bowel. I have also had to take an amazing amount of drugs, including large doses of cortisone. It's a wonder drug but has some very serious and disturbing side-effects. Within the very recent past, however, I have been put in contact with a professor of surgery at a London hospital. He has a fairly revolutionary approach to Crohn's disease but his method appears to be helping me and the others under his care. And I am off cortisone.

I mention my Crohn's disease, however, for a reason. No medical person will deny that, like many other illnesses, it involves an element of stress. I was not helped by the fact that for years I didn't take holidays or proper days off. So after my big operation I decided to change my way of life. Most weeks, I now disappear for two days. It is good to get away from the doorbell and the telephone and the constant barrage. But even when away I study and read. I keep in touch with my answering machine at base in order to deal with the regular emergencies.

My working week is very varied and I like it that way. I occasionally interview couples who want to be married during the week although I see most couples at the week-end. I also celebrate a number of marriages during the week, although Saturday is the favourite day. On some Saturdays in the Summer I can have up to six marriages in the one day! I jokingly say that I am the Gretna Green of Northern Ireland. Occasionally I travel during the week to conduct a wedding in Dublin, Cork, Scotland etc. I have travelled to France to conduct a marriage.

On a regular basis I visit Northern Ireland's prisons, either to see a prisoner or to perform a marriage there. Most of our prisoners in Northern Ireland are 'political prisoners'. But generally speaking, conditions in the Northern Ireland prisons are quite good. I found

Portlaoise Prison in the Republic a much stricter and more restrictive prison to visit. I have usually found the prison officers in Northern Ireland to be friendly and helpful. You will get the odd bigoted officer who will refuse to call Catholic priests 'Father' and who will give you a very frosty 'Sir' instead. But I have found those types to be rather rare. Nowadays on prison visits in Northern Ireland one is served tea, coffee and biscuits.

My most painful prison visits occurred during the dreadful hunger-strikes of the early 1980s in the Maze Prison, Long Kesh. I started going in because the leader of the first of the two hunger-strikes, Brendan Hughes, known on the Falls Road as 'The Dark', was from my Belfast parish. That first hunger-strike was called off after some 50 days. The Republican prisoners claimed that they were deceived by the British Government. I agree with them as I believe that I was present when the deception occurred. So the second hunger-strike started – the one that was led by Bobby Sands and ended in the death of the ten famous hunger-strikers.

One Sunday morning, early in that second hunger-strike, I happened to be in Long Kesh celebrating Mass in one of the compounds. These were the part of Long Kesh now gone, where the prisoners who had 'political status' were housed in compounds and controlled their own lives and days much like military prisoners do in military prisons during a war. After one of those Masses, by the way, I was once offered a choice of beverages – tea, coffee, minerals or vodka and orange! Thinking it a joke I opted for a vodka and orange. One was produced! Apparently some of the relatives had the habit of injecting the oranges with vodka before leaving them into the prisoners. All the prisoner had to do then was squeeze his orange and he had vodka and orange!

After the Mass one Sunday, a prison officer asked me would I mind bringing communion to one of the prisoners in the hospital. Of course I agreed. The prisoner turned out to be Bobby Sands. After I gave him communion I asked him if I could sit and talk to him a little. He answered: 'You can sit and talk if you don't start preaching to me about suicide and hell.' I wanted to do no such thing, of course. We had a long talk about everything and I was quickly convinced of his absolute sincerity. He told me: 'When I die I will close my eyes in this world and when I open them I will be staring into the eyes of Christ. I will be able to explain to him exactly what I did and why I did it. He will understand in a way that no-one else can understand.' There was no arguing with that. Bobby Sands believed, sincerely, that he was putting into practice the words of Christ in the Bible: 'No greater love has any man than to lay down his life for his friends.' Sands asked me if I believed that he was committing a sin in doing what he was doing. Having listened to him, I had to say: 'No, I don't believe that you are committing a sin. I don't believe that your death is suicide.' And I don't. A person committing suicide is usually in despair and wants to die. The hunger-strikers were not in despair and they did not want to die. They wanted to live. But they felt that their physical life was the last weapon they had to use against the might of the British Empire. It took great courage and bravery to do what they did. I said other Masses in the prison hospital for the dying hunger-strikers. I heard some of their confessions. I held one of them who wept over his coming death. I attended their funerals. It was one of the saddest few months of my life as a priest.

Sometimes when I visit the prisons I feel that the atmosphere there is like that in a monastery. There is an air of quiet, an air of discipline, an air of study and an air of reflection. The political prisoners I know have all come out of prison deeper and more spiritual than when they went in. In a way prison can be a crucible in which some people, especially people with intelligence and high motivation, are refined.

Every week I get calls from people who are in difficult circumstances. Occasionally I get involved in counselling someone who is homosexual. I often have to talk to families and to very conservative parents and get them to love and accept a son or daughter who has just announced that he or she is gay. This work sometimes involves coming into contact with people who are ill or dying from Aids. I've had to be a priest for a number of such men and women during their last months and weeks. And then I've celebrated their funerals. In the same circumstances, I've celebrated death-bed marriages in hospitals. This, too, is sad work but very rewarding work. It is nice to be able to offer comfort to people in such tight corners. It is good also to be able to reassure people that God cares about them and that if they are soon to meet him that they have everything to look forward to and nothing to fear.

There are many other things that happen in one of my weeks. I might be invited to take part in a debate or a discussion. And I have a fair number of calls from people in the media pursuing stories on the Church. As I write these lines today, I've already had contact with the *News of the World* in London, *The Sun* in Dublin, Carlow/Kildare Radio and the BBC in Belfast. Many priests are afraid of the media which they regard as the enemy. But the media, of course, can be used for both good and bad and if you have something to say, something you believe in strongly, then you shouldn't be afraid to proclaim it from the house-tops. The media have come to recognise me as someone who will not hang up the telephone on them, someone who will comment and comment truthfully. Added to the various other activities, I am a part-time student at Queen's University, Belfast. A few years ago I completed a Master's degree in Irish Studies and am at present researching a Ph.D. degree on the life and work of Archbishop John Charles McQuaid of Dublin. So my weeks are very varied. I'm very busy. I never suffer from either boredom or depression

In the Summer of 1971 I went with my grandmother on a pilgrimage to Rome. It was her life's ambition achieved. We attended a Papal audience. Paul VI was Pope. As he was being carried on his ceremonial chair from the audience hall I happened to be beside the aisle. I had my prayer-book in my hand. I reached out. The Pope grabbed my hand and book and spoke one strange word to me: *'Coraggio'* – courage. I'm not so foolish as to think that the Pope was telling me to have the courage to oppose the hierarchy. But it was, at least, significant for me. I think that I have had to show a certain courage. A kindly critic once said: 'Buckley, I don't ever doubt your courage; but sometimes I doubt your wisdom.' It is not easy to be in opposition. I do try to be constructive. There has to be a place for constructive opposition and criticism within the Catholic Church. At present the Pope, John Paul II, and the Vatican and hierarchy won't tolerate opposition. When Cardinal Suenens was a professor in a seminary one of his students who was struggling with doubts about the Church said to him: 'Professor, I am opposed to the Church.' The future Cardinal replied: 'Of course you are, my friend. Who isn't?' Cardinal Suenens was later one of the four Cardinal moderators of the Second Vatican Council.

CHAPTER 4

My Spirituality

And ye shall know the truth and the truth shall make
you free.

John: 8:32

IF, TWENTY YEARS AGO, someone had suggested to me that in the 1980s
and 1990s I would be living in Northern Ireland and would be an
ecclesiastical 'dissident', I would have laughed them out of the room.
I did not plan my present position. It simply happened. It was a
process. However, it is a process and a position I do not regret. There
are, of course, ways in which it is unpleasant to be an outcast.
Occasionally when I am walking through Belfast and a priest I used
to know and talk to spots me, he blushes and dodges into the nearest
shop – even if the shop sells only ladies' underwear! One time in Belfast
one such priest crashed his bike into a lamp-post as he attempted not
to have eye contact with me. I cannot understand why I inspire such
fear and confusion in grown intelligent men.

Recently in Dublin I was browsing in Veritas, the Catholic book
shop in Abbey Street. I noticed a priest and a nun in the street outside
watching me and pointing at me through the window. The priest came
in and whispered something to another priest who was also browsing.
They both turned and stared at me as if I had two heads. I suppose
that it is nice to belong to a group. I don't belong to the priestly one
any more. Sometimes I miss that a little. It was good to be able to say
Mass in a large church with a full congregation and in the atmosphere
such an occasion engenders. It was nice to be invited to presbyteries
for meals, to feel part of the clerical fellowship. I have had to sacrifice
that. I miss it a little. But it is a price worth paying to have my freedom.
And, anyway, I've always preferred the company of 'normal' people
to the company of priests!

A few years ago I visited my birthplace, Tullamore, Co. Offaly. I
happened to meet the parish priest at a function. He invited me the
following day for lunch at the presbytery. I was pleasantly surprised

and, of course, I accepted. I purchased two reasonably good bottles of wine and made my way to lunch. But it was a most painful experience. The wine was never opened. It was to be 'kept for a feast day'. And the conversation was terribly stilted and full of stress. The other priests kept their eyes from meeting mine. The talk was of sport, politics, the weather. All controversial matters, indeed all serious matters, were totally avoided. It was a very embarrassing two hours for everyone. If only it had been more natural. I would have loved it if one of the priests had challenged me directly. If only one of them had said: 'Buckley what are you doing breaking all the rules, rocking the boat and embarrassing us and the Church?' I would have loved the opportunity to explain myself and even to argue issues back and forward. But no, that would have been too real. 'If you see a pig with two heads – say nothing!'

I can hear the reader ask: Why is this man not like other priests? Why is he different? It is a very fair question. The answer is complex. Firstly I feel that I'm not like other priests. I feel that I do not fit into the clerical club. As my description of my seminary days in Clonliffe College has already demonstrated, I'm very much an individual. And individuals do not do well in a Church that sets out to destroy individuality in its students and priests.

My individuality was never broken. My personality was not capable of changing so drastically as to allow me to become an unthinking functionary. So by nature I was destined for trouble in an authoritarian Church. From my earliest days my father had encouraged me to read, to think and to question. He brought me up on a diet of Charles Dickens and Mark Twain. I identified with characters like Little Dorrit, Oliver Twist, David Copperfield, Tom Sawyer, Huckleberry Finn and Uncle Tom. Very early on I learned about the struggles the 'have-nots' had to engage in with the 'haves'. I had learned to have a scant respect for 'superiors' who look down upon and abuse their 'inferiors'. So I was schooled in that way and by the time I was eighteen and entered the seminary I was far too formed in the ways of thinking for myself and questioning to abandon my own intellect (such as it was) and to hand it over as putty in the hands of Holy Mother Church.

And from my earliest days in the seminary I noticed and disapproved of two things – the upstairs/downstairs discrimination between priest and students, and the abuse of authority – authoritarianism. In order to make it through I had to accept a certain amount. But I never owned these things in my heart and by engaging in the iconoclastic pranks described earlier I was symbolically thumbing my nose at the whole system, which to my mind was straight out of a Gilbert and Sullivan opera.

To get on in the Church – to become a parish priest, a canon, an archdeacon, a monsignor and a bishop – you have to cease to be an individual. It is rare to find an individual in the hierarchy. Bishops like Archbishop Helder Camara of Brazil and Archbishop Tutu (a Protestant, of course!) are scarce. Very many priests take refuge in dogma and Canon Law and don't think for themselves. Most of the thinking ones only go so far or keep their thoughts to themselves. How often a priest has said to me: 'Buckley, what you're saying is true – but you shouldn't be saying it!' They seem to have forgotten the words of Christ: 'The truth shall set you free.'

After ordination in 1976 I got a very rude awakening. In dioceses I worked in I saw the double standards, the double talk, the corruption, the abuse of power. I was constantly put down for being myself and expressing my true inner feelings. I had a choice. I could have given in. I could have become like the rest and joined the clerical club. I might even have been a monsignor today! I could have left the priesthood as many of the best priests have and gone away disillusioned. Or I could stay, on my own terms and in my own way, following my conscience. This is what I have done. Therefore I am still a Catholic and a priest and happy to be so. But I am a free Catholic and a free priest. And I don't have to worry unduly about Canon Law. I have the Bible. I find that a better guide.

I'm always being challenged about this approach. I'm accused of breaking my vow of obedience. Well, I never took a vow of obedience. I did make a simple promise to obey my bishop and his successors. But from the earliest times in my Catholic life, even in the old catechism, we were told that were not bound to obey commands we felt to be wrong, immoral or against God's law. The New Testament reminds us that obedience to God comes before obedience to men. I believe that my present life and ministry is pleasing to God. If some men don't understand that, then there is very little I can do about it. To me, God's will, which I know in my conscience, is more important than the will of a Pope, a bishop, a parish priest. And God's law comes before man-made Canon Law. God's law is there so that we can grow in every way. Canon Law is there to protect the *status quo* in the Church and to keep us all under subjection.

Ignorant people or bigoted Catholics shout at me: 'If you can't stand the heat then get out of the kitchen.' I have to remind them that the Church is God's family. It's not a kitchen. They say: 'If you don't like the rules then leave the club.' Again I remind them that the Church is not a club. It's a family. In every family there is diversity. There should also be tolerance. We should be able to have diversity in unity. When we don't, then it is the organisation that is to blame and not people like me who simply want to be the individual that God created them to be.

I have always thought deeply and prayed about all these matters. I have asked God to guide me. And the things I reject in the Church's policies are the things that I cannot find supported in the Bible, God's word, and in my own quiet times before God. Too many Catholics and too many priests are enslaved by the institution and by Canon Law. I am free of that particular type of slavery. And that's why I'm different from many other priests. That's why I don't fit neatly into the clerical club. That's why I find myself in the position I am in today. A few years ago, a nun friend gave me a lovely poster which depicted a young chick breaking free of its shell. The inscription on the poster was: 'Jesus sets you free to become all you were meant to be.' I believe that today I am where God wants me to be. And I'm trying to bloom where I'm planted. That means that to some I am a flower and to others I am a weed. I'm just grateful that it's God who is the gardener!

I think that the single biggest insight I've had since I joined the Church was to distinguish between the Church as God's family and the Church as an institution – the distinction, if you like, between the basics and the accidentals. Before I went to the seminary I was like many other Catholics. I saw the Church as a pyramid – with God at the top, the Pope next, then the bishops, the priests, the brothers and the nuns. The laity were what is jokingly referred to among priests as 'the lowest form of ecclesiastical life'! At that time I regarded every priest and especially every bishop and the Pope as being perfect, as being God's absolute representatives. Then I believed that when the Pope, the bishop or the priest spoke it was God who spoke. I was brain-washed into thinking like this as I went through the normal

Catholic schools. I remember my first teacher in Carlow was a big nun called Mother Carmel. I was convinced that Mother Carmel and all nuns were such other-worldly creatures that they didn't even have to go to the toilet! Later in puberty I thought about priests in the context of sexuality and I think I believed that priests didn't have any problems with sexuality. It was almost the old notion that priests had an operation the night before they were ordained which removed the sexual struggle or that God removed the urge in some other way. Wouldn't it be great and easy if that were the case!

And then I went into seminaries and entered the priesthood and the presbyteries. It came as a shock to me to see just how human priests were. They were not gods after all! I saw priests being angry and abusing people. I saw priests being pampered by nuns and laity and demanding that pampering. I knew personally of one college professor, a priest, who had a bath every Saturday night at 7 p.m. He was a very legalistic man who lived his life by the clock – right down to seconds. When he went to the bath at 7 p.m. the nun in charge of catering had to go to his bedroom, remove a vest and underpants, take them to the laundry-room and heat them with her iron and leave them back on his bed so that the minute he stepped out of the bath he could step into heated underwear! What husband would get away with treating his wife like that?

I saw priests abusing alcohol. I began to know of seminarians and priests who were sexually weak in both heterosexual and homosexual ways. I saw priests being greedy for money. Some parish priests were famous in the diocese for chasing wealthy widows, for taking unrecorded loans from them and for not revealing those loans to relatives after the death of the unfortunate widow. Other priests were famous for asking parishioners for items from their homes during their pastoral visits. Antiques are often requested by priests under these circumstances. Embarrassed parishioners, not liking to refuse a priest, often hand them over. And so I realised that priests and bishops and popes were just like the rest of us. They were human and weak. Often they didn't practise what they preached. I realised then that I should not regard the clergy as I regard God. That greatly helped me to distinguish between the basics and the accidentals.

I also realised that in this life there are more questions than answers and that the doctrines and dogmas of the Catholic Church – or any church for that matter – do not answer all questions. As a priest, I was dealing with people with very great personal problems – people in marriage breakdown, people struggling with homosexuality, women who were going to have or who had had abortions, etc. I was never able to throw the book of Canon Law at them. I always listened and hope I always had compassion. But all the time I felt trapped by Canon Law and the rules of the Church. I felt I needed to approach people and their problems in a broader way. When I looked at the Bible, particularly at Jesus in the New Testament, I did not find there the narrowness of Canon Law and Church dogma. So I began to question Church rules and dogma. I felt that the laws and doctrines of the Church had good in them and that I should not throw out the precious baby of the faith with the dirty water of the wrapping it comes in. But I also felt that something more was needed. In the New Testament Jesus interpreted the religious rules of his own day with liberality and flexibility. He ate with sinners, he picked corn on the Sabbath, he talked to outcasts. In doing so he angered the Canon lawyers and hierarchy of his day – the Pharisees. So there was my precedent and a great precedent for a Christian priest. And that led me to to approach Canon Law and dogma with a very healthy scepticism. Rules were important to Christ but people were more important and love was the greatest rule and the greatest commandment. So now when I have a problem I reach for the Bible and not for Canon Law. And I also reach inside myself. When confronted nowadays with a problem I simply ask myself, 'What would Christ do if he were here?' Then I try to do that. Sometimes what I do is in accord with Church law and teaching. Sometimes it's not. But if I sincerely strive to act in accord with God's will as I understand it, how can I go wrong? If our hearts are in the right place then we cannot go wrong. God will be pleased with and reward us for the positive things. He will give us both healing and forgiveness for our 'mistakes' and make everything all right. One of the philosophical statements from the Church that I do agree with says: 'God can bring good out of all things – even out of evil.'

I never actually sat down and decided to be a dissident. It just happened. But living as a priest in the Church and among other priests in presbyteries did radicalise me. Initially, I found I would get on reasonably well with the clergy in the presbytery. But I eventually came to see many of them as tired, and at a great distance from the parishioners. I didn't want to be like them or to become like them. For a while I tried to be diplomatic and to play a double game. I tried to please the priests and at the same time to be close to and work with the people. But that didn't succeed for reasons I've explained previously. Eventually I had to choose. I chose the people.

But I also drew very close to the parishioners. I loved them very much and became very, very deeply involved in their daily problems and struggles. That made the people love me and of course sing my praises. Comparisons were drawn between myself and other clergy and that led to difficult relationships. I suffered so much hurt during these years that it has scarred me very deeply. I know that those scars make it very difficult for me to relate well to other priests. I'm not saying that they were totally guilty and that I was totally innocent. But I do believe that I was handled very badly. So I am now a people's priest. I am not a priests' priest. I can, however, deal very well with priests on a one-to-one basis, particularly if they need me to minister to them. For instance, I have chatted in recent years to several priests who came to see me because they were involved with women. I liked helping those handful of priests. I think they found me helpful to them. They seemed to find it easy to confide in me and even use me as a confessor. It has consoled me a little that even a small number of priests like and trust me enough to let me minister to them. The priests I like best are those who have been very honest and human with me. I cannot cope with priests who play games with me.

If I were to be asked: 'What is your ambition as a Catholic and a priest?' I would have to answer: 'To live out the Gospel with my life as best I can in spite of my sins and weakness.' That means, I think, that I have to try to be a bit like Christ for those I meet and work for. In the old Catholic theology the priest was described as the *alter Christus*, another Christ. All of us as Christians and ministers should ideally, I suppose, strive to be other Christs.

I believe that Jesus was God, the Son of God. But I also believe that he was utterly human. He had a great need of people. He spent 30 of his 33 years at home. So he must have been very deeply into family. He had very close friends. St. John is described as the 'beloved disciple' and at the Last Supper John lay affectionately on Christ's breast and Jesus obviously was comfortable with that affection. So Jesus needed the deep warm friendship and companionship of his male friend John.

Jesus was also very much in need of close female contact. For rest he used to retire to the home of Martha, Mary and Lazarus. There Christ had Mary sit adoringly at his feet and from the gospels we see that their conversations must have been warm and personal. He obviously enjoyed the cooking and catering of Martha. Even in Jesus's case the way to his heart was sometimes through his stomach. And when Lazarus died, Jesus wept at his grave to the point where the crowds said: 'See how much he loved him.' Christ's other great friend was the female sinner (possessed by seven demons) Mary of Magdala. He obviously had a deep emotional, physical and sexual (I don't say genital) relationship with Mary of Magdala. She must have been rather used to 'clinging' to him. When he met her in the garden he told her: 'Do not cling to me as I have not yet ascended to my Father and your Father, to my God and your God.'

We human beings, we Christians, we priests, should be prepared to be as human and, therefore, as vulnerable as Jesus was and as expressive of our feeling and affections as he was. Too many priests are afraid of close friendship and involvement with their people. In the seminaries 'particular friendships' are discouraged. One of our professors in college, for instance, gave us the following advice: 'The priest is a mystery man. The more of a mystery man he is the more the people will respect him. I'll put it bluntly. If on the day you leave a parish after seven years ministry there and the people know less about you on the day you leave than they did on the day you arrived then your ministry there will have been successful!' So there is this great gulf between priests and people that did not exist in Christ's life that needs to be changed.

I was once reprimanded by a parish priest for bringing young parishioners to my family home to stay. He felt that if those young parishioners saw that I came from a human family with problems, if they saw me in my pyjamas or shaving, then it would lessen their respect for me as a priest. I ignored that parish priest's counsel and many other pieces of advice like that and continued to associate very closely with my parishioners. I found that it increased their respect for me. And, more than that, I found that it made them love me. If I had a choice between being respected and loved I would opt for love. You are far more likely to influence people in favour of the Gospel if the people you are trying to influence love you. Far too many Catholics respect priests out of fear. What a terrible contradiction it is for people to fear their priest – the man who is supposed to be one of their best friends, the man who is supposed to love them like God loves them.

For me, living the Gospel very much involves me in using my very humanity to touch people. I can think of a simple example. If there is a death in a house, a tragedy, I as a priest can go to that house. I can feel a bit awkward and, like the many other sympathisers, I can shake hands and say those meaningless words: 'Sorry for your trouble.' My visit will be appreciated. But I will not really get through to those in grief. But if I go and don't say meaningless platitudes but physically embrace the bereaved or sit and hold their hands and let them talk and cry then my visit will be all the more meaningful and helpful because I used my humanity and my power of affection to comfort them. That is the kind of thing that Jesus did and would have us do. I knew an old parish priest in Wales, a man in his eighties, who was called to the house where a child had died. The old Canon just sat with the mother and cried with her. Big tears streamed down the old cleric's face. Later I asked the woman what helped her most to get through the time of her child's death. She had no hesitation in answering: 'It was the fact that the Canon sat with me and cried with me and shared my grief. It was as if Jesus was sitting crying with me.' That old Canon, who happened to have an alcohol problem and who had no pastoral training in his seminary days, knew instinctively that the best way to help your people is to share your humanity with them.

So I believe that I must live the Gospel by being a friend, a best friend or a big brother to the people I serve. That means I can stay in their homes with them. It means that I can eat at their table. It means that I can go to the pub with them for a pint. It means that I can sit unshaven in my pyjamas around the breakfast table with them. It means that I can hug them, embrace them, particularly when they are in trouble. It means that I can go and sit with them when they are in hospital or when they are in prison, even if they are guilty.

I must also share my inner thoughts and experiences with others. Far too many priests behave like modern psychotherapists. They counsel people as 'clients' but never reveal their inner selves to those clients. In some circles this is regarded as the proper way to guide and counsel. It's the psychological equivalent of the priest/mystery man theory. But I don't feel this to be a legitimate approach. I know it would be important as a priest not to burden people with things about yourself that they couldn't handle. But there has to be some room for a bit of self-revelation as a way of letting people see that you understand what they are talking about. For instance, if I am talking to a parent of a mentally-handicapped child about their child it always helps to let them know that my little sister Sandra is mentally handicapped and in care in Dublin. I heard recently of a person who runs a group for the parents of mentally-handicapped children. The group organiser has a mentally-handicapped relative himself but has never revealed this to the group! Apparently this is encouraged in psychotherapy circles. I regard this approach as insincere and uncaring and unintelligent. You must share yourself with others if you are to help them without making them feel inferior to yourself. Many priests have not learned this. Of course they have not been taught it.

Another vital part of living the Gospel is to be relevant and to respond to the real needs that people have and not just some imaginary or purely spiritual needs. Father Michael Keane, the founder of the Knock Marriage Bureau, is very strong on this point. He says that when a priest is working in a community he should, with the community, identify the community's 'felt needs' and respond to those needs.

Each parish and each place has its own needs. When I was in Wales the need was to have a priest close to the community. So I organised things like prayer-meetings for the adults and camping trips for the youngsters. I also did my couple of nights in the parish club as the barman where five other priests played the music and did the singing. In Divis Flats in Belfast the needs were very different. So I became involved in the agitation for better housing and with the young people who were stealing cars. I also went out in my boiler suit to sweep the streets. In Kilkeel a big need was the need for young people from the rural areas to have something to do, particularly at the weekends. So we organised Saturday night discos for the young ones and brought 500 of them by bus to the discos every weekend. Even now, ten years later, I am always moved when passing through Co. Down to have some former disco-goer, no longer a teenager, wave at me and give me a thumbs-up salute. By celebrating the marriages for the divorced and for mixed religion couples as I do at present, I am responding to a huge felt need of people from all over Ireland, the United Kingdom and the world at large.

Gone are the days when priests can be sacrament machines. Of course we still need the sacraments. But now we must find new ways of reaching out and touching people where they find themselves at. As Father Keane says, we should identify the felt needs and respond to them. By so doing we also lead people to the sacraments, to spirituality, to the Church and hopefully to God. We could preach at a hungry man and tell him about God and his very physical hunger will render him unable to listen to us. But if we feed him without strings attached he will eventually ask: 'Why did you help me?' If we can say I did it because I am a Christian and God tells me to help my brothers and sisters, then that man is much more likely to want to know about the God who motivated us to reach out to him.

In order to live the Gospel one must also be a prophet. In popular misunderstanding a prophet is a man or woman who can foretell things that are going to happen in the future. But that's not what a prophet truly is in the Judeo-Christian tradition. A prophet is a person, who can also be a sinner, but who is in close touch with God in some way and is inspired by God in some way for some reason. The prophet has an insight that the community does not have and feels moved to share that insight with the community.

In our Catholic baptism ceremony, the priest invites the child to share in Christ's role as priest, prophet and king. We are all priests because we all offer worship. We are all kings because we are heirs to God's kingdom. But we are all also prophets. We need to be bold. We need to have something to say and say it. We need to be able to challenge and to rock the boat in order to make things better. There is very little talk in the Church about a Christian's call to be a prophet. That kind of talk is too threatening to a hierarchical patriarchal Church that wants its people to 'pay, pray and obey.'

I believe that my dissidence is a type of prophecy. I know better than anyone that I am a sinner. But I am not discouraged by that. Most of the prophets in the Bible were both sinful and neurotic. But God has told us that he chooses the weak to confound the strong and that he uses what the world considers foolish to confound the wise! If I want to speak out or to act in order to challenge the Church to change and be more compassionate, then I am fulfilling my baptism call to prophecy. But prophets are never welcome, at least not while they are still alive. What did Christ say: 'Woe to you when the world speaks well of you. That was the way their fathers treated the false prophets. Blessed are you when the world speaks ill of you. That was the way their fathers treated the prophets.' Most Catholics would agree that change is needed in our Church. But if there are not some individuals to call for change that change will not happen or not happen as quickly as is required.

THE GOD I BELIEVE IN

If you say that you are a believer or a Christian, then a god has to be at the centre of your thinking. I believe in God. I have never had a problem believing in him. I have, however, terrible problems understanding how he works.

As a child I was told in my catechism that God had no beginning. I cannot grasp that with my intellect but I have no problem accepting it. After all, to be God he must have had no beginning. Otherwise whoever made him would be God instead. Then I was told that there are three persons in one God. That's hard to understand too. St. Patrick's three-leaf shamrock is an attractive and helpful symbol. There is God the Father, the Creator, God the Son, the Saviour, and God the Holy Spirit – the spirit of Love. I don't understand, though, why we need a Trinity. Could not the one all-powerful personality have done it all? But I don't trouble myself about these matters. I do believe in God and I have no problem accepting that the Godhead has a number of manifestations – be it three or three million.

God the Father seems very remote. The image of the old man with the long white beard helps the mind slightly but he is still hard to get at. It is almost as if God the Father is like the Pope – at the top and very far away, very inaccessible to us. Jesus, the Son who came to us, is a bit more like the local parish priest. He is easier to understand and get at. The Holy Spirit is represented as a dove. He, too, is mysterious and hard to grasp. It seems that Jesus, the one who came as a man, is the easiest one to understand and relate to.

I believe in a personal God, a God who is intimately involved with each and every one of us, who listens to us and who knows even the little things that are happening to us. But he seems to be more of a 'know-er' and 'listener' than he is an actor. I cannot understand why God allows terrible tragedies to occur, why he allows children to be hurt, abused and killed, and why he allows evil people to prosper and often allows good people to suffer. If I were God I would want to use my unlimited powers to stop awful things happening, to be kind to good people and to punish bad people.

But then I think that God has an overall plan. And if he were to intervene in the world every second we would be mere robots, mere pieces in God's great chess game. I believe that in the beginning, God had a plan for the universe. I believe that that plan involved no evil, no pain and no suffering. I believe that God made mankind free and that, in some way, we abused that freedom and distorted the original plan. Hence, we now have to live in a place less perfect than God had originally planned and through our lives here we are making our way back to him and to the originally planned happiness.

But what about all the pain and suffering in the world? I got some insight into how that fits into God's plan of things by watching the film *Oh God*, which stars John Denver as an atheist and George Burns as God. God appears to the atheist in his bathroom and allows the atheist to ask questions. One question is: 'What are you doing about all the suffering in the world?' God answers: 'I have done something about it. I have given you each other.' There is a great truth in this. Much human suffering is caused by the weakness or evil of others. A great deal of that suffering could be solved if men and women did less wrong to each other and helped each other more. For instance, in the economy of God would it not be better for the European Union to send its unwanted grain to those dying of hunger rather than burn it to keep prices up? Who is responsible for those who die – God who has given us the earth to cultivate or those who burn the grain the earth produces?

I don't believe for a minute that God is a Catholic or a Christian or that he loves only Catholics or Christians. I think that your religion is merely an accident of your birth or a gift of God's providential diversity. Men and women have always searched for God. Who are we to say that we are more pleasing to God in our search than the Buddhists are? There are many names for God but there is one God. And that God loves his Muslim children as dearly as his Roman Catholic ones. And there will be room in Heaven for them all.

But what of hell? I believe that hell exists but that it is relatively empty. There is a lot of weakness in the world but not too much real evil. Many of the wrong things that are done are not done because people are evil but rather because they are weak and misguided. Weakness never brought anyone to hell. Only truly evil people go there. And when God judges, he judges by the heart and not by externals like we do. God can see the things in people's lives that have made them the way they are and God can excuse and forgive on the basis of such things. We cannot say that even Hitler went to hell. There may have been things in Hitler's life that explain why he became the monster he did. And, of course, people can repent and be forgiven in the last seconds of their lives. My dad used to quote a story to me of a terribly unjust landlord who all his life mistreated and tortured his tenants. One day out riding he fell from his horse and was killed. The people all said that he was in hell. But the story says that a little bush grew up at the place where he died and when the breeze blew through it a voice was heard saying:

> Between the stirrup and the ground,
> Mercy was asked and mercy found.

GOD'S UNDERSTANDING AND FORGIVENESS

I completely reject the God of fear that I was introduced to as a child. That God was an invention of the Church and of the churchmen. He was invented so that the Church could control people by filling them with fears and by playing on their guilt. The parish missions and retreats I attended as a child, were entertaining and awesome. Redemptorist and Passionist priests banged pulpits and convinced us all that we were bound for hell. The preaching was mainly about sin, mortal and venial, and about the occasions of sin. There was very little to uplift or make you feel good and positive about yourself or about life.

There was a special emphasis on sexual sin. Impure thoughts and impure actions, both with yourself and with others, were condemned. Those priests and confessors drove us literally around the bend with guilt. I went to confession at least once a week and always went with fear and trembling. I always felt very dirty and unworthy. All my prayers were about begging God's forgiveness. It was a very black and negative spirituality. No-one ever really told me about the unlimited understanding and forgiveness of God. I have now been liberated from this concentration on God as a policeman and a judge and executioner. For years now I have been helped in that regard by the verses written by the famous Father Faber:

> There's a wideness in God's mercy like the wideness of the
>   sea,
> There's a kindness in his justice which is more than liberty;
> There's no place where earth's sorrows are more felt than up
>   in Heaven,
> There's no place where earth's failings have such kind
>   judgement given.
> For the love of God is broader than the measures of man's
>   mind,
> And the heart of the Eternal is most wonderfully kind;
> But we make his love too narrow by false limits of our own,
> And we magnify his strictness with a zeal he would not own.
> If our hearts were but more simple we would take him at his
>   word,
> Then our lives would be all sweetness in the sunshine of Our
>   Lord.

OUR HUMAN WEAKNESS

Many people who try to lead a spiritual life regard their weaknesses as the things that lead them away from God. I see it very differently. I believe that our weaknesses, more than anything else, lead us to God and can keep us close to him. There is a huge distinction between weakness and badness. There is, of course, some of both in us all. But if we are sincere in our relationship with God, then he forgives us our badness and gives us healing for our weakness.

The greatest sin of all, or so we are told, is the sin of pride. Those who think that they are without sin are guilty of pride. But they are not the only guilty ones. What greater pride could anyone have than to think that one is capable of committing a sin so big that God would not be capable of forgiving it? We are all sinners. But as soon as we ask God's forgiveness then we are immediately forgiven. When we human beings forgive we sometimes say: 'I'll forgive but I'll never forget.' But when God forgives he forgets. If I committed a murder on a Saturday afternoon and sincerely repented at teatime and then died on Saturday night and went before God, I might tremble and say to him: 'What about the murder, Lord?' God would answer: 'What murder? There's no record of any murder here.' God's forgiveness is absolute.

Our weaknesses do have very positive fruits when we handle them properly. St. Paul had a weakness – his famous 'thorn in the flesh'. Three times he asked God to take it away and three times God refused. God told Paul that he would give him strength in his weakness. Paul later declared: 'Of what shall I boast? I shall boast of my weakness. For when I am weak then I am strong.' Our weaknesses, properly handled, make us more humble; they make us realise that we must depend on God and not on our own strength. Our weaknesses also make us more compassionate to others. Who understands an alcoholic better than another alcoholic?

Some years ago, sitting in a church and reflecting on the great weakness within myself, I wrote the following lines:

> Father, be an eagle to me
> My wilderness is not sand or moor or marsh
> It is not a place of withered bushes
> Blowing wildly in a howling wind;
> It is not a region of dead trees, rocks,
> Or barren crusty soil.
>
> My wilderness is more frightening,
> It is within;
> A desert of desire, temptation, weakness, self-indulgence and sin
> It holds me spellbound.
> I want to leave it and I don't
> I am trapped.
> A prisoner.
> A slave.
> Like the Israelites, I enjoy the fleshpots of Egypt.
> Father in Heaven, Divine Eagle,
> Swoop on me.
> Snatch me in your claws.
> Drag me screaming from this living hell.
> Pierce me.
> Shake me to the roots
> With all the violence of your love for me.
>
> Throw me on your back
> And carry me away to your place.

Make me the apple of your eye.
Watch over me.
Hover over me.
Guide me.
Be with me as there is no other God.

Father, Heavenly Eagle,
Until you snatch me I shall be imprisoned.
Until you claw me I shall be torn.
Until you carry me I shall be paralysed.
Until you crush me I shall be broken.
In your great love,
Force me
To be my real self
And to love you.

There is a huge difference between evil and weakness. Evil will bring you to hell but weakness never will. There are, thankfully, a limited number of evil people in the world. We are all very weak. But somehow our weakness is our greatest strength!

PRAYER

As Catholics we have been given a most awful introduction to prayer, which has made prayer boring and impossible for most Catholics. Through traditional praying God was inaccessible. We were all trained to pray by saying hundreds and thousands of Hail Marys, Our Fathers and Glory Bes. We were also trained in the use of novenas, rosaries and prayer-books. We were told that the Mass was the great prayer. All of this was very mechanical. It led to boredom and eventually many people gave up praying or trying to pray. Most people feel a failure at prayer and this worries them. People often say to me: 'Father, I can't pray. But I do talk to God for a few minutes at night when I get into bed.'

They don't realise it, but their bed-time chats with God are real prayer – much more a prayer than the rosary in many ways. Prayer should be a conversation with God. That involves talking. But it must also involve listening.

I like to say Mass or attend Mass. When I am there I am very conscious that I am communicating with God – saying prayers to him and listening to him speaking back to me through the readings, sermon, etc. I also like to read the breviary – the Prayer of the Church. I can talk to God and listen to him through the psalms and the readings. Very occasionally I like the rosary. I sometimes say it for old times' sake. I also occasionally like to make novenas or to do the stations of the cross. All of this is prayer. But there is no alternative to holding a conversation with God.

I try to set some time aside to go to a church or a quiet place where I will just sit and talk to God. Or I will bring in a note-book or a piece of paper and write God a letter. I find writing to God particularly helpful. I communicate best in writing. So why not use that method with my friend, God? A conversation has to be two-way but it must also be free and spontaneous. If I decide to talk to God at 3 p.m. on a Monday why should I assume that God should have to answer me at 3.05 p.m.? I should say what I have to say to God and then be silent. If he wants to speak to me then, he will. If he wants to be silent and communicate with me later, he will do that and that will be fine. We can never force communication out of anyone – and especially out of God. No-one loves us more than God. But no-one refuses our attempts to manipulate as much as God does. Sometimes God will answer us immediately. But often he will delay for his own reasons. People complain that God never answers their prayers. But that's not true. God always answers. But we are not always listening. We should stay tuned into God – 24 hours a day. We should keep our receiver turned on. And then God, often in a surprising way, will communicate with us and answer us. God is the God of surprises. I have learned some lessons in this area.

Every day, when I was a curate in St. Peter's in Belfast, overworked and unhappy in the presbytery with the other clergy, I went and sat in the cathedral to pray, to communicate with God, to have my batteries renewed. One day in particular, I was feeling especially sad, vulnerable and needy. I sat about five rows back from the front of the cathedral. I prayed for an hour and begged God to give me some little sign, some little touch, some little consolation. But nothing came. I was answered with a great silence. I was revolted by God's lack of response. I was thirsty and I wanted to turn on God's tap there and then. But nothing came. As I left at the end of the hour I was revolted with God. When I thought about it, I felt that I wanted to vomit at the thought of this God.

An hour later I went downtown in Belfast to play a game of squash with one of our youth club workers. I had a good game and afterwards had the gents' changing room to myself. I was in the shower. And then something happened. Words are very inadequate but I will try to describe the experience. The shower suddenly became somewhere else and nowhere in particular. There was a great brightness that came from no light I know. I suddenly felt warm, relaxed and very peaceful and happy. It was as if I was transported to a bit of heaven. A voice spoke – not into my ear but into my heart. The voice said: 'You wanted to be touched and consoled. I am now touching and consoling you. You see that water flowing from the shower refreshing you and falling from your hands. Well, my love for you is the same. It falls on you, refreshes you and falls on others from your hands.' That's all that happened. But I had tears in my eyes and goose-pimples as big as duck eggs. As I drove home I was on air. God had answered my prayer, not in the cathedral but in the sports complex changing rooms. He had not talked about the things I had talked to him about. But he had squeezed my heart with his hand. I learned that evening to wait on God who will respond in his own way and in his own time. Psychologists and atheists will say that the whole experience was a concoction of my own mind and needs. They are wrong. In the shower I encountered God and it made all the difference.

Of course, not all conversations between friends are friendly. There must be a place for disagreement and anger. If we are truly praying then there must be times when we can express our anger with God to him. Otherwise we have a very unreal relationship with God.

The prayer of anger once worked for me in a rather spectacular way. When I was a curate in the parish of Briton Ferry in Wales, my uncle telephoned me one night. My cousin was in trouble with the Garda for some petty crimes. Would I take him to Wales and get him a fresh start? Of course, I agreed. But it was very difficult. We had a very small presbytery of only three bedrooms and we had two priests and a housekeeper. But my cousin came over and we squeezed him in. The situation was tense. For three full weeks I did little or nothing else but try to find my cousin a job and a place to live. I failed miserably. Each day, too, I prayed hard for a solution but none came. One morning after three weeks I went back into the church after Mass and stood in front of the tabernacle. I was very angry with God. 'Thanks for nothing.' I said. I bitterly complained to God about the fact that I was doing my very best for him as a priest but that he had totally ignored my prayers about my cousin's needs. I was very aggressive in my prayers and used the 'fuck' word more than once! I stomped off into the presbytery for my breakfast. The telephone rang. It was a local hotel. They had an interview for my cousin for a job as a part-time barman. I drove him for the interview. He emerged from the hotel and I jumped out of the car and enquired: 'Did you get the barman's job?' 'No,' he answered. I was totally downcast. 'But they offered me a different job,' he said. 'They want me to be trainee manager and there's a flat going with the position!' My problems were solved. In one fell swoop my cousin had a good job and a good place to live. I went back to the church and stood once again in front of the tabernacle. thanked God for helping. But I also said: 'I can't feel sorry for being angry with you and for swearing at you. After all it seemed to take that to get you to swing into action. So, if that's what it takes, you can expect more hassle from me!' Seriously, I feel that God sometime allows us to get to the end of our own rope before he intervenes. But he respects those who believe in him enough to talk straight to him.

Prayer should be conversation with God. You can talk to him or write to him. You must listen and he will always answer. Sometime he will surprise you by the way he answers. There is room in prayer for expressing to God your frustration and anger.

But, above all, our relationship with God is sweet and comforting. On 6 June, 1981, I attended the ordination of a friend in Cleator Moor in Cumbria in the Lake District. It was the fifth anniversary of my own ordination. When the crowd left, I stayed for a while in the church just to reflect on my own priesthood and on my relationship with God. took a pen in my hands and these words flowed – without hesitation or correction:

> ### Tingling
> Jesus, Lover, precious brother friend,
> Human words seem all in vain;
> Place your saving ear to sinful lips,
> Let me kiss and whisper to your heart.
>
> Pleasure fills my body as I think
> On you, I desire your body Lord;

Eucharist thrills, as does my brother,
Your holy flesh all around the globe.

Sometimes you are far away,
And I feel that I am going to sink;
I talk about you all out there,
But now you are everywhere on me.

Jesus, Jesus, passion to me now,
The thoughts of you are tingling me;
Tears of happiness I want to have,
Hold me close and squeeze me whole.

I must end as I cannot show,
The things you mean to me today;
This moment now belongs to heaven,
A sun is a gap between two clouds.

At times I have felt very barren and empty at prayer. At other times, like in the Belfast shower or the Cleator church, I felt touched by an indescribable love. The good times in prayer, rare as they are, more than make up for the long hungry journey of the rest of the time. My favourite 'set' prayer is one I found some years ago in a Passionist monastery in Co. Down.

I Kiss The Wounds

I kiss the wounds on your sacred head
With sorrow deep and true
May every thought of mine today
Be a thousand acts of love for you,
Of love for you, dear Lord.

I kiss the wounds on your sacred shoulder
With sorrow deep and true,
May every cross I bear today
Be a thousand acts of love for you,
Of love for you, dear Lord.

I kiss the wounds on your sacred hands
With sorrow deep and true,
May every task I do today
Be a thousand acts of love for you,

Of love for you, dear Lord.

I kiss the wounds of your sacred feet
With sorrow deep and true,
May every step I take today
Be a thousand acts of love for you,
Of love for you, dear Lord.

I kiss the wounds in your sacred heart
With sorrow deep and true,
May every beat of my heart today
Be a million acts of love for you,
Of love for you, dear Lord.

I have always made contact with God best through suffering – either through contemplating on the sufferings of Christ or by reflecting on my own sufferings and their possible meaning.

DISCOVERING GOD WITHIN

Most human beings are on a spiritual journey even if they neither know nor admit it. St. Augustine said: 'Our hearts were made for you, O Lord, and we shall find no rest until we find it in you.' Every human being is in search of meaning, in search of his or her God. As Catholics, adherents to a religion of dogma and externals, we have been trained to look for God 'out there'. And so we try to find God in dogmas, in ritual, in hierarchy, etc. And no doubt these things are reflections of aspects of God. But very often they lead us to know about God rather than know God.

God can certainly be known through external things – particularly through other people and through nature and the environment. But the really close encounter with God comes when we encounter him within the agonies and the ecstasies that exist within our own hearts and heads. Mankind's trips into outer space have certainly let us know more about God's wonderful creation. But it is only the voyage into our inner space that really introduces us to God. Most people, sadly never make this journey and are not encouraged to.

I have always been interested in the inner space. As a shy and self-conscious child and teenager, I spent a great deal of time on my own reflecting about myself. I found that very lonely and very painful. But it did introduce me to a way of connecting with myself and with

God that I might have otherwise missed.

Some years ago, I went on a two-week course in Primal Therapy with Dr. Frank Lake of Nottingham. Using his own controversial methods he brought me back to experience my time in the womb and to relive the experience of being born. I learned a lot about myself and the darkness that was within. I was able to return home and tell my mother things about my birth that she had forgotten! I can make a very definite connection between the panic I experienced in the womb at being thrust out into the world and the panic and insecurity I sometimes feel in my so-called adult life. The singer Sinead O'Connor has been criticised for talking about the wounded child within herself and others. Primal Therapy put me in touch with the wounded child within me. It also put me in touch with aspects of God and spirituality that only suffering can. I have continued throughout my life to take counselling and spiritual guidance. It is only by engaging in this journey that we can really find God.

For instance, there is a suffering involved in being a first-born child. Most first-borns will know about this. While with Dr. Lake I discovered a poem by David Boadella that dealt with the pain of the first-born. I can identify with it very strongly:

> *First Born*
> When a child walks alone, it may not be only, but older.
> Whoever was first born was only, once,
> No matter how many came after,
> And sometimes colder,
> Due to exposure perhaps
> Pushed out in front, sometimes severe
> As a pioneer.
>
> Why do we treat our first born so?
> Wearers and bearers of all our errors,
> Of all we did not know.
> So perhaps they are right, these older children,
> Thrust,
> First,
> Solemn as outcasts,
> Into the tangled world where dreams cannot comfort,
> And cuddly bears are clung to,
> To scorn their poor, their apprentice mothers.

The late-born are rosier.
Their months at the breast were less experimental.
Something resembling home had begun to grow
Out of earlier failures, when they were still toddlers.
The cuddly bears were more dispensable.
So they remained young even in old age,
And kept hopping from day to day as a child will,
Crossing a river on bright stones.
They are not in our debt still.

Pity our grown-up babies who were never quite young,
Those we carried too long or too wrong,
Whose tears are stuck,
Who are married to a kind of hard luck
Where even success may not be a blessing;
Who took the first breath, but are nearer to death.
They may live to be blazers of trails,
Seared perhaps with the mind's flame,
Or pale with fierce desire.

But it will not come easy,
Nor ever so cosy
For them,
Round the fire.

I have discovered God by wrestling with many of the thing
mentioned in this poem. If anyone asks me now how they can fin
God, I tell them to begin to look within themselves and to be prepare
to continue looking within for the rest of their lives. My father was
wrestler with God. As I have written earlier, he went to Mass sometime
and at other times stayed away for years. He prayed sometimes an
at other times railed against God. He was a spiritual man but not
pious man. When he died, I specially chose for his funeral Mass th
Old Testament reading describing Jacob wrestling with God's messe
ger for a whole night. God respected Jacob for his honest wrestlin
God respects us too when we lock horns with him in our feeb
attempts to communicate with him and believe in him.

SUFFERING

We get close to God either through reflecting on the sufferings of Jes
or by reflecting on our own sufferings in the context of Jesu

sufferings. Jesus suffered in four basic ways. He suffered physically, mentally, spiritually and socially.

Jesus's physical sufferings lasted over his whole lifetime of 33 years. He was born in a stable. To be deprived of a decent place in which to leave the womb was to my mind a great physical suffering. Then King Herod wanted to kill him and he and his parents had to flee to Egypt. To be deprived of your homeland is also a great physical suffering. Jesus lived in poverty and simplicity at Nazareth. Poverty, as the poor know, is a great physical suffering. Jesus was homeless – Foxes have holes and the birds of the air have nests but the Son of Man has nowhere to lay his head.' Homelessness is a great physical deprivation. Finally, in the last days of his life, Jesus suffered physically in a most intense way. He was arrested. He was given a mock trial. He was beaten, jeered, spat upon and finally murdered in a cruel way. What greater physical suffering is there than to have your very life cruelly removed?

Because he suffered so much physically Jesus understands our physical sufferings. Therefore, we can identify with him in our homelessness, our poverty, our hunger, our sickness, our pain and eventually our death. I have spoken already of my own illness. Since 1986, I have had daily pain and bleeding. I have been to hospital for surgery. I have had drugs with dangerous and ugly side-effects. For the rest of my life I will have to live with daily diarrhoea and all the social problems that involves. I am very positive about my illness and anxious to co-operate with the doctors for help and an eventual cure. But knowing that Christ suffered physically helps me to cope with my illness. Everyone can do that – people who are more ill than I am and those who are less ill.

Jesus suffered mentally, and mental suffering can be more painful and more isolating than physical suffering. Even in physical suffering you can find peace of mind. But when the suffering is in your mind it can be most terribly distressing. Jesus suffered mentally. He was so tense, nervous and afraid in the Garden of Gethsemane that we are told he sweated drops of blood. On that occasion, he was afraid to be on his own. So he brought friends with him to keep him company. Those friends fell asleep and so Jesus knew the mental pain of intense loneliness and isolation. There were other times in Jesus's life when he experienced intense mental pain. For instance he knew grief. When his friend Lazarus died Jesus wept openly. On Calvary, Jesus's mental suffering was far more intense even than his physical suffering. One can only imagine the mental horrors that attend that kind of death.

So Christ, from personal experience, can identify with us in our mental sufferings. In my life to date, I have experienced panic, anxiety, fear, insecurity. Knowing that Christ went through the same and more helps me to cope with those mental sufferings when they happen to me. Jesus's mental sufferings give us courage and meaning in our panics, fears, depressions, nervous breakdowns, etc.

Jesus suffered spiritually. He was at once both God and man. We cannot even imagine the pain and the contradiction of being both God and man. And Jesus was absolutely human. He found it difficult to fulfil his spiritual mission. In the Garden of Gethsemane he prayed: 'If it be possible, let this chalice pass me by.' He was afraid of what God the Father was about to ask of him. On the cross of Calvary, Jesus teetered on the brink of despair. He felt abandoned by God and man. He prayed: 'Father, why have you forsaken me?' Jesus was in the desert of forsakenness.

When we suffer spiritually through doubts, inability to pray, despair, the feeling that God is far away and doesn't really care, we can take courage from the fact that Jesus went to the very spiritual limits. The film, *The Last Temptation*, which shallow fundamentalists have condemned, is a great parable about the suffering human Christ. Watching that film strengthened my faith. It introduced me more to the real Jesus that any statue or gaudy painting could.

Jesus suffered socially – through rejection. His rejection began in the womb. There was no room at the inn for him to be born. He had to flee to Egypt to escape death as a baby. During his ministry his own people in Israel rejected him. Family members, the Gospels tell us, thought that he was mad. He was rejected by the religious leaders of his day.

When we are rejected – by our families, our communities and by our churches and religious leaders – we are sharing in Christ's own lot. The fact that he was rejected helps us to cope with the many rebuffs we experience. In that sense to be rejected, especially by the religious leaders, is a sign of God's favour! Dietrich Bonhoeffer, who suffered greatly for his faith and who was executed for it has said: 'Jesus makes it clear, beyond all doubt that the "must" of suffering applies to his disciples no less than to himself. So the disciple is a disciple only in so far as he shares his Lord's suffering and rejection and crucifixion.'

Suffering makes us closer to God. Through suffering we share in Jesus's lot. Suffering reduces our pride and makes us realise that we depend on God and not on our own strength. Suffering also makes us more compassionate to others. When we struggle ourselves we share the lot of suffering humanity. Jesus said: 'No man can be my disciple unless he takes up his cross everyday and comes after me.'

One of my favourite saints is St. John Vianney, the Curé d'Ars, and the patron saint of priests. He suffered greatly, physically, mentally, spiritually and socially right throughout his life. On one occasion he said: 'Contradictions [sufferings] place us at the foot of the cross. The foot of the cross is the gate of heaven. To get there we must be trampled upon, vilified, despised and broken.'

One time there was a meeting between the bishop and the priests of the diocese where John Vianney worked. One of the cynical priests complained: 'My Lord, Father Vianney is mad.' The Bishop thought for a moment and replied: 'I wish the rest of you were half as mad!'

Many books have been and could be written about suffering and how it bears fruit in the spiritual life. Some years ago I found a poem by Stephen Phillips that says it all. Suffering is a sign of God's favour on us:

> Unshunnable is grief; we should not fear
> The dreadful bath whose cleansing is so clear.
> Who gave unto the Moon that hopeless quest?
> Condemned the wind to wander without rest?
> He, as I think, intends that we shall rise
> Only through pain into his paradise.
> Woe! woe! to those who placidly suspire,
> Drowned in security, remote from fire;
> Who under the dim sky and whispering trees
> By peaceful slopes and passing streams have ease;
> Whose merit is their uncommitted sins.
>
> Who watched the falling, yet who never fell,
> Shadows not yet ascended into Hell.
> No sacred pang disturbs their secular life.
> Eluding splendour and escaping strife.

They die not, for they lived not; under earth
Their bodies urge the meaner flowers to birth;
Unstung, unfired, untempted was their soul,
Easy extinction is their utmost goal.
To those whom he doth love God hath not sent,
Such dread security, such sad content;
Young are they carried to the font of pain,
In coldest anguish dipped again, again,
Or else unto his burning they are led,
Desirous of his glory to be dead;
When he ascends like Semele they die,
Proud to be shrivelled in his ecstasy.

But he hath branded on such souls his name,
And he will know them by the scars of flame;
As Christ, in the dark Garden, had to drink
The brimming cup from which his soul did shrink;
As Dante had to tread the world of fire,
Ere he approached the rose of his desire;
So fear not grief, fear not the anguish, thou
The paining heart, the clasped and prostrate brow;
This is the emblem, and this is the sign,
By which God singles thee for fields divine;
From such a height he stoops, from such a bliss,
Small wonder thou dost shudder at his kiss.

PRIESTHOOD

I like being a priest as much today as I did when I first started. I ha
been very hurt and rejected by the clergy and the hierarchy. But th
does not take away my love for the priesthood and my faith. I ha
been horrified by all the bad things I have found in the church
particularly by the terrible cynicism and unkindness I have seen.

Nowadays, the romantic shine has gone off the priesthood for m
My motives for staying are probably more pure than my motives
entering. I have a lot of problems understanding how God works k
I do feel that I love him and want to serve him, whatever that mea
I also love people, especially people who are in difficulty and I w:
to love and serve them too. So I want to stay a priest to love and ser
God and others. I'm not totally unselfish in this. I am aware that I
a lot of kicks and satisfaction by helping others. But should one st

doing good because one enjoys doing it? There must be very few people in the world who do good for absolutely pure motives.

I see my life as a priest as a call to be everybody's big brother. One of my great inspirations in life and in the priesthood has been Charles de Foucauld, a young French Catholic from a reasonably wealthy family. By the time he was fourteen years old he was orphaned and had lost both his parents. He was brought up by his grandfather. But he lost his faith in God and for many years devoted himself to a life of extreme sensuality. By the time he was 26 though, he was to declare: 'I am a young man for whom it is all over.' He was totally depressed and disillusioned with his life of materialism and sensuality.

He found a priest in Paris who heard his confession and led him back to his faith. Charles then became a monk and finally a priest. He went to the Sahara desert and spent the rest of his life ministering to the famous Tuareg tribe. He had a little hermitage at Tamanrasset. He received up to 160 visitors a day – the hungry, the spiritually hungry and the curious. Charles received them all. His spirituality revolved around two simple things – worship of God through prayer and the Eucharist and offering hospitality to every man and woman who came his way. He contended, and I agree, that in prayer and hospitality he had two ways of worshipping the same God. If Charles was at prayer and a needy brother or sister came to his door, Charles left his prayer to help the caller but regarded his prayer as having being unbroken. So kind and compassionate was he that the locals nicknamed his hermitage: 'La Kawah' – 'the place where everybody's brother lives'. I believe a priest should be everybody's brother. Being the oldest of 17 children has given me an ideal training to live like that.

The Apostles' Creed and the Creed we recite at Mass are limited. I can summarise my spirituality, the spirituality that inspires all I think, say and do, in my own personal Credo:

I Believe

I believe that in this world it is impossible to understand God.

I believe that God made this wonderful universe and all that exists.

I can find God in nature, in animals, in birds and the environment.

I believe that God made all men and women,

That he made them all equal
And that he loves and cherishes them all equally.
I believe that the whole human race is the family of God.
I believe that there may be intelligent life on other planets
And if so they too are part of God's family.
I hold that religion and faith are two different things,
That religion can be both good and bad
And that it is spirituality that counts.
For me your religion is an accident of your birth
Or a gift of God's great providential diversity.
There is no one true church.
All churches and all religions contain aspects of the truth.
But only God is Truth.
No man in infallible.

A Buddhist or a good atheist is as acceptable to God as a
    good Catholic.
I believe that sex is good and so is the body.
The only sexual act that is sinful is the one that uses or abuses.
I believe in people, especially suffering people.
I believe in the power of weakness.
I believe that all men and women will be saved.
I believe in a packed heaven and an empty hell.
And even Satan might get another chance.
I believe in the freedom of God's sons and daughters.
I believe that dogma is often evil.
I believe that life is a journey towards God,
And that no one has the right to insist you go a certain road.
I believe that God and reality are too big for my poor words,
I believe therefore that I am only at a beginning,
    Only knocking at a door,
    And I believe that the best is yet to come.

We can all get spiritually lazy. Keeping ourselves spiritually fit and healthy is a lifetime's work. It's easy to dry up and to become cynical. Real human beings and real Christians live with a passion right throughout their lives. I have always been inspired by these words of Josiah Holland:

God give us men!
A time like this demands strong minds,
great hearts, true faith and ready hands;
men whom the lust of office does not kill,
men whom the spoils of office cannot buy,
men who possess opinions and a will;
men who have honour,
men who will not lie,
men who can stand before a demagogue
and damn his treacherous flatteries without winking!
Tall men, sun-crowned,
who live above the fog
in public duty and in private thinking.
For while the rabble,
with their thumb-worn creeds,
their large professions and their little deeds,
mingle in selfish strife,
lo! freedom weeps,
wrong rules the land
and waiting justice steeps.

I hope that throughout my life I will try to become like Josiah
Holland's men.

CHAPTER 5

The Catholic Church –
an Inside Perspective

His creed no parson ever knew,
For this was still his 'simple plan',
To have with clergymen to do
As little as a Christian can

Sir Francis Hastings Charles Doyle

UNTIL RECENTLY THE IRISH and Polish Catholic churches were regarded by the Vatican as the two flag-ships of the Catholic world. The Church had a strong hold in each country and their hierarchies were the most obedient to Rome. Things have come a little unstuck in the flag-ships though. Poland is now known to have carried out 600,000 abortions a year and there are few things as abhorrent to the Vatican as abortion. It has also emerged that many Polish priests are not as faithful to clerical celibacy as had previously been thought and now there are many so-called 'nephews' and 'nieces' hanging around Polish presbyteries. On top of all of this Poland's strongest link with Rome, Pope John Paul II, has cancer and, in his 70s, is on the way out one way or the other.

In Ireland, the writing is also on the wall. There is a huge push on to liberalise Irish society. Contraception is more available. Abortion is a contentious public issue and is not without considerable support. Divorce is on the way and the Irish government liberalised its legislation on homosexuality. The speed towards change was accelerated in May 1992 by the unexpected bombshell of the Bishop Casey affair.

This affair was the death-knell for Irish bishops pontificating on sexual matters. More than anything else, it undermined the hierarchy's claim to moralise to the rest of the population. The news of the Casey affair will be seen by history as the catalyst that removed the Irish bishop's moral monopoly and, in that respect at least, it was a happy fault.

THE POPE

Voltaire said that if God did not exist it would be necessary to invent him, because of humanity's need of a god. If the Catholic Church did not have a Pope, it might also have had to create one because of an organisation's need to have a unifying figure-head. Pope John Paul II is the worst kind of Pope the Catholic Church could have at this time in its history. The Catholic Church was a bit spoiled with Popes since the late 1950s. There was John XXIII who began the renewal of the Second Vatican Council and who was universally loved by Catholics and non-Catholics alike. The son of a peasant from rural Italy, he exuded compassion. People knew in their hearts that he cared about their human problems and that he was not at all like the sub-human cardinals and other clerics who surrounded him in the Vatican civil service, the so-called Curia.

When John XXIII went we got Paul VI. Paul was very different from John. But he was not an arrogant dictator by any means. He seemed to worry about the responsibilities of being Pope, a lonely man in a job he found agonising. In 1968 he disappointed the Catholic world with his encyclical *Humanae Vitae* on contraception. Many Catholics, from theologians to laity, had expected a relaxation of the Church position. The commission of experts assembled by the Pope to advise him recommended a change. But it did not come. The Pope took his own lonely and crazy decision. Many people were shocked. Some left the Church. Many of those who stayed behind continue to ignore the teachings of *Humanae Vitae* and quite right, too. Pope Paul VI didn't make a big impression on ordinary Catholics. He was there and that was simply it. In fairness to him he did bring John XXIII's Second Vatican Council to a conclusion.

After Paul VI we had Pope John Paul I for 30 short days. He captivated the world by his smile. The Church seemed to be getting another, if somewhat slimmer, John XXIII. He didn't last. Within a month he was dead. In Rome, the rumours were flying. He was supposed to have written 'Ireland deserves better' on the file proposing to make the then Archbishop Tomás O Fiaich of Armagh a cardinal. Another rumour had it that the night before he died he issued a list of those who would have to go, cardinals included, from the Vatican. Several versions of who found the dead Pope were circulated. One said it was the nun-housekeeper bringing him his breakfast. Another said that it was his secretary, Monsignor John Magee from Newry in Co. Down and the present Bishop of Cloyne in Cork. There was no post-mortem. Popes don't have them. That fuelled further suspicion. David Yallop published his book *In God's Name*. The Vatican never responded. I was impressed with the Yallop book. It certainly left me wondering if the Pope had been murdered. I believe that something strange happened. A few people know the truth but I doubt if they'll ever tell. Truth is a very regular casualty in the Church of Rome.

And then another kind of disaster struck. We got John Paul II from Poland. In the beginning, we all liked and loved him. I personally brought four bus-loads of young people to see him in Galway. At that Mass I was standing near a crowd of skin-heads from Dublin. After John Paul said: 'Young people of Ireland I love you,' one of the skin-heads was crying. He turned to me and said: 'Did ye hear that? He fuckin' loves us.' John Paul was young for a Pope. He swam and walked and climbed mountains. He began to travel. He was good at touching people and lifting and hugging babies.

But soon we discovered the real man behind the globe-trotting public relations facade. He reiterated traditional teaching on contraception. He demanded the removal of altar girls from the altar before he went out to say a Mass in the US. He condemned homosexuality. He was opposed to the ordination of women. He stopped priests getting dispensations to leave the active priesthood to marry. He retained the strict obligatory celibacy laws of the Church. He came out against the Church becoming involved in politics except, hypocritically, in Poland. He shouted his congregation down in Nicaragua when they demanded radical liberating Catholicism. He lectures the starving and poor exploding populations of Africa and India about the evils of contraception. He is opposed to liberal theology and has had his inquisitors in the Vatican put several world-famous theologians on trial.

The globe-trotting charismatic Pope is at heart a dictator who demands absolute obedience and blind faith. He behaves not like God's representative but like a tyrant-god. One of the Pope's titles is 'The servant of the servants of God'. Pope John Paul II is no one's servant but demands that all serve him without question. In my opinion he is a walking example of power and authority gone wrong, living proof that absolute power corrupts absolutely. I find his style of papacy totally repugnant. If I were to meet him I know I wouldn't agree with him for three minutes. I know he'd start lecturing and waving his finger and I wouldn't take it from him. Thankfully these last few years I have lost all fear of bishops and popes. I only wish that more priests and Catholics would do likewise.

IS THE POPE INFALLIBLE?

The nuns and the Christian Brothers taught me that the Pope was infallible. But now I know that he is not. Simple blind-faith Catholics think that everything the Pope says carries the infallibility tag to it. These people don't even know the traditional teaching of the Church on infallibility – not that I agree with that teaching.

Many ordinary Catholics think that Papal infallibility goes back to the beginning of the Church. In fact, it was not exercised at all during the first ten or twelve centuries of the church's existence. Only Ecumenical Councils made such statements. And the first eight of these Councils were summoned not by Popes but by Kings and Emperors. It was not until the First Lateran Council in 1123, after the split with the Eastern Orthodox Church, that councils began to be summoned by Popes.

Secondly, in the past 140 years, only two statements claimed to be infallible have been made by Popes. Both concern Mary. The first is the dogma of the Immaculate Conception, proclaimed by Pius IX in 1854. The second is the dogma of the Assumption, proclaimed by Pope Pius XII in 1950. Each of these dogmas was strongly opposed by some of the leading theologians and cardinals in the Church.

Indeed, Papal infallibility itself was not defined until 1870 during the First Vatican Council. This Council had to break up in a hurry when the Italians seized the Vatican States during the Franco-Prussian war. The result was abandonment of the plan to add counter-balancing statements stressing the infallibility of the bishops when acting as a body and in union with the Pope. If this had been done it might have stopped the spread in the last 120 years of what some commentators have called 'creeping infallibility' – the tendency of Catholics to believe everything the Pope says is infallible. Needless to say, the Curia in Rome did nothing to stop this false idea taking hold.

For instance, *Humanae Vitae*, Pope Paul VI's 1968 encyclical reiterating the Church's traditional teaching on contraception, is not infallible. Don't take my word for that statement, which might surprise many Catholics. You have the assurance of the Vatican's former press director, Monsignor Fernando Lambruschini. When briefing journalists on the day the encyclical was issued, he told them it was authentic but not infallible. (It may be no coincidence that he was transferred soon afterwards.)

The precise Church teaching on Papal infallibility, for those who are interested, is that only those statements concerning faith and morals to be held by the whole Church made by the Pope when speaking *ex cathedra* (that is, exercising his office as the pastor and teacher of all Christians) are claimed to be infallible. And in defining the Pope's infallibility in these special and rare instances, the First Vatican Council said the Pope is possessed 'of that infallibility wherewith the divine Redeemer wished His Church should be endowed in defining doctrine concerning faith and morals.' The Church itself puts strict limits on the exercise of Papal infallibility. It is the Curia and the bishops who have tried to push these limits as far as they can.

Personally, I don't believe the two Marian dogmas mentioned above – the Immaculate Conception and the Assumption. As Christians we believe that Jesus came into the world to take upon himself our sinfulness, 'that he was like us in all things but sin.' We are told that he was fully human. Why, then, would it be necessary for God to create a specially 'clean' woman to allow Christ to come? If he were going to come the way we all came, then surely the woman who bore him had to be the same as all our mothers. The Church says in the doctrine of the Immaculate Conception that God allowed Mary to be born free from the 'original sin' with which all his creatures are tainted. What a lot of nonsensical theological juggling!

The other Marian doctrine is the Assumption, which holds that Mary's body, after she died, was assumed directly into heaven. In other words, because Mary gave human flesh to God's son, it was inappropriate that her body should be consigned to a grave to rot. Again, we are trying to make something unnecessarily special about Mary. Jesus came to share our humanity. Why, if he wanted to be like us, would his human mother have to be conceived in a special way and to be miraculously taken to heaven by angels? Even Jesus, God himself, had to die and be laid in a grave. Why should a human, albeit his mother, not have to go to heaven through a grave too? Was she to be greater and to do better than her divine son?

I believe that the doctrines of the Immaculate Conception and the Assumption spring from the extreme Mariology of the Catholic Church. There is little or no basis for them in the Bible. They are supposed to be infallible. I do not accept them, not indeed that they affect ordinary practical everyday life.

I have a lot of time for Mary. I believe that she was used by God as an instrument. God asked her to co-operate with him in his plan for the world. Mary said 'yes' to God in spite of the great misunderstanding that she might have to endure. But I don't believe that she was either conceived or died in any strange way. Nor indeed is there any reason to say that God, in placing his son in the womb of Mary, could not have used Joseph's seed to achieve his plan. Did God use Mary's egg or was the human Jesus created somewhere else and Mary's womb used merely as a baker uses an oven to bake the bread? Certainly such a mysterious way could have been God's way. But why would God have gone to the trouble of creating the marvellous human reproduction system and then by-passed it when he wanted to send his own son into the world in fully human form? When it comes to the Immaculate Conception and the Assumption, we are, I think, dealing with one of the many absurd side-roads that the Catholic Church has wandered down over the centuries. The two Marian dogmas are really intended to display Papal power, foster excessive Mariology and create an anti-Protestant theology after the Reformation. The Pope is not infallible.

The fundamentalists will immediately cry: 'What about Christ's promise in the Gospels,' the 'Whatsoever you bind on earth shall be bound in heaven' lines? Here, I think, Christ was telling us in his Church that the life of faith is a journey. If we travel sincerely, he will guide us as he guided the Israelites through their desert with the 'cloud by day and the pillar of fire by night.' But that does not mean that we in the Church don't make mistakes and don't take wrong turnings at times. What about the teaching that it was a mortal sin to eat meat on Fridays? Did all the poor buggers who had their sausages and rashers at that time go to hell? And now you can eat all the meat you want on Fridays and still go to heaven. Which teaching was right – the one which forbade eating meat on Fridays or the one which lifted the ban? Was the Church which ordered the murderous Crusades right and infallible? Were the Cardinals and bishops of the Inquisition who ordered witches and heretics to be burned at the stake following right doctrine? Was the Pope who ordered that the Mass should be said for all time in the Latin language right or was Pope John XXIII who allowed the Mass in the vernacular guided by the Holy Spirit?

Many blind-faith Catholics have the notion that in the Pope's study in the Vatican there is a red telephone on his desk which is his hot line to heaven. The Pope gets infallible messages from God on this line and passes them on to the rest of us who are the ecclesiastical peasants. For a Pope to make an infallible statement there is a procedure. The Pope must take an issue and see what the world's bishops think of it. He must then see what all the world's Catholics believe. And then, and only then, can he, exercising the infallibility with which Catholics believe Christ endowed his Church, make an infallible statement. In practice, I think that infallible statements are most dangerous. If the history of the Catholic Church proves anything it is that the Popes and the hierarchy are most fallible indeed.

THE CURIA

The Curia in the Vatican is the Catholic Church's civil service. It consists of cardinals, archbishops, bishops, monsignors, priests and nuns from all over the world who are specially trained over years to administer the world-wide Church. The Curia is a collection of conservative and power-crazy celibates who are there to see to it that everybody keeps in step. When liberal Popes like John XXIII and John Paul I took over as Pope, their greatest opponents were the members of the Curia. A liberal Pope like John XXIII achieved his Church changes in spite of the Curia and not with their help and co-operation.

The Curia in the Vatican is carved up into various congregations, just like ministries or portfolios in a civil government. There is a congregation for bishops to keep the world's bishops in check. There is a congregation of the clergy to keep an eye on the world's priests. There is a congregation for religious to supervise the world's religious orders. Religious orders are more likely to be liberal, and therefore 'trouble-makers' in the eyes of the Vatican, than are priests who are under the control of bishops in dioceses. All of these congregations are presided over by a cardinal or by an archbishop who reports regularly to the Pope.

There is another department in the Vatican supervised by the now infamous Cardinal Ratzinger. He is a German theologian who scrutinises the teachings and writings of theologians throughout the world. If a theologian dares to write something that is contrary to the official teaching of Rome he is sent for and carpeted by Cardinal Ratzinger. The theologian is presumed to be guilty until he proves himself innocent – a nearly impossible task in front of Ratzinger and his crew of inquisitors. When a theologian is found 'guilty' he is silenced and not allowed to write or teach again in a Catholic institution. A number of prominent liberal theologians have passed through Ratzinger's hands recently – Charles Curran from the United States, Leonardo Boff of South America and Hans Küng, a professor of the University of Tübingen in Germany. Ratzinger's department is the modern Inquisition and if we were not living in the 20th century, with the international community watching, the Church would be sentencing people to life imprisonment in the Vatican dungeon or to burning at the stake in front of St. Peter's in Rome.

We all know of the great powers that civil servants can have in secular states. The power of the Curia is even greater. Some readers will not believe me. Others will call me mad or paranoid. But the Roman Curia is one of the most dangerous and cynical group of men on the face of the earth. They have 2,000 years of experience behind them and they could teach the FBI to suck eggs. Shortly before his death I had a long interview with Cardinal O Fiaich of Armagh. He told me that he had a very open mind on optional clerical celibacy, on women priests, on contraception, etc. 'But,' said Cardinal Tomás to me in almost a whisper, 'I cannot say these things publicly. I have to report to Rome regularly. They hear everything. The boys in the Curia would have my guts for garters.' The Cardinal Archbishop of Armagh and Primate of All Ireland was afraid to speak his mind. He was looking over his shoulders for fear of the Roman Curia.

BISHOPS, DIOCESES AND PARISHES

The world-wide Catholic Church is divided up into several thousand dioceses. Each diocese is presided over by a bishop or archbishop. Sometimes, as in the case of Armagh in Ireland, that Archbishop is also a cardinal. In the case of large dioceses Rome will appoint auxiliary bishops to assist the diocesan bishop.

How is a bishop chosen? The answer is – most secretly. Every few years the Papal Nuncio, the Pope's representative or ambassador in a country, circulates the priests of each diocese with a document inviting their suggestions as to who might be a good bishop. The priests receiving these requests are bound to secrecy. They are not allowed even to mention to other priests in their dioceses that they have been contacted. These consultation documents are returned to the Nuncio who keeps them on his file and who, of course, keeps Rome fully informed. So for every diocese there are a number of names of possible bishops floating around all the time.

When a diocese becomes vacant the Nuncio sounds the priests out specifically. He may also consult a few well-connected and wealthy lay people. The bishops of the area and the country are also consulted. Eventually a list of three names is forwarded to Rome by the Nuncio. The congregation for bishops brings these names to the Pope who normally appoints the first-named person on the list, though he need not appoint any of the three. The Nuncio will then send for the selected candidate and tell him of his appointment and bind him to absolute secrecy. No-one will ever really know how the successful candidate has been selected. The results of the vote among the priests will not be made known. In fact, Pope John Paul II has been imposing conservative candidates on dioceses throughout the world to stop the wave of liberalism. Nowadays, we are told, if a candidate is the popular choice of the priests of a diocese, it is a black mark against him. John Paul wants conservative bishops who will crack the whip and get the foot-soldiers strongly into line.

For instance, when Dublin required a new archbishop some years ago the Vatican appointed Desmond Connell, a philosopher from the Department of Philosophy at University College, Dublin. When Cloyne in Cork needed a new bishop the Pope sent them John Magee, a religious order priest from Northern Ireland who had been on the Vatican staff for many years. When Cardinal O Fiaich died the Vatican imposed the 73-years-old Cahal Daly on the clergy and people of Armagh. Nowadays to be a bishop you have to be a well-proven conservative hard-liner – a safe pair of hands that John Paul and the Curia can trust to impose the party line. And so, when it comes to the episcopate, we have an awful lot of square pegs in round holes, often out-of-touch academics who have little or no real pastoral experience.

Irish bishops traditionally live in 'palaces', large houses in leafy suburbs well-removed from the ordinary people. Someone has said that in Ireland we do not have 40 bishops but we have 40 popes! And certainly bishops are most powerful within their own dioceses. Bishops get a big salary, much larger than they would admit to. Recently the Catholic Church in Ireland tried to float the notion that a bishop had £7,000 a year! A lot of rubbish! How could you run a palace, keep secretaries, have telephones, fax machines and desk-top publishing, keep a large car, go on regular holidays and commute to Rome on £7,000 a year? If an Irish bishop can really do all of this then I suggest that that same Irish bishop be immediately appointed the country's Minister for Finance. Clergy are supposed to be good with money. An anecdote tells of a hysterical lady observed running down a Dublin street with a child in her arms. A neighbour asked her what was wrong. 'The child has swallowed a five-pence piece,' screamed the distraught mother, 'I'm taking him to the doctor.' 'Bring him straight to the parish priest,' advised the neighbour. 'He'd get money out of anything!' My experience in the Church tells me that an Irish bishop has in the region of £50,000 per year as a salary. Bishop Casey, for instance, could never have maintained his famous life-style of wining, dining and fast cars on £7,000 a year.

In spite of the fact that the New Testament advises bishops 'Never be a dictator over any group of whom you are put in charge,' bishops wield absolute power and authority in their dioceses. The Church's rule book, the Code of Canon Law, suggests that a bishop should have a diocesan council to advise him, a priests' council to help him and a finance committee to assist him. In practice, bishops do as they please. Diocesan councils and priests' councils are only consultative and are generally composed of devout Catholics and priests who are merely 'yes' men and women. And a bishop has total control over diocesan finances. Who dares question the bishop?

A bishop has complete control over his priests. He can move a priest from post to post as often as he wants and with only a few days' notice. The priest has no say. Some bishops 'consult' priests on such shifts. This, in practice, means that instead of getting a letter ordering you to shift you are summoned to bishop's house. You probably get a cup of tea, five minutes of small talk and are then ordered anyway to your new setting. Moving priests is often a nice subtle way for a bishop to punish a disobedient priest. In the mid-1980s, when Cahal Daly wanted to teach me a lesson or two, he moved me twice in less than a year-and-a-half. This is most unsettling and can lead to great psychological and emotional problems for priests. Some dioceses have what they call personnel committees. But many of these are just a charade and in the end the bishop can do what he wants. One of the stories that circulates among the clergy of the Diocese of Down and Connor concerns the late Bishop Mageean. He was a great poker player. One night a curate beat him into a corner and the Bishop had nothing left to wager. The curate suggested that the Bishop put the next promotion to parish priest on the table. The Bishop agreed and lost but kept his word and appointed the curate to a parish at the next vacancy.

Most Catholics only see the bishop once a year at the time for confirmations. The bishop comes, confirms the children, checks the parish books and then spends hours having a huge nosh-up and sometimes a boozing session with the clergy. Many stories of the consequences of these confirmation nights abound. One Irish bishop a few years ago was returning from a clerical booze-up and was sleepy at the wheel of his car. He came to a sharp bend in the road, missed it and drove straight through a shop-window. The local Gardaí were called to remove the dazed prelate to the Garda station. The car was removed and the shop-owner sent for. The bishop was sobered up with good Garda coffee. A cheque was given to the shop-owner and the Gardaí saw the bishop home safely. Needless to say there was no prosecution or publicity. Another Irish bishop, who is famous for being fond of the drop, was discovered recently directing traffic outside the palace. And, of course, Bishop Casey was in the news previous to the Annie Murphy saga. He was stopped in London by the police and convicted of drinking and driving. He apparently appeared in court in a polo-neck sweater and gave his occupation as 'clergyman'. His excuse to the police and the court was that he had been dealing with a waiter who had, in the words of the bishop, 'a heavy hand'. Of course, not all bishops behave like this during and after confirmation dinners. My last confirmation dinner was in Larne and Cardinal Daly, who does not drink alcohol, had a cup of tea, a leaf of lettuce and a tomato. Maybe he was making reparation, as all good pioneers do, for the sins of others?

We are getting away, thank God, from that awful habit of calling bishops 'My Lord'. That was a hang-over from the days when bishops, as well as being lords spiritual, were also landlords and feudal lords.

The kissing of the ring was from that stable too. One time on a visit to Belfast's Divis Flats, where I was curate, Cardinal O Fiaich was asked to leave the flat of a friend where he was enjoying a drop of the craythur, to come downstairs where a bevy of elderly Catholic ladies wanted to kiss his ring. At a time there was an indulgence for kissing a bishop's ring! O Fiaich didn't want to leave the chat or the whiskey so he removed his ring and gave it to the messenger with the instruction to return it to him when the ladies were finished kissing it.

Gradually over the years Irish bishops have been undergoing a process of being demythologised. This is very healthy. All of us are getting less and less afraid of the bishops. I have lost my fear of them completely. As I explained recently to a journalist: 'I burned my ecclesiastical bra years ago.' The Irish bishops have less and less of a hold on Irish society. This is all to the good. And of course Bishop Eamonn Casey of Galway did more than anyone else has done in hundreds of years to show us that the bishops are just like the rest of us – human sinners who are struggling to get through life.

PARISHES

If every bishop is an emperor in his own diocese then every parish priest is an emperor in his own parish. In the old pre-Vatican II days, some parish priests were 'irremovable'. In other words they were there for life. That situation has gone now and bishops move parish priests with nearly as much ease as they move curates. But parish priests are still a force to be reckoned with.

Once again, in Canon Law, a parish priest is supposed to have a parish council and a finance committee to advise him. But many parish priests prefer to run a one-man band. If they do have such committees they often fill them with their own nominees! In every parish you get that small number of devout Catholic men and women who are only too happy to be the parish priest's pets and slaves! A small number of Irish parish priests do run their parishes with an element of democracy. But those are in the minority. A friend of mine was once asked by his Belfast parish priest to come on to a school committee. 'What would that involve, Father,' asked my friend. 'Quite simply this,' answered the priest, 'watch how I vote and vote accordingly.' My friend, a man of principle, told the parish priest that he would have no interest whatsoever in such an arrangement.

Parish priests generally do what they want in their parishes. They often don't tell the people anything much about parish business. If they are preaching and looking for money, they tell the people: 'This is your parish, your church or your school.' But when these buildings are built and paid for and when there is money in the bank there is no question of the people having any say or asking any questions. In one parish I know of, an elderly devout Catholic gave the parish priest £15,000 to install an automatic belfry. It was duly installed. Some time later the bells stopped ringing. The old man noticed and after some months rang the parish priest's door-bell to make enquiries, but he got no satisfaction. Later, he repeated the story to me in tears. I comforted him by reminding him that he had given the belfry as a gift to God and not to let the priest upset him. The old man had loved and idolised priests all his life.

Many Irish bishops and parish priests have vandalised parish churches up and down the country since the Second Vatican Council. Of course, these churches had to be modernised to fit in with the new liturgy. But the people should have been consulted instead of decisions being taken in palaces by bishops, parish priests and well-paid architects. After all, the people had to pay for the renovations. In many churches there were marble altar rails, pulpits and altars that had been donated by the deceased relatives of the parishioners. These materials should have been maintained and somehow woven into the fabric of the renovated churches. If people were consulted and if donated materials were recycled, then the very same renovations could have been achieved with less hurt and heartbreak to genuine people. But no, we were dealing with dictatorial bishops and parish priests and opportunistic architects. A great number of parishioners, particularly in country parishes throughout Ireland, have been hurt and disaffected by the iconoclasm of these ecclesiastical vandals. It is the people of a parish who remain. Bishops and parish priests are just passing through and we are supposed to be servants, are we not?

Many parish priests not only treat the people badly. They treat their curates worse, particularly if those curates have to live with them. I have sworn that no matter what happens I will never again live under the same roof as a parish priest. More than 90 percent of curates will tell you the same thing. Even if you're not getting on well with a parish priest the situation can be bearable if you don't have to live with him.

But imagine having to have every breakfast, dinner and tea with him. It is worse than a bad marriage. And a curate dare not complain about his parish priest to the bishop. The bishop will always back the parish priest. Thousands of poor curates have been driven to drink, despair and suicide by parish priests. It is an untold tragedy, believe me.

RELIGIOUS ORDERS

Priests in parishes are generally members of the 'secular clergy'. (In Dublin they called them the 'circular' clergy!) Alongside the secular clergy system you have the religious orders. A secular priest has, contrary to common belief, no vows. When ordained, he merely promises the bishop obedience and respect and promises not to marry and to read his prayers (Divine Office) every day. And I'm often accused of breaking my vows. I never took any!

However, in religious orders, the priests and brothers take three solemn vows – poverty, chastity and obedience. Poverty means that they can personally own nothing. All property is commonly owned by the order. Chastity means what it says – no bad thoughts, no abusing yourself and no sex of any kind. Obedience means that the orders of our superiors are to be interpreted as direct orders from God.

Are these vows kept? They are not! A nun, a brother or a priest might have a vow of poverty. But they have a good roof over their head. Their meals are cooked for them by a chef or cook and laid in front of them. Charladies clean their monasteries and make their beds. The Order buys them all their clothes, provides them with a car, insurance, tax and petrol. They get their annual holidays paid for and pocket money when they're going. If they want to study, the Order pays all their fees. If they are sick, the Order pays their way in the best private clinics and hospitals. And that's holy poverty for you! If I could get someone to pay all my bills, provide me with the highest standard of living and give me pocket money as well, I would take a vow of poverty in the morning. Wouldn't you? I'm reminded of the big conference of clergy that was convened to discuss poverty. It was held at a five-star hotel. All week the delegates had top-class treatment. On the Friday night, two old Canons were sipping their vintage port and nibbling their Stilton cheese in the hotel dining-room. They both looked as if they were heading for a serious attack of gout. 'Well, Mick,' says one Canon to the other, 'if this is the conference on poverty I'm really looking forward to the one on chastity.'

Many of our religious orders do not observe true poverty at all
Instead they simply give away to their organisation their own right to
make ends meet and are rewarded with a comfortable life free of any
worry, any bills or any responsibility. The poverty thing is a 'con'! There
are exceptions. Some enclosed religious, orders like the Cistercians or
the Poor Clares, do live lives of poverty, penance, work and fasting
But your average religious priest, brother or nun wants for absolutely
nothing. A large percentage of them are spoiled rotten.

What of chastity? For a start I don't believe that there is a person
alive who has never had a sexual thought or fantasy. Maybe there is
but I've never met one and I've met a lot of people. In religious life
you do come across some men and women who certainly give the
impression that they are passionless, all dried-up. But are these people
really holy or are they just so repressed as to be almost sub-human
Whenever I meet these types I think of the old advertisement for vodka
SO PURE IT'S WICKED. I think that it is possible to be so 'chaste' and
'pure' as to be thoroughly wicked. Maybe some of the Christian
Brothers and nuns who beat us black and blue in school were chaste
and pure to the point of sadism? Somehow I have visions of them
alone in their cells tortured by sexual thoughts, perhaps masturbating
and then beating themselves with their flagellation whip for punishment.

But what is true chastity? Is it not to be at peace with your sexuality
and to be an integrated person? Most of the religious I know and have
dealt with have found their chastity a great burden – a cross to be
struggled with each and every day. Many religious, men and women
enter full sexual relationships with other human beings at various times
during their religious lives. A few years ago our very own Gay Byrne
had two former nuns on his *Late Late Show* who had lived active lesbian
lives while in the convent. I know lesbian nuns. I know nuns who
have had and are having full sexual relationships with men, sometimes
married men. I know religious brothers and priests who are actively
sexual in both the heterosexual and homosexual arenas. I certainly
believe that it is possible, if rare, to find religious who are totally 'chaste'
and happy in their chastity. But for the most part the chastity vow
a great cross for most of those who try to live it.

And what of holy obedience? Perhaps obedience is the easiest vow of the three to keep. These days religious superiors are not too oppressive. And the religious orders have democracy. Religious superiors are elected by the rank-and-file every three years. In religious orders they say: 'Be careful how you treat people on the way up. You may have to meet those same people on the way back down again.' If a religious superior is bad, the foot-soldiers can vote him out next time around. That probability can temper the abuse of authority. And religious superiors can do no more than two three-year terms. Then they must return to the ranks as a private. That, too, has a sobering effect. Would that bishops and parish priests had the same restraint placed upon them! There are a great number of weak-minded people in religious life, people who hate taking decisions and who find it easier to have someone else make all their choices for them. These people love obedience and regard it as a virtue. They would, wouldn't they? But what about the call to disobey? Christ had to disobey the religious leaders of his time in order to do his father's will. The prophets and some of the saints had to do likewise. Obedience can be a vice. At Nuremberg some of the world's greatest criminals used the obedience card as their defence. They should have disobeyed. Where is the courage to disobey when obedience is obviously an evil?

One of the most awful aspects of religious life has now, thankfully, disappeared. In religious houses, particularly convents, up to not so long ago you had a class system. If a young lady brought a good dowry with her (money from her family) she became a 'choir sister'. If, however, she came without a dowry she was a mere 'lay sister'. The choir sisters were the first-class nuns. The lay sisters were the domestic slaves of the choir sisters. They were not allowed to sit in the same part of the church as the choir sisters and they spent their lives cleaning, scrubbing and cooking for the first-class nuns. This was apartheid not unlike that of the southern states of the United States or South Africa, and of course it was all done in the name of God! Another horrible practice in the Catholic Church was the establishment of a special order to care for women who had been immoral and had children out of wedlock. They were no better than unpaid slaves who spent their lives doing penance for their terrible sins. In men's religious orders the distinction was between those members who were ordained priests and those who stayed 'only' brothers. A friend of mine, Brother Gerard Collins of the Carmelite Order, was always embarrassed about this right to the end of his life. So ashamed and upset about being 'only a brother' was he that he wore a big priest-like collar and when anyone asked him what he was he became extremely uncomfortable and answered 'a clergyman'.

Ordinary lay Catholics will not realise it either but there has always been a tension between the secular clergy (those in parishes) and priests from religious orders. Somehow the secular clergy regarded the order priests as second-class. Part of this was to do with the fact that in Ireland to get into a diocese you and your people had to have money. If your family were prepared to pay your way the local bishop took you and sent you to Maynooth and you could become a priest near home. But if you were poor, you had to go to a religious order or to a diocese in England, America or Australia. They were short of priests in these places and the bishops there took young men without family dowries. Because of this situation a lot of Irish priests were the sons of wealthy farmers or pub-owners. The tradition on the Irish farm was for the oldest son to inherit, marry and stay at home. The second son was sent to the priesthood and the later sons were sent to the professions, like teaching. Daughters, of course, were dowried off either to other farmers' sons or to the convents as nuns. One time there was an argument in the priests' dining-room of an Irish seminary. The priests around the table were saying how the best priests were the sons of farmers and publicans. One priest, not from such a background, became very angry. He banged his fist down on the table. 'You're all talking a heap a' shit,' he screamed. 'What about Jesus, the first priest? His father was a bloody carpenter!'

In bygone days the local diocesan bishop had a lot of control over religious and how they dressed and behaved in public. Archbishop John Charles McQuaid was a strict bishop. It was forbidden, for instance, for nuns to be on the street after a certain time in the evening. One evening two nuns were out rather late and the Archbishop's black limousine with the blacked-out windows drew up. The door opened and the nuns were ordered in. They were dropped off home after a lecture about their late wanderings. Archbishop McQuaid's house was sandwiched in between two convents on Military Road, Killiney, Co. Dublin. Clerical circles recall how John Charles sent for one of the Reverend Mothers one day to complain that one of the convent windows facing his palace had no curtains on it and that he could see the nuns within. The Reverend Mother, a feminist somewhat ahead of her time, quickly retorted: 'Your Grace, you should not be looking.' We used to joke that John Charles used to fill his pipe with a blend of two famous tobaccos: 'Three Nuns' and 'Parson's Pleasure'.

People will have noticed that nuns' habits have become rather less elaborate over the years. Some nuns have discarded the habit completely. The French Sisters of Charity used to wear the big starched 'swan' on their heads. If a shower of rain came they returned to the convent with the swan drooping and clinging to their faces and shoulders. The same nuns used to have 14 yards of material in their skirts. I gather a little under two yards would make a skirt for the normal female. As for this extra protection we used to say that the skirts of the French Sisters of Charity were like the famous Donnelly's sausages that had two skins – 'double wrapped for double protection'!

CANON LAW

The law of the Catholic Church is called Canon Law. It consists of some 2,000 rules or canons for the governing of the Church. It is one of the most medieval and unjust legal systems in the world and the Church tolerates within its own rules the things it condemns in secular societies. This is hypocrisy.

For instance, one Canon says that no-one can judge the 'First See', in other words, the Pope. According to Canon Law he is answerable to no-one but God. So if the Pope does someone in the Church a terrible injustice the victim has nowhere in Canon Law to go. He or she can, of course, appeal to the Pope himself. But whatever happened that important old legal precept which says that no man can be a judge in his own cause?

Canon Law has been constructed by the Catholic hierarchy and their servants to protect the *status quo*. Pope, cardinals and bishops have all kinds of rights. Parish priests have some rights. But if you're not a parish priest you have no rights – save the right to a Christian burial.

My own case will serve as a good example of what I mean. Bishop Patrick Walsh of Down and Connor Diocese wants me to stop performing confessions, confirmations, but particularly marriages, without his permission. I am willing to be reconciled with him and that reconciliation will involve sorting out my celebrating of marriages without his permission. As I read Canon Law, three canons require

Bishop Walsh to be reconciled with me. But the Bishop has refused. Why? Because he wants me to drop everything I'm doing and ask for nothing – no work, no security, nothing. He fails to grasp that a true reconciliation involves two sides to a dispute making concessions to each other!

So Bishop Walsh's answer is to suggest the possibility of a Church court and put me on trial for breaking Canon Law. And this is what would be involved:

1. He, the Bishop, a party to the dispute, will appoint the judge!

2. That judge will appoint the prosecutor.

3. That judge will invite me to appoint a defender. That defender must be a Canon lawyer and acceptable to the Bishop!

4. Every Canon lawyer in the local church here is a priest with a vow of obedience to Bishop Walsh, some other bishop or a religious superior!

5. How am I to get an objective defender then?

6. I cannot hear the evidence of witnesses against me!

7. Bishop Walsh has a file on me. I cannot see it!

8. I am permitted to argue only on the basis of Canon Law. I can't bring the Bible, God's Word, into it!

9. If I am unhappy about the proposed court to whom can I appeal? To the bishop or to the judge appointed by the bishop?

10. I can appeal to Rome ! What chance would I have – a dissident priest appealing to Rome against a bishop Rome has appointed and supports!

This is a typical Catholic Church court. I have said that I would prefer to face a Provisional IRA kangaroo court up the Falls Road. I believe I would have a better chance of getting justice there. The Irish Catholic bishops run courts like this and then have the gall and hypocrisy to lecture the British Government about the injustices of the 'Birmingham Six' and the 'Guildford Four'.

When Canon Law was being revised in 1983 the world's Canon lawyers, conscious of the problems I highlight here, suggested that a new section be inserted into Canon Law – a 'due process' section whereby a person in the Church, like me, might get a fair hearing before the Church's courts. This, of course, would have had the effect of making the Vatican, the Pope and the world's bishops accountable.

John Paul would not have it and drew his pen through the proposed 'due process' section. And we are still left with Catholic kangaroo courts! Think of this the next time you hear a cardinal or bishop lecturing the state about justice!

The poor quality of justice in the Catholic Church is proven by the case of Father Michael Keane, a priest of the Archdiocese of Tuam in Galway. After he was ordained he inherited a large sum of money. The Archbishop of the time, Dr. Walsh, was anxious that Father Keane donate all or part of his fortune to the Church. It was hinted to Father Keane that a man with his kind of money might very well become a bishop! Father Keane, wisely, declined. Over the following years and decades Father Keane, a strongwilled and sometimes uncompromising liberal, disagreed with two Tuam Archbishops over a host of issues. It culminated in Father Keane leaving Tuam and being given a position in the Archdiocese of Dublin as a curate. After a while, Father Keane and a fellow-curate managed to incur the wrath of their parish priest. There was a dispute and Father Keane told the people about it at Mass. He was immediately suspended by Archbishop Dermot Ryan. For well over a decade, Father Keane has been without priestly work. He was eventually evicted from his presbytery by Archbishop Ryan.

Father Keane is, wrongly I feel, determined to have a public apology. No bishop will give him this even if he deserves it. But he has committed no real crime. He has been treated most unfairly and has been left sitting year after year while at the same time the Catholic Church complains about a shortage of priests. But Father Keane, like myself, has committed the greatest of sins. We have challenged the power! A priest will be forgiven for having sex with women or men. They will be forgiven for sexually abusing children. They will be tolerated for stealing or having a drink or drug problem. But they will not be forgiven for daring to challenge the power. Canon Law is there simply to protect the power and to punish those who dare challenge it.

THE BLIND FAITH

Too many Irish Catholics have regarded their bishops and priests as gods. They did things, not because they were right, but because Bishop so-and-so or Father so-and-so told them that it was right. Contraception is a good example. Women have often come to confession to me and asked me if they could use contraception. They did not themselves want to take responsibility for their own decisions. They would use contraception, not because it was the moral thing to do but rather because Father Buckley said it was all right. I always threw the decision back over to them. I told them the teaching of the Church and I gave them my 'opinion' but I told them that the decision must be their own.

Soon after my row erupted with Cardinal Daly I had a telephone call from a lady from a very posh part of Belfast – the Malone Road. It was a Sunday afternoon and she was raging with me. Why? Apparently there had been a big argument over Sunday dinner about my case. She and her husband were on Bishop Daly's side. Her children were on mine. 'I hope that you are proud,' she screamed, 'to have caused a row in a good Catholic family.' I told her that I thought it was a very healthy sign that a Catholic family should discuss religious issues over dinner and even feel strongly enough to disagree. She didn't see it that way. She finished the call with a classic statement: 'If Bishop Daly told me to jump into the Lagan [Belfast's river] my fur coat would be found on the banks tomorrow morning!' If that's not blind faith I don't know what is.

People will realise, perhaps, that the Catholic Church is not what they think it to be. It is a very human organisation pretending to be divine. We must learn to distinguish between the essentials and the accidentals, between the baby and the bath water. I am happy about the essentials – the Bible, the Sacraments, the priesthood, and so on. But I am most unhappy about the accidentals – the abuse of power, the oppressive hierarchy, the priestly caste and a host of man-made and foolish dogmas. I want to be a free and thinking Catholic.

CHAPTER 6

Women and the Church

'You are the gate of Hell. You are the first deserter of
the Divine Law '

Tertullian

THE ABOVE WORDS WERE addressed to women by the early Church father,
Tertullian. Another Church father, St. John Chrysostom, followed
through with: 'Among all savage beasts, none is found so harmful as
woman.' St. Augustine was not going to be outdone. He declared: 'Any
woman who acts in such a way that she cannot give birth to as many
children as she is capable of makes herself guilty of that many murders.'
The Council of Macon in the early Church was attended by 43 Catholic
bishops and 20 men, representing twenty other Catholic bishops.
During the Council a vote was taken to decide whether or not women
were human beings. 32 voted that women were human and 31 voted
that women were not human. So women were declared human beings
by one vote at that early Church Council! With that negative attitude
to women, sex and birth-control, the Catholic Church got off to a very
bad start in its thinking about sexuality. It has never, to this day,
recovered from those bad beginnings.

It all starts, for Christians anyway, in the first book of the Bible, the
Book of Genesis. Here we have God creating a man first, Adam. The
point is immediately made that the male was God's first choice, first
love. That stands to reason, of course, since God is, according to
traditional Christianity, a male himself and one who favours males. But
Adam was lonely. So God brought him all the animals to see if any
could provide companionship. None could. Adam, I suppose, must be
admired for his lack of interest in beasts! Then God hit on an idea. He
put Adam to sleep, removed one of his ribs and created a woman. Eve,
the first woman, came to be. Adam and Eve were then, if you follow
the Genesis story, happy in the Garden of Eden. They had all they
wanted. There was only one rule in the Eden society – they were not
to eat from the tree of life. And then along comes Satan, disguised this

time as a snake. He decided to approach the weak woman rather than the strong male. The apple was taken and Eve tempted poor Adam to have his bite. They immediately knew that they were naked and so they hid from God. All of this led to their fall from Eden to earth. The whole implication of this story is sexual. As they say: 'It wasn't the apple on the tree; it was the pair on the ground!' Adam was all right until the woman came along. The Devil used the woman. Adam had his bite. Nakedness became a problem. They were ashamed of their little bits.

There is a tendency, more with Protestants I must admit, to take the Bible literally. But Catholics also fall into the trap. Christians too often forget that the Bible is a book composed of some facts but also of many parables and much poetry. I do believe that it is the inspired Word of God. But I know that God used human authors. And those human authors didn't mind taking full advantage of artistic licence. The Genesis story is an attempt by fairly primitive man, early sexist man, to explain the inexplicable mystery of creation. And it doesn't even fit. We are told in the Bible that Adam and Eve had two sons, Cain and Abel. Where did the rest of us come from then? Scripture scholars tell us that sons were important enough to mention but daughters were not. Even if you accept that, you must then believe that we all came from Adam, Cain or Abel having sex with Eve or her daughters and producing more daughters capable of child-bearing. So we all came from rampant incest, did we? It is hardly a great compliment to God to contend that incest was the cleverest way he could find to create the human race. No, I think evolution is a more believable theory. And it does not take away from God's role as Creator. Could not God have devised and implemented evolution? Evolution sounds more intelligent and noble than universal incest. And anyway did you know that Cain couldn't have children? Why, you ask. Because he wasn't Abel!

If I were God and had the choice of having either incest or evolution attributed to me, I think I'd opt for evolution. And if God chose incest, then incest can't be wrong and that slogan we've all heard: 'Incest is best' is eternally true! Northern Ireland fundamentalist Protestants will insist on the literal truth of the Genesis story. They make a laughing-stock of God, creation and the Christian message. People have pointed out to such folk that if you accept the Genesis story you've got to believe that mankind has been on earth for only a few thousand years. When others point out that human bones have been found going back hundreds of thousands of years these Christians reply: 'God hid those bones there to test our faith.' It is blind and simple-minded believers who really test our faith and our patience and get Christianity a bad name. When Bishop Daly 'sacked' me from Larne, I was besieged by Elim Pentecostal Christians who wanted to convert me and make me into a new little Moses who would lead Catholics out of the slavery of Rome into the promised land of Elim. I had several arguments and discussions with them about taking the Bible literally. One day I asked them if they had ever sinned with their hands. They confessed that they had. 'Well', says I, 'the Bible says: "If your hand causes you to sin cut it off".' I told them that if they wanted to convince me that the Bible should be interpreted literally they should return for our next discussion minus a hand. I never saw them again!

Built on all of this narrow-minded and negative belief and theology is the idea that the woman's body is dirty and bad. In Old Testament Judaism, a married man could not touch his wife when she was having a period. She was dirty then and would defile him. The woman whom Jesus cured in the Gospels had been bleeding for twelve years and was not only suffering physically. She was also suffering mentally and socially. Her female haemorrhage was, to the Jews, a curse from God. She was another kind of leper. We continued this horrible attitude in Ireland up until recently with the practice of 'churching'. After having a baby, a woman could not attend Mass and the Sacraments until she had been 'churched' or cleansed by the priest. How crazy and unjust it was for us men to make a woman pregnant and then consider her unclean and banished from church for giving birth to the baby we had helped to place inside of her. In recent times, Irish Catholic priests have tried to explain away the churching phenomenon by saying that it was misunderstood by the laity. A Father Colm Burke, the parish priest of Islandeady in Mayo, wrote in this vein to the *Irish Times* on 28 July, 1992. He argued that the churching ceremony was all about welcoming the woman back into the church community after her physical absence for the birth. I do not accept Father Burke's argument. Women in Ireland up to thirty or forty years ago often had their babies at home and were allowed or demanded very little time to lie and recover from the birth. Very often a farmer's wife had her baby in the morning and was up within hours cooking, cleaning and continuing her domestic and farming duties. So she was not absent. Why should the church have waited for weeks to welcome her home from an absence she had never had? People like Father Burke want us to believe that churching was a kind of a welcome-back party given by the local parish. Nonsense! It was widely taught and widely understood as a cleansing. That's why women had to sneak up to the church, shamefully and at a quiet time, to be churched by the parish priest in a dark corner. No amount of theological gymnastics will take away from the fact that this was a savage practice by a Church that regarded sex and its result, pregnancy, as a dirty business.

In this theology, genital expression became the second-class way of living. Even in marriage, sex was merely tolerated. It was a way of populating the planet, a way of getting new members for the Church and a way for tying a man to one woman and stopping him wandering – the 'cure for concupiscence'. Women were told by the Church that even if they didn't like or enjoy sexual intercourse they had to submit and give their husbands their conjugal rights. It was a sin to refuse. Women coming to me in confession in Belfast in the late 1970s and early 1980s used to confess: 'Father, I refused my husband his jungle rights.' Virginity was superior to sex. This fed the cult of the Virgin Mary who was placed before women as the ultimate model. In time, the Catholic Church declared that Mary was forever a virgin. And yet the Gospels tell us that 'Joseph did not come to know Mary until after Jesus was born' and also talks about the 'brothers' of Jesus. If Catholic women were bound under pain of sin to submit to their husbands, then why should the Blessed Virgin Mary be honoured for having refused Joseph his conjugal rights for a lifetime? The Church would answer that Mary had a special role and that Joseph was given an unusual strength of character and became a life-time abstainer. On the one hand, the Catholic Church puts before us the Holy Family of Nazareth as the ideal model, a family in which the wife refused her husband his conjugal rights, and tells wives since that if they do the same they commit a sin. Is a sin not always a sin? What was a virtue for Mary is a sin for a Catholic woman today. Catholic nuns were the new Virgin Marys, the brides of Christ. Celibacy was a higher state than marriage. The spirit was good, the body bad. Heaven is good, the earth is bad. Men are good if they are not led astray by women, the new

Eves. God made women, the earth and the body. Does God create that which is evil and bad?

CONTRACEPTION

Canon Padraig Murphy, the parish priest of St. John's parish on the Falls Road, built a new parish church during my time in Belfast. He had a huge multi-coloured billboard outside the church showing the state of the church debt and fund-raising. The billboard showed a massive circle coloured black and red. Each week the arrow went from the red further into the black as funds came in. We all joked that Canon Murphy was raising money for his church by the so-called 'rhythm method' of fund-raising. His billboard was marvellously reminiscent of the chart for the rhythm method.

Officially the Catholic Church allows only three methods of contraception – the 'rhythm method' (which gave rise to the joke: 'Where would you get a band at three in the morning'), the Billings method and the oldest method of all – abstinence. These three methods satisfy the Pope, the Roman Curia (the Church's civil service) and the hierarchy. But no-one else is satisfied. The rhythm method is about using a calendar, watching your dates and avoiding intercourse on those days when the female partner is likely to conceive. The Billings method is about watching dates too, but also about testing female secretions and examining them for tackiness, etc. Abstinence is about saying 'no' and going without. Most modern Catholics do not agree with the official Church teaching on contraception. Many bishops, priests and theologians do not agree with the Vatican position. And so you have a small segment of the Church, the conservative section of the hierarchy, saying one thing and the rest of the Church, the more enlightened part, doing the opposite. Some bishops, priests and theologians have openly disagreed with the contraception teaching. Other priests simply tell women and couples in counselling or confession to follow their own conscience. And quite right, too!

The Vatican teaching on contraception is really a hang-over from the days when the official Church teaching was that the first and primary end of marriage was the procreation of children. The official teaching is not logical. In the rhythm and Billings methods, the Church allows you to use calendars, charts, thermometers and whatever things you use to test tackiness. The Church objects to the pill and the condom because you are using 'artificial' means. But what's the difference, morally speaking I mean, between rubber or chemicals and paper, pencils and thermometers? You don't find calendars, thermometers and pencils naturally inside a female body, do you?

In the 1960s, Catholics throughout the world – bishops, priests and laity – were expecting the Vatican to change its laws on contraception. Pope Paul VI brought together an international commission of experts theologians, philosophers and medical experts – to examine the issue and report to him. That commission favoured a change. The world's Catholics and clergy expected a change. However, the Pope, under the influence of the Roman Curia, went against the commission and produced an encyclical, *Humanae Vitae*, outlawing artificial birth control. The world was shocked. Many theologians publicly disagreed with the Pope. Many priests left the priesthood and many Catholic married couples either stopped practising their faith or ignored the papal teaching. Today, the Church still officially bans artificial contraception but the majority of the world's Catholics use it. Cardinal Suenens of Belgium on a number of occasions asked Pope Paul VI to reconsider both the contraception issue and the issue of allowing priests to marry. He begged the Pope to make a decision on birth control in consultation with the world's bishops. The Cardinal wrote to the Pope:

> I believe that what is at stake here is the manner in which pontifical primacy is exercised and thus the very future of the Church. The sense of unease which surrounds this problem can be felt throughout the world. It arises with particular intensity in the context of two burning issues: that of birth control, which affects countless couples; and that of optional celibacy in the Latin Church, which continues to trouble the clergy . . . All that misunderstands, or, in practice, ignores episcopal collegiality is felt to be, at present, a danger for the Church; it makes obedience more difficult, both for the faithful and for the clergy; and it sets back any progress we may have made in the area of ecumenism . . .
>
> The good of the Church would be dramatically endangered, in my opinion, if the Holy Father were seen to take upon himself the role of sole defender and guardian of the faith and of moral

standards, if he were to stand before the world alone, cut off from the college of bishops, from the clergy, and from the faithful.

(Memories and Hopes, Suenens, pp. 190-191).

The Pope chose to ignore his commission, the world's bishops, the clergy, the faithful and the constructive warning of the Primate of Belgium, Cardinal Suenens. He stood alone. And from that time the Pope lost his sheep on the contraception issue and indeed on the wider issue of sexual morality. Cardinal Suenens had sent the Pope papers and studies on the contraception issue. According to the Cardinal: 'All of these studies, each from a different perspective, addressed the global and personal aspects of conjugal life, and warned against any position that would miss or ignore its complexity on the pastoral level.' The Pope opted instead for the rigorous and Canon Law position of the Roman Curia and the curial Cardinal Ottaviani. Cardinal Suenens had argued at the Second Vatican Council that if the right approach were not taken on the birth control issue the Church would produce a teaching on it that had no credibility. 'One Galileo affair should be enough,' Cardinal Suenens had declared. But Pope Paul VI preferred the 'flat earth' approach to contraception and since then this particular teaching has received neither credibility nor acceptance from the vast majority of Catholics.

Of course, there is a world of difference between married couples using contraception responsibly and in the context of love and someone using it because they want a new BMW or prefer poodles to babies. Couples should only have the number of children they feel they can look after properly. Given that, how they limit their family is their own business and that of their doctor. There is a place for Church teaching and for couples including the spiritual dimension in their decisions. But there is no place for the Church invading the bedroom, particularly by forcing legislators to enshrine Roman Catholic moral theology in law or Constitution. Recently a relative of my own opted to have a vasectomy. His wife had four living children and had several miscarriages that threatened her health and life. That vasectomy, although against Vatican teaching, was a true act of love. When I was a curate in a Welsh parish a lady with eight living children approached me. Her drunken husband raped her twice or three times a week. She didn't want to leave him. I would have left him. 'Was it a sin,' she asked me, 'to take the pill?' I very strongly told her that in her case it would be a serious sin NOT to take the pill. The Catholic Church has won and lost many battles in its long history. It has definitely lost the contraception battle and a lot of credibility too. The Irish Republic, in restricting the availability of contraceptives, was behaving incredibly and weakly. We should have condom machines in all our public toilets.

We all know that condoms do not absolutely prevent AIDS. But we do know that condoms or 'safer sex' can help prevent AIDS. We need better sex education in our schools, and part of that better sex education has to include advice on the proper use of condoms. If condoms prevented even one death from AIDS then I would be in favour of them being delivered automatically every morning by the milkman!

ABORTION

Abortion is never a 'good' thing. If it was a good thing the advertisers would be trying to get us all to have one. Abortion is, at best, a necessary evil. But at times it may be necessary. If I were a married man with five children and my wife were expecting our sixth child and the doctors told me that, due to medical complications, they could not save both, then I would choose my wife. In the process I would be aborting a baby. I would do so very sadly and with deep regret. I know that I would not be choosing a good thing. I know that I would be deciding between the lesser of two evils – the death of my wife and my five living children's mother or the death of my sixth baby. I know that these choices are extremely rare in modern medicine. But they can occur and their possibility reminds us that we cannot be absolute on any moral issue. As the husband and father I should be allowed by the law of the land to make this choice with my wife. The state medical services should also facilitate my choice. I should not have to whip my wife away to England to save her life. I know that in practice this would not happen because Irish doctors apply the law with a certain flexibility, even at present.

The official teaching of the Catholic Church allows 'abortion' in certain circumstances. If a pregnant wife has a cancerous growth and is also pregnant, the Catholic Church allows her to have her womb removed or receive treatment even if this results in the death of 'abortion' of the baby. In allowing this the Church says that the death of the baby is only a secondary and accidental effect of the treatment. If the woman were not pregnant she would have the same treatment. The fact that she is pregnant is 'accidental'. This teaching is based on the belief that you cannot directly take life but that you may be entitled to pursue a course of action which is moral even if one of the accidental effects is the taking of life. So the Catholic Church, in allowing for this type of case, is also admitting that the prohibition of 'abortion' is not an absolute one.

With the exception of such 'accidental' abortions, the Catholic Church is very firmly anti-abortion. It is entitled to hold this belief and to preach it to those who wish to listen. Many people, including non-Catholics, agree with Roman Catholic teaching on abortion. But the Catholic Church is not entitled to have its teaching on abortion enshrined in the Irish Constitution or in Irish law. It is the people of Ireland who are entitled to decide whether or not there should be abortion in Ireland. They should be allowed to decide this freely and without the Catholic Church putting huge moral (or immoral) pressure on them or their politicians. The Catholic hierarchy are entitled to be a pressure group. Every democracy tolerates pressure groups. But they are not entitled to any more say or sway than any other pressure group. Nor are they entitled to threaten or intimidate. It is a freedom of choice issue. The Catholic hierarchy should follow their founder's example. Jesus never forced anyone to accept his teaching or follow him. He invited people to think and live in a certain way. If they responded he received them. If they said 'no' he let them go. Any Church that has to depend on the law of the land to force people to accept its message is a very weak and unconvincing Church. You cannot legislate people into believing. The Irish Catholic Church has made the great mistake of trying to legislate people into being good Catholics. Now that that legislation is changing the Church has a crisis. What should it do? It should have integrity and an appealing message and it should invite people to follow its doctrine and then leave them free. It might have fewer people in the pews but those who are there will be convinced. Maynooth surveys may boast an 80 percent church attendance. But I wonder how many of them are there because they really want to be?

Abortion is for some necessary but for many not desirable. It is, however, a matter for public morality and a question of choice.

Religious leaders, whether Catholic, Christian, Jewish or Muslim, are entitled to instruct their followers. But no church and no religious leader is entitled to lay down the law to the Irish people. No church should intimidate or dictate to the politicians. No decent politician should allow himself or herself to be intimidated. The Irish Catholic Church has done this and has been allowed to do this by weak politicians. That must change. That is changing.

From my own experience I know that some women live to regret having had an abortion. These women need our love and care. I have noticed that some women who have had abortions as young women regret the abortion when they come to the menopause. I often wonder about that. Is it because they are losing their ability to have children that they regret having disposed of one child? Or has it to do with the hormonal and psychological disturbances that occur at menopause? But the Church has a duty to offer these women pastoral care. There is an organisation in Dublin that offers this kind of care – Women Hurt by Abortion.

PRIESTS AND WOMEN

To many priests women are mysterious and fascinating creatures from another planet! There can be a great gulf between priests and lay-people. There can be an even greater gulf between priests and women. Knowing priests as well as I do, I can see that many of them cannot relate very naturally to women. For example, I knew a priest who was in his middle years by the time I got to know him. He had little or no experience of dealing with females in his family life. He was sent to an all-male boarding school and later entered an all-male seminary. By the time he was ordained he was both fascinated by and awkward with women. He was heterosexual by inclination. His ordinary everyday conversation was punctuated by talk about women. He particularly liked to tell blue jokes about heterosexual sex. Nearly every time I was in his company he talked about ladies' underwear.

A great part of the problem lies in the fact that in their seminary training priests are relatively cut off from lay-people and particularly lay-women. This is probably less true today than in previous times but it is still fairly common. Some of the religious orders whose priests are trained in missionary institutes come into more contact with women than do secular priests who are trained in diocesan seminaries. Some seminarians attend university at Maynooth and Dublin and this helps them to have more contact with females. But the seminaries themselves are male worlds where there is little or no attention given to either sex instruction or advice on handling relationships. Seminarians go through six or seven years in an all-male world where women are more or less never mentioned. Then they are released as young priests into parishes. They begin to experience things like loneliness. They encounter women for the first time at close quarters. They get attracted and fall in love sometimes. Young priests, like all young men, have strong sexual desires and are in their prime. Put all of these things together and you are bound to develop problems.

Women were mentioned in passing during some of the retreats we attended during our training for the priesthood. But they were mentioned always in a negative way. Sex was mentioned in the context of sin. Women were mentioned mostly as 'occasions of sin'. The idea was that if you avoided women you would probably avoid sex and therefore you would avoid sin. So many priests are left with that legacy of viewing women as creatures that can lead you into sin and away from God.

Another serious aspect of this situation is that while women make up more than half the population and the vast majority of church-goers, priests get no special training in ministering to women or to women's special needs. Women obviously have a very distinctive make-up. They are often much more obviously spiritual than are men. And yet there is no attempt in seminaries or in the Church in general to develop a pastoral strategy for ministry to women. Traditionally women in the eyes of the Church and the clergy are housewives, mothers or housekeepers. They are there to make the tea and sandwiches after the males have concluded the serious business.

WOMEN, POWER AND ORDINATION

The Catholic Church is a patriarchal institution and women do not really count in it, especially when it comes to the question of power. There is no decent reason, either from the Bible or from genuine tradition, for banning women from ordination or exercising power in the Church. We don't have them ordained or put in positions of power for one reason – prejudice. We are a patriarchal Church that discriminates against women. The time has long since passed for that to change.

A number of years ago the Portadown Jesuit priest, Father Declan Deane, wrote to the Irish newspapers saying that he belonged to an organisation called Priests for Equality which is campaigning for the ordination of women to the Roman Catholic priesthood. Priests for Equality was founded by an American Jesuit, Bill Callahan of Maryland, and it has some two to three thousand priest members world-wide. Apparently a number of the American bishops support its aims. Father Deane says that the reforming Pope, John XXIII, had something to say in his famous Encyclical *Pacem in Terris* that throws light on the question of the ordination of women: 'Human beings have the right to choose freely the state which they prefer. They therefore have the right to set up a family with equal rights and duties for men and women and also the right to follow a vocation to the priesthood or religious life.'

At the time of his letter to the Irish papers I interviewed Father Deane for the Belfast Sunday newspaper, the *Sunday News.* Father Deane told me that there are very good reasons why the Church should change and is changing. The Church has to recognise the 'signs of the times.' There is a changing vision of the role of women within the Church. Many of the Church Fathers saw women as inferior and submissive to men. They said that women and slaves were both inferior and unfitted for ministry. The great 12th century theologian-priest Thomas Aquinas had written: 'It is not possible for the female sex to signify eminence of degree as that sex is characterised by the state of submission.' So for centuries the Church regarded women as inferior. But today in the Church it would be an evil and sinful thing to say that women are inferior or submissive.

In the 'old Church' priesthood was about power, authority and eminence. But today in our 'new Church' priesthood is supposed to be about service, compassion and healing. These are qualities usually attributed to women. Through these 'signs of the times' the Holy Spirit is conveying to the Church that it will have to open up all of its ministries to women. Fr Deane continued:

> In my experience many Catholics and priests are in favour of the ordination of women. I would say that over 50 percent of my age group in the Jesuits would be in favour. In 1986/87 a national survey in Ireland was carried out that asked ordinary

Catholics if they would be in favour of the ordination of women. Of those who replied 54 percent were in favour, 31 percent were against and 15 percent were undecided.

For the Catholic Church to ordain women will take a great moment of conversion. It will take a moment of conversion similar to that St. Peter had when he was in the house of Cornelius, the Roman official. Peter had been convinced that only Jews could be Christians. But in the house of Cornelius, Peter had a vision in which the Holy Spirit conveyed to him that all men and women, including Gentiles, could follow Christ. A similar conversion experience is needed for the Catholic Church to realise that women can be priests as well as men.

The Catholic bishops, backed up by conservative and right-wing Catholics and priests, are opposed to the ordination of women. They offer no good arguments from Scripture to back up their view.

They say that Christ didn't ordain women or have a woman among his twelve apostles. But that is a very simplistic and inaccurate argument. The priesthood as we know it was a development of some centuries after Christ. Christ had no formal 'ordination' ceremony for any of his disciples. He had twelve chosen followers, the apostles, and there were many women followers to whom he was very close. The Gospel tells us that several women went about with Jesus and ministered to him out of their own resources. Mary of Magdala was a close friend and disciple as were Martha and Mary and, of course, his mother Mary. If women were good enough to minister to Christ himself, then surely they are good enough to share in his priestly ministry to others?

The Catholic Church makes it clear that one of a priest's main functions is to celebrate the Eucharist and feed the community on the body and blood of Christ. It was Mary, Christ's mother, a woman, that first gave the world the body of Christ. If Christ could take his flesh from a woman then why cannot a woman be used by Christ to continue to give his flesh – sacramentally – to the world? And while the Bible does not explicitly say that women should be ordained, it most certainly does not say that women should not be ordained!

Conservative people appeal to tradition. They say that we cannot do now what has not been done for 2000 years. But why not? I believe that God is revealed through tradition, the history of the community. But we also believe that tradition is an on-going thing. Christ is, to Christians, the fullness of God's revelation. But Christ's message is not completely contained in the Bible. St. John tells us that his Gospel is only a small part of what Christ had said. St. John says that if all that Christ said was to be written down the world itself could not contain all the books that would need to be written. So even today, after 2000 years, we are still only at the beginning of teasing out Christ's revelation.

Professor George Tavard, a Catholic priest-theologian, has written about women in Christian tradition. He welcomes the changes in the attitudes of the Church to women. But he points out that we still have a long way to go:

> I would suggest now that the liturgical reforms, the canonical adjustments, the institutional updating that have taken place in the last few years, and that are not yet completely effective, will be looked upon as elementary in comparison with the infinitely more thorough self-reform implied in the accession of women to the full freedom which they should enjoy in the Church. Even such a step as the introduction of a married clergy in the Latin rite would mean very little in terms of a reform of the Church as a whole: married men tend to be no less one-sided in their views and projects than single men. Sharing initiative, responsibility, and spiritual power with women would bring about much more altered ways of acting and thinking in both clergy and laity. It would undoubtedly have a cathartic effect that the half-hearted reforms of the last few years cannot possibly equal.

Father Tavard is telling us, I think, that in time to come we will see changes involving women in the Church that perhaps we cannot now even imagine! He is right. I believe that there will be women priests, bishops and, in time, a woman Pope. I would welcome this. The male authorities I've had to deal with are so harsh. I would much prefer the structures of the Catholic Church to incorporate the qualities of the female – the listening, the gentleness and the emphasis more on the heart than on the head.

In seminary one of our professors who did mention women did so in a very negative way. He was warning us about women and about how hard it is to deal with them. He summed up his advice with the words: 'Don't try to understand women. You will not be able to. Women are not like men. Women think with their womb!'

There is a great fear of women within the Church and the clergy. It may come from centuries of prejudiced thinking. It may come from some of the strange psychological forces within men. It may be a mixture of those and other things. But it is unrealistic and unhealthy.

At times, of course, women themselves have not helped their own cause. Some are brain-washed. I have found that some women I've spoken to are more opposed to the ordination of women, for instance, than are most men! Servile women and servile nuns have spoiled men and priests over the years and have often unwittingly contributed to their own enslavement. Mother Teresa is a good example. No-one can doubt her good work. It is a holy thing to give the homeless a home, to feed the hungry and to nurse the sick. But Mother Teresa is very submissive to the Vatican and the Pope. She obviously is like this because she believes that she should be obedient to the Vicar of Christ in Rome. But why does Mother Teresa not challenge the abuses in the Church the way she challenges other abuses she finds? And why, when she came to Ireland, did she allow herself to be used by right-wing Catholic elements who oppose social change, secularism and pluralism?

There was a joke going the rounds after the Second Vatican Council that might yet turn out to be prophetic. It went: 'At Vatican Three the bishops will bring their wives and at Vatican Four their husbands.' Thirty years ago conservative Irish Catholics never imagined that they would see lay men and women distributing Holy Communion. If they are around long enough they will see their new female parish priest. Personally I look forward to the day when every role in the Church, whether it be a ministerial or power role, is open to women. We will then have a better and more human Church.

CHAPTER 7

Sex – the Gateway to Hell

'There was no sex in Ireland until the television came'
Oliver J. Flanagan, TD

WHEN THE IRISH POLITICIAN, Oliver J. Flanagan – 'Blessed Oliver' as he
was called – made the above statement on RTE's *Late Late Show* we
all had a good laugh. We were all tempted to say: 'Oliver, if there was
no sex in Ireland until the television came, then where the hell did
you come out of?' But while we might have a laugh at Blessed Oliver's
expense we also have to realise that in a way he was speaking for the
whole of Ireland. For up until fairly recently we were all ignorant about
sex. We all talked about it in hushed tones. Inside we all had our own
feelings and our own struggles but somehow these were not to be
acknowledged to others and certainly not to be acknowledged publicly

Sex was just not talked about in the Ireland of the 1940s, 1950s and
1960s. When I was a 12-year-old in primary school with the Christian
Brothers at St. Canice's on the North Circular Road, Dublin, another
boy whispered to me one day in class: 'There's five facts of life.' I had
heard something about these fantastic 'facts of life' and I was now
absolutely curious about them. Who would I ask? I decided to ask my
father. So I waited my chance. The following Saturday afternoon we
were alone in the kitchen. 'Daddy', says I, 'can I ask you something?'
'Of course you can, son', was the reply. 'What is it?' 'Daddy, will you
tell me the five facts of life?' I might as well have thrown a hand-grenade
into the poor man's lap. He jumped out of his chair and looked away
from me. I could see him blushing very deeply and I couldn't
understand what I had done. We were quite poor at the time. But my
Dad put his hand into his pocket and handed me a new red ten-shilling
note! He told me to go to the shops and buy myself a nice new toy. I was
delighted with the present. But my curiosity about the five facts of life
grew stronger. And I also got the feeling that I was asking about something
'dirty' and unmentionable. I know that I'm not unusual in all of this. Very
few people of my generation and before had any sex education, either

at home or in school. We learned what we learned at the street corner or from school-mates. Sex was taboo in that Catholic Ireland.

I spent fourteen years in school, mostly at Catholic schools run by the Sisters of Mercy and the Christian Brothers. I had the old catechism drummed into me. But I never had any sex education and I never had any instructions on sexual morality. When we dealt with the sixth and ninth commandments, the Christian Brothers and priests passed very quickly over them. Many of those religious were obviously uncomfortable with these areas and communicated their discomfort to us, making us more curious and more confused. I can remember as a teenager having one priest for class who, when we asked about sex, used to blush deeply, sweat and shake all over. I never asked questions about sex in class. I would have been too embarrassed. But one or two of the 'hard men' in the class always liked embarrassing this poor priest. Looking back now I can see how cruel it all was.

Even in the seminary I had no sex instruction, apart from the strange interview with Archbishop McQuaid. There we were, scores of normal young men, with all the normal feelings and desires, supposed to be preparing for a lifetime of celibacy and chastity and nobody told us what was what, what to expect or how to handle the difficulties. The whole attitude was one of ignoring sex in the hope that it might go away. And of course it didn't.

But why talk about sex? Why consider it an issue? Well, of course it is an issue. We all know that the reproductive drive is one of our strongest instinctive urges. Sex is an issue for nearly everybody at some stage of life. And for some people it is more of an issue than for others. To ignore something important is always wrong. It never works. And there is something wrong about the Catholic Church ignoring and neglecting proper sex education when later on it imposes such huge restrictions on adults with regard to their sexuality. Recently, I had a visit from a lady teacher who teaches biology in a Catholic secondary school. As a natural part of her subject her students began talking about the human reproductive system and about masturbation. The teacher answered questions honestly and professionally. She is a young married woman. The next day the priest-principal reprimanded her for giving the 15-year-old boys and girls information on sex. 'They will have to know about the sleazy side of life soon enough,' the cleric said. The teacher was threatened with the sack if she repeated her offence. The same priest-principal recently detained a young 13-year-old boy for two hours after school. The kid had brushed against a girl-pupil in the scramble for the bus. The priest accused the confused young kid of having brushed against the girl's developing breasts. These stories say something rather sad about the view of sex that often exists within the Church and its clergy, schools and institutions.

It might not be as important for me to talk about sex here if Irish people did not have such a terrible guilt about the subject. They do have that guilt though. And they do need to be liberated from it. I used to have a lot of guilt myself about sex. I was too afraid to do very much about my sexuality as I was growing up but I had my desires and my fantasies. I regarded these as 'bad thoughts', as sins, mortal sins that kept me away from communion unless I had been to confession. I got my guilt from my ignorance and lack of information about sex. I got it from watching Catholic teachers, religious and priests being awkward about sex. I got it from listening to missioners coming to my home parish banging the pulpit about bad thoughts, impure actions and fornication. I got my guilt from being quizzed in confession by priests about every little detail of sex. Like others I was asked such questions as: 'What exactly were you thinking? Describe the picture. Had you an erection? Did you lose the seed? How often?' One priest told me when I was fifteen that every time I committed an impure action I murdered hundreds of thousands of innocent human beings. On a number of occasions, I have had to comfort and counsel women who were solicited in confession by priests. In one case, the priest had the young woman kissing him on the lips through the confessional grille and in another case the priest had a lady suck his finger through the grille. One can only guess what was going on in the priest's mind. In these cases the women are victims of the priest's immature or disturbed sexuality. But the priests are also victims – victims of an inadequate and distorting education and training.

In the past, the Church tried to control these situations, not by re-thinking its training and system, but by handling the 'symptoms' when they popped up. For instance, a priest was allowed to hear a man's confession outside the confessional but not allowed in the case of a woman. So ingenious priests got around this in various ways. One priest used to up-end his bike and put it between him and a woman so that the spokes of the front wheel formed a confessional grille

Another priest was reported to have heard a woman's confession through the cabbage colander in her kitchen!

Many Irish Catholics of my generation and before carry terrible guilt about sex because of Church teaching and because of confessional quizzings. Many Irish Catholic couples felt that they always had to make love in the dark and in the missionary position, because they regarded their partner's nudity and more adventurous positions as pleasure-seeking and as sinful. They were taught that sex was for having babies. The Church never told them, and still doesn't, that they should enjoy sex with each other. The Catholic Church, run as it often is by repressed celibates, has always had a most begrudging attitude to sex. And that's why it's important to talk about sex. It is an issue for a lot of people. A lot of people need to be liberated from their guilt and other hang-ups.

I now have a very different attitude to sex. I regard it as one of God's greatest gifts to the human race. It is there, not just for having babies, but to be thoroughly enjoyed – ideally in the context of love and respect. I have seen the harm that can be done by the negative attitude to sex. In 1994 I still get very sad and agitated letters from rural bachelors, spinsters, widows and widowers, asking me to reassure them that they will not go to hell because they masturbate. One such letter in November 1993 went:

Dear Father Pat,

I'm writing to you because I've read about you in the papers and I think that you are an open and understanding priest.

I have a small farm that I do not work any more except for a few sheep.

I never married as I never met a girl I liked enough to ask and I also felt that no-one would ever have me.

All my life I have been plagued with bad thoughts and impure actions against myself. I have even had impure thoughts at Mass about Our Lord on the Cross and about His Blessed Mother. I have also wondered about priests and their housekeepers.

Some priests I have been to confession to are very kind. Others have been very cross. I sometimes worry about going to Hell for my impurity. I'm afraid that I will not get to confession before I die and if I die impure I will be lost.

I know that you are very busy and that you have a lot of people to see after. But I would be very grateful if you could put my mind to rest. I enclose a donation for you to say a Mass for me that I might get the grace of purity.

Yours faithfully . . .

You would be surprised at how common such a letter is and how common such feelings of guilt and despair are. I always reply with a long and reassuring letter to such people. I point out that sexuality, masturbation and fantasies are normal. I tell them that the God who made them, sex and all, understands. I tell them that what they are talking about are not sins at all. And, depending on the level of their guilt and despair, I promise them, as a priest, that they will be all right and that God will take them to heaven when they die. But how sad it is to have lived your life in such moral slavery and misery! I don't know what heaven will be like. But people who have been so damaged by the Church's teaching on sex deserve to have God provide them with an out-and-out orgy as their part of being in paradise!

I have mentioned earlier the interviews about sex which Archbishop McQuaid gave me and my fellow-students when we entered the seminary. Looking back now, with the benefit of experience, how do I view that first interview with McQuaid? I am confused. Was it genuine pastoral care on his part ? Or was it a way for him to work out his own repression and frustration? I don't know the answer. If I was forced to make a judgement I think I would say that I feel it was a mixture of both. McQuaid was a good man in so many ways and did a great deal of good for troubled people. From my knowledge of him I know that there was no badness in him, whatever about weakness. But the interview shows the extreme forms of guilt, repression and fear that existed in the Catholic Church in Ireland with regard to sex even in the 1970s.

In Clonliffe we seminarians were locked up a great deal of the time and were therefore reasonably safe from women. We did have some nuns doing the catering but they were of an age and disposition that was certainly a 'cure for concupiscence'! We attended the Mater Dei Institute which was next door and which had a majority of women students – nuns and lay women. I became friendly, nothing else, with a young novice nun from Tipperary. The nearest we got to committing sin was having a coffee together. I was reprimanded by the Clonliffe Dean, Father Conway. Some older nuns had reported us. We were giving scandal! But if we were safe from women, we were not safe from ourselves and from each other. There were incidents of homosexuality in Clonliffe when I was there from 1970 to 1973. But I think they were rare. We were all very idealistic and had terrible hang-ups and guilt feelings about sex. But who could protect us from ourselves and from masturbation? Not even Father Conway and his nocturnal trips with his torch could stop that. And of course it happened.

CELIBACY

St. Paul, in his letters, said that a bishop should be the husband of one wife. From the 4th century there was a growing tradition in the church which called for celibacy. But this tradition was not universally imposed until the 12th century. We had married priests in Ireland until much later. That's where we get surnames like MacEntaggart, (the son of the priest), MacAnespie, (the son of the bishop) and McNabb, (the son of the abbot). So what's new in the Casey affair? The late Cardinal O Fiaich told me during a meeting I had with him sometime before his death that there was a parish in Co. Tyrone where the priesthood passed from father to son for some two hundred years and that that family were some connection of his own. In the beginning, therefore, clerical celibacy was optional. And it still should be. One day soon it will again be optional.

Already we see the thin end of the wedge. The Church has allowed converting Anglican vicars to become Catholic priests and retain their wives. These men are generally deployed in the more liberal United States. The Church has also allowed two married Catholic men in Brazil to be ordained. The men can stay married, continue to sleep with their wives but must promise not to engage in intercourse! This makes both the priesthood and the sacrament of marriage a laughing stock. And how does Pope John Paul II hope to implement this unrealistic ruling? He is a major obstacle towards progress in the Catholic Church. He has outlived his time. The Church will not make progress until John Paul goes to his heavenly reward. When that happens we will have married priests and we will be a step nearer having women priests too. Someone said quite wittily: 'John Paul kisses the ground and walks on women. He would be better kissing the women and walking on the ground!' Another story concerns John Paul praying some time ago in his private chapel. God appears to him and allows the Pope to ask three questions. 'Will there be married priests in the Church?' John Paul asks. 'Not in your time', answers God. 'Will there be women priests?' 'Not in your time,' says God again. Finally John Paul enquires: 'Will there be another Polish Pope?' Quickly God answers: 'Not in my time.' I hope God is right. I hope there won't be another John Paul. My only fear is that if John Paul dies too quickly they'll give the job to Cahal Daly! 'But he's seventy-five,' I hear the reader protest. 'I know,' I answer, 'but who thought he'd succeed Tom O Fiaich when he was seventy-three!' No, I think I have more faith than that in the Holy Spirit although I'm not sure he gets much say in papal elections.

Celibacy is not working for the Church. In the last few decades 120,000 priests have left the active priesthood, many to marry. That's one quarter of the world's priests. The sad story of this phenomenon is told in that excellent book by David Rice – *Shattered Vows*. David is a former Dominican priest from Newry, Co. Down. It is estimated that up to a thousand Irish priests have left. That's one-seventh of all the priests of Ireland. The sad thing is that those who leave are often the best priests. Their only crime was to fall in love. Many of them would have liked to stay married and also stay in the active ministry. And why not? How stupid it is of the Church to have literally thousands of ordained priests out there willing to serve and not to allow them to do so. Instead the Church is closing parishes and leaving people without the Eucharist and the other Sacraments.

At the same time, among those priests who stay, many cannot cope with celibacy. An unknown, but certainly substantial, number of priests and even some bishops are caught up in illicit affairs of both the heterosexual and homosexual kind. The strain of celibacy causes others to be unhappy and repressed. It leads some priests to have nervous breakdowns and into abuse of alcohol and drugs. The cost of clerical celibacy to the Church and to the people of God who make up the Church is incalculable.

It was in 1992 that this whole question burst into the open in Ireland when the story of Bishop Eamonn Casey of Galway hit the international headlines. The Bishop was found to have had an affair some 17 years before, when he was then the Bishop of Kerry. The affair had remained a secret until the woman, in an effort to get the Bishop to acknowledge his son and pay for his education, broke the story to an Irish newspaper. The Bishop made a hasty departure from the country and sought refuge from the publicity in South America. It was later discovered that he had taken some £70,000, later said to have been refunded, from the diocesan funds to give to his former mistress and her son. In that same year, an Irish priest on loan to a parish in England, ran away with a 17-year-old female parishioner. And the ITV *World in Action* programme (20 July, 1992) gave a lot of publicity to the number of priests, some of them Irish, who sexually abused children.

In Ireland, the Bishop Casey affair triggered repercussions, the full extent and force of which cannot yet be assessed. Certainly it demolished the episcopal pedestals from which Irish bishops liked to lord it over their priests and their flocks. They were thrown into such confusion and embarrassment that several of them, unwilling to face the media, felt it opportune to leave the country on hastily-arranged holidays and on pilgrimages to Lourdes. One cartoonist showed the VIP lounge at Dublin airport with a notice on the wall: WOULD THE LAST BISHOP OUT PLEASE PUT OFF THE LIGHTS. At the airport, RTE's Charlie Bird tackled Cardinal Daly. 'Were there other bishops and priests out of line sexually?' he asked. The Cardinal lost his cool and blew a gasket. These were evil rumours, the Cardinal insisted. But his disclaimer did not kill other rumours to the effect that Eamonn Casey was not the only bishop in the country with a sexual skeleton in his cupboard.

It would, however, be wrong to suggest that the Irish clergy are especially remiss in their observance of celibacy. In fact, for all I know, Ireland could be very well down the league. One hears of the many South American, African and Italian priests who do not consider themselves bound to a celibate life. And, in the past few years, the incidences of concubinage and sexual abuse of children among priests and brothers in the US and Canada provide an indisputable indication of the fact that the man-made law of clerical celibacy is not being seen by a growing number of North American clergy as binding on them. I'm sure that if we had optional celibacy in the morning there would still be priests committing fornication and adultery and abusing children. But if we took away obligatory celibacy and all this dark repressive guilt priests have, there would be far fewer instances of them doing something illicit about their sexual needs.

What does a priest who falls in love do? I have occasionally been consulted by priests in this position. If the priest wants to leave the priesthood and marry, I encourage him to do so. However, the present Pope will not dispense priests unless they can get a medical certificate saying they are either mentally ill or a pervert! That is downright evil. Often when a priest leaves, the local church authorities will positively see to it that he cannot get a job. That is evil too. But some priests leave and do well. Without a dispensation they cannot marry in church. They often have to go to a registry office. This means that the Catholic Church believes they are 'living in sin' and cannot go to communion. Traditional Catholic teaching would have it that if they died in their 'sin', they would go to hell. Where is charity? I am always happy to celebrate marriages for these priests. As I write this, I am, in fact, preparing to do such a marriage tomorrow. How does the hierarchy's attitude to priests who want to leave square with the parable of the Good Shepherd which they preach to us? Why can't they, if they are good shepherds, leave the 99 'good' sheep and search for the 'lost' sheep as the Lord told them to? Why the hypocrisy? And why do the rest of us not call this hypocrisy what it is? Is it because we think that the bishop or the Pope is God? If a priest comes to me and does not want to leave the priesthood and if his partner is happy for him to stay, then I believe that he is morally entitled to continue as a priest and to continue in the relationship. The celibacy law is a bad law. People are not bound to obey bad laws. Even the old catechism told us that we were not bound to obey our parents or our superiors if they asked us to do something sinful. To force a man to live the celibate life when he is no fit to do so is a real mortal sin. It is not the poor priests who break their celibacy promises but those who place that unbearable burden on every priest's shoulder who commit the greater sin. Ignorant people say: 'He had six or seven years to make up his mind. He has made his bed; let him lie on it.' Nonsense. Who knows everything at 18 or even 24 particularly if you have been sheltered from the world? And how can you make a promise at 24 and be sure that you can still keep it at 54 when you and the world will both have changed? Those priests who can do this are to be congratulated. Fair play to them! But those who cannot are not to be condemned. They are to be loved and helped. If celibacy were optional, this problem would be solved.

And what of the women who are involved in sexual relationships with Irish priests and bishops? In the wake of the Eamonn Casey affair I have been contacted by 57 such women. Six of them had babies fathered by priests. Four have had abortions at the insistence of the priests concerned. One was asked to have an abortion and refused. In all the cases I've heard from these women to date, it was the priest who initiated the relationship. It often happened when the woman went to the priest to discuss a personal or a marriage problem. I also get the very strong picture that the women in these relationships are mature, committed and, if you like, in love, whereas the priests seem more immature, less committed and more interested in sex than in an emotional relationship and bond. I came across a case where one priest was having a sexual relationship with six women at the one time! We discovered this only when I put two women, who had contacted me because they were in a relationship with a priest, in touch with each other for mutual support. At their first meeting, they discovered they were in love with and sleeping with the same priest! When they did a bit of detective work, they discovered there were four other women sleeping with him too! The priest's name must remain confidential for now. Many of the women who have contacted me are in relationships with a priest who has another relationship going – often with a nun!

SOME STORIES OF PRIESTS AND THEIR WOMEN

To give the reader some grasp of how priests can treat women with whom they are involved in a relationship, I will recall four stories I have heard from women who have been in touch with me. To protect confidentiality, the names, places and small details have been altered. But the stories are true.

MAIRÉAD

Mairéad is a nurse. She works in an institution over which the Catholic Church has a fair amount of control. Though married, she has had a seven-year relationship with a priest, former chaplain at her workplace.

Mairéad and her husband, it seems, cannot have a child. They have both been tested extensively and nothing has shown up. Mairéad went to the priest to discuss her inability to have a child and the emotional strain that this was placing on her marriage and her own mental and emotional life. He was very understanding. He listened for two hours. When Mairéad's voice shook he held her hand. When she broke down and cried, he sat beside her and squeezed her tightly. When she was leaving his house, he left her to the hallway. He pressed her against the wall and kissed her passionately on the mouth. Mairéad, still upset and tear-stained, was confused. She had not thought of the priest as a lover or as someone who was physically or sexually attractive to her.

Mairéad's relationship with her husband was poor. He was a moody young man who found it difficult to express his feelings. He was a bit uncomfortable with sex and love-making. Since he found out that Mairéad and himself could not have children he was even more uptight. He talked even less and he hardly ever made love to Mairéad.

Mairéad had occasion to meet the priest nearly every day. He started to seek her out. He would come and sit with her in her office for hours, drinking tea and eating toast. A few times he brought wine or champagne for their meetings.

Within a fortnight of Mairéad going to see the priest, they were having a full sexual relationship, which Mairéad admits she enjoyed. But she was a little bit surprised at his sexual appetite. They had sex four and five times a week – nearly always in his house. But they did organise a few weekends away as a Mr and Mrs. The priest produced a number of pornographic magazines and a number of pornographic videos. He said that he had got these from a priest-friend. He would ask Mairéad to watch the videos with him and then do to him what she saw the women doing to the men on the videos. At first Mairéad was reluctant but agreed and, after a while, 'kinky' sex, as she calls it, became a normal part of their love-making.

One Christmas Eve Mairéad approached him after Midnight Mass with some news: 'I'm pregnant!' At first he was shocked. He brought her to the presbytery and showed her a new video he had got his hands on. They then made love. That particular love-making session was very violent. He hurt Mairéad badly.

A week after Christmas the priest spoke to Mairéad about the pregnancy. He wanted it terminated. Mairéad was shocked. 'Is that not killing?' she asked. 'No, it's not, Mairéad,' he said. 'It is just a bundle of cells at this stage. Let's do it early.' Mairéad told her husband that she was going to London on business.

She and the priest flew to England and she had an abortion. The priest paid for the whole trip and for the medical expenses. He sat with her in the abortion clinic while she had the abortion. He told her that she had done nothing wrong. After the abortion they had four days together in a London hotel. They went sightseeing. They had meals and drinks. He purchased a generous supply of condoms for himself. He asked Mairéad to think about going on the pill.

When they returned to Ireland he and Mairéad continued to see each other and make love. They exchanged monies and gifts. Her husband accepted that they were just good friends. But the priest was very jealous of her husband. He used to say to Mairéad: 'I can't stand the thoughts of that creep near you. Don't ever have a baby with him, please!'

Mairéad became more and more involved with the priest and started to love and want him more and more. She even suggested that he would leave the priesthood and that she would leave her husband. But he refused. There was something else about him that Mairéad didn't like. He had a ten-year friendship with a nun. The nun used to ring him every day. He was never able to tell the nun about Mairéad. The nun used to visit him for a weekend every month. During that weekend, he did not see Mairéad and she was not allowed to visit or ring his house. He said that the friendship with the nun was only a friendship. But Mairéad feared otherwise. On one occasion she found the nun's panties among his washing in the bathroom. On another occasion she found the nun's sanitary towels hidden in his wardrobe. On two occasions, she found used condoms in his toilet.

Eventually Mairéad couldn't cope with the nun's presence in his life. They fought about it. The nun seemed to have a terrible hold on him. Mairéad eventually gave him an ultimatum – 'It's me or the nun.' He stopped seeing Mairéad. Mairéad rang the nun and asked to meet her. The nun told Mairéad that they had nothing to talk about, that he was hers and that she, Mairéad, was a slut and an adulteress.

At the same time Mairéad found out that she was pregnant again. She told him. The priest replied: 'Are you sure it's mine?' Mairéad was devastated and went into an emotional flap. He ignored her and told her that their affair was over. For a while Mairéad kept ringing him and calling at his door. He refused to let her in. Mairéad confided in her GP who sent her to a specialist. She also told some friends. Eventually she told the whole sorry tale to her husband. He was devastated. But they have stayed together and are bringing up the baby as their own.

All this time Mairéad was meeting the priest every day at work. He either ignored her or sneered at her. Mairéad and her husband felt that it would help them get their lives back together if the priest was not in their orbit and if Mairéad didn't have to meet him every day. They both went and asked him to seek a move from the bishop. He laughed at them and slammed the door in their faces. They decided to approach the bishop themselves. The bishop saw them briefly but was very cold and non-committal with them. His Lordship described the priest as a great priest. They asked the bishop to move him and promised that that would end the matter. The bishop refused to say whether or not he would move the priest. The couple left it for two months and nothing happened.

Eventually Mairéad and her husband wrote to the bishop threatening that if the priest was not moved they would begin legal action and would go public. He was moved within a week. He never contacts Mairéad now about his son. Mairéad and her husband are receiving counselling and hope to have a better marriage so that they can provide their 'son' with the love he needs.

DEIRDRE

Deirdre is a married woman with grown children. She has had a terrible life. Her husband has always been very neurotic and has always abused with alcohol. He is and always has been an angry, violent man. For 20 years now they have lived totally separate lives. She has no feelings left for her husband. He claims that he has always loved her.

Ten years ago, Deirdre was feeling particularly down and went for counselling. The counsellor she approached happened to be a Catholic priest. She poured her heart out to him. He was a great listener. He began visiting Deirdre's home and said he wished to befriend the couple and the whole family so that he could facilitate healing and reconciliation. From the beginning Deirdre's husband hated him.

The priest started taking Deirdre for walks, drives and meals. She found the listening, sensitive company exhilarating. She hadn't ever had this. He rang her every day. He brought her little gifts and flowers. He sent her little cards. They had pet-names for each other. They held hands, embraced and kissed. They fondled each other's genitals. And after a while they started going to bed together. They never had full intercourse. The priest felt that they could go quite far with each other but they could never go to the point where he would 'lose the seed'. This, he said, would be a sin. So Deirdre had to be content with the withdrawal method of contraception.

But there was another problem. The priest had a 20-year relationship with a nun. According to the priest, he and the nun had been to various spiritual directors together. These directors had told them that they were spiritual husband and wife. And he told Deirdre that because of this it was all right for him to 'lose the seed' with the nun. The nun was his primary partner. Deirdre was to be woman B. And apparently there may have been others.

There was a great deal of tension and jealousy between Deirdre and the nun. They were both vying for the priest's love and attention. He seemed to be happy to have two women fighting over him or wanting him. He also had the occasional bout of scruples and guilt about it all. When he felt guilty he would go to confession and have either the nun or Deirdre serve Mass for him. He had been on courses in various parts of Europe and the United States and he assured Deirdre that priest/women, priest/nun relationships were the norm in the universal Church. 'In America,' he told her, 'they have the "Third Way", where priests and nuns have spiritual marriages with each other.' But Deirdre felt no guilt anyway. The priest was the guilty one at times.

At present Deirdre, the priest and the nun are still in their triangle. There has been no resolution. Their situation is not unusual. The nun in this case has been open with her religious superior. But her religious superior is also involved amorously with a priest. So the Reverend Mother is not really in a position to rap sister's knuckles!

FIONA

Fiona is a middle-aged widow. Her husband was killed in an accident at work some years ago. He was wealthy and left her very well-off. She got a large sum in compensation for his death. They had no children.

When Fiona's husband died, a local priest came to comfort the widow and to make the funeral arrangements. He was very kind. He saw Fiona through all her trauma. They became friends. He would call to Fiona for a meal. He would have her to his presbytery for tea.

Fiona and the priest knew each other for a year before they even touched or held hands. He was very, very shy. Eventually Fiona took the initiative and held his hand. It was she who placed a kiss on his cheek for the first time. It was another year before he and Fiona got around to making love. He was very afraid and very guilt-ridden.

He is a very good priest. He is a great preacher and the people love it when he comes out to say Mass. He is very good with the children in the parish schools. The priest himself comes from a very wealthy family and is very well off. He gives away a lot of money to the poor and to charities. But he spends some of his money on himself and Fiona too. He likes nice clothes, cars, regular continental holidays, good food, fine wines and a well-kept and decorated home.

Fiona and he meet three or four nights a week for a meal, a few drinks and to spend the night together. Sometimes the venue is Fiona's home and sometimes it is his presbytery. They take short breaks together every year and spend a month abroad together each summer.

The only cloud in their sky is his terrible scruples and guilt. Fiona has no such problems. She feels that they are both adults and that they are hurting no one. The priest loves Fiona and could never give her up. But he is tortured by his conscience which has been formed by traditional Catholic teaching. He is convinced that he is living in sin but sees no way out. He does not want to leave the priesthood. Sometimes to cope with his guilt he drinks too much. He has talked to one bishop and several priests about his dilemma. They have all told him that he is not doing wrong, that the Church's celibacy laws are unjust and that God understands. This reassurance helps him at the time but he always slips back into his guilt track soon again. He will not give Fiona up. Nor will he give up the priesthood. It casts a cloud over their fairly happy relationship. He feels it is the price he must pay. There is no-one else in his life or in Fiona's. I met this couple because Fiona felt that I might help him with his scruples. I did, temporarily. I have offered to celebrate their marriage – a marriage that would remain our secret. He is still thinking about it.

JANE

There is no better way to see and understand the working of the Catholic Church than when it is challenged by a crisis. It is then the system appears in its true colours. One of the women who approached me after the Bishop Casey affair was a woman I will call Jane.

Jane was married to an alcoholic and aggressive husband and was the mother of several children. She lived in a settled city suburb. One of the parish curates, newly-ordained, began calling on her home. It seemed that priest and family became good friends. But gradually Jane began to realise that the priest's friendship was not just platonic and harmless. He was beginning to show a deep interest in her. He visited her when she was ill and a relationship began between them.

It continued for many years – well over a decade. It was a very loving relationship, Jane says, and also deeply physical and sexual. They made love often. Occasionally the priest would grab her and throw her on the bed and make passionate love to her. 'I cannot live without a woman,' he told Jane often. He asked Jane to wear black lace underwear and other 'kinky' clothing. He liked to photograph her in the nude and in her different underwear. But he never got the films developed. He always left that to Jane.

Eventually the priest and Jane decided to set up home together. She left her husband and moved to a new house which they both paid for but which was in Jane's name. They opened a joint bank account – often giving or lending each other hundreds, if not thousands, of pounds. Jane lived in their new home as a housewife. The priest continued to work as a priest and commute to the love-nest. Jane says that she could have had ten children but she had had a hysterectomy and was therefore 'safe'. The priest knew that and he had a field day.

Eventually things came to a head and the bishop found out about the relationship. The priest was put under pressure to break it off. He was weak and succumbed to hierarchical pressures, although he still kept in touch. The Church authorities then sent him abroad. This kept him out of the way. While away he became involved with other women. Jane knew, forgave him and continued to offer him moral and financial support.

The Church authorities brought in some clerical 'heavy guns'. There are a few such priest trouble-shooters like this in Ireland. They are reasonably well-known clerics who pretend to be liberal but are really reactionary hit-men. They put pressure on Jane. They convinced her to leave her house and go to the US. She was told that she could live there in a presbytery with her priest-lover. An American bank account was opened for her. The priests in Ireland tried to get her to sell her home by giving them power of attorney.

Above all Jane was asked to keep quiet. She did so for a while in the hope of rejoining her priest-friend. But hope of this receded. She eventually talked to some journalists. She was put in touch with me. I wrote to the priest involved. He ignored my letter. I rang his presbytery and left a message for him to telephone me. He never did even though his parish priest assured me that he would. I simply wanted him to tell Jane where she really stood with him and to support her financially and through counselling until she could cope with all that had happened.

Jane spoke to a number of senior clergymen and bishops about the situation. Some of them agreed that she was treated in the most awful way. Others, it was obvious, were trying to protect the priest who had fled. They were also interested in saving the 'good name' of the Catholic Church. They were not really concerned about her and what the whole affair was doing to her and her health. She was asked how much money it would take to buy her off!

Jane has not only lost her faith in the Church and in priests but she has lost her health and peace of mind. She is a sad, lonely and abandoned woman. The Church cynically ignores her plight and hides her lover. When she challenges them they contact her doctor to see if he will say that she is mad.

Jane's story is not unique in Ireland. I have heard a similar story at least 56 times this past year. This is as yet an untold tragedy. The Pope, the world's bishops and the Irish Catholic hierarchy know what's happening. But no man among them is prepared to stand up, admit the truth and call a halt to the tragedy. All the bishops are concerned about is preventing 'scandal'.

There are hundreds of Janes in Ireland. They need our love, our understanding and our help. They do not need our denial, our condemnation and our cynical neglect. When I meet people like Jane I see how the Catholic Church has failed in Ireland. I see the emptiness of all the sermons and feel the hypocrisy of all the fine public statements. And when I hear cardinals and bishops lecture politicians about low standards in high places, then, on behalf of all the Janes in Ireland, I scream: 'Physicians, heal yourselves!'

Women who have drifted into relationships with priests need the Church's help. Many of these women became involved with priests quite innocently. Sometimes it began when they went to the priests for counselling. These are not bad women. I was shocked by the attitude of many Irish people, especially Irish women, to Annie Murphy – Bishop Casey's girl-friend. These people excused and forgave Casey and wrote Annie off as a loose woman. That's more Irish Catholic hypocrisy. It takes two to tango. Annie Murphy was in her twenties. She was just getting over a bad marriage and a divorce trauma. She was in a strange country. Bishop Casey had told her father to send her to him for help and healing. Bishop Casey was an experienced priest and bishop with vast social work skills behind him. He was old enough to be Annie Murphy's father. Casey was at least 50 per cent responsible for what happened and only our Irish Catholic hypocrisy and prejudice can stop us seeing that. Women who become involved with priests are, like the priests, victims of the unjust celibacy law. These women should have our support and understanding. The Church should pay their counselling and other expenses. And if there are children involved, the Church has responsibility to the children, particularly if the man remains in the priesthood. In a very real way, these children are the children of the Church.

As a direct result of Cardinal Daly's Dublin airport contention that liaisons between clerics and women were 'rumours', I was contacted by a lady who was very angry with the Cardinal. She had been in a relationship with a priest. She felt very hurt at the way the priest had treated her. The Bishop Casey affair brought all her pain back to her. She was now having her hurt compounded by hearing the leader of the Catholic Church in Ireland write her off as a 'rumour'. She contacted five priests for help. They were uninterested. She then sent a message to the bishops to say that if the Cardinal continued to write off as rumours her and those like her she would go public.

Since she contacted me we have set up a very loosely-organised support group for women involved with priests. We have called it Bethany Revisited. Bethany was the place in the Gospels where Jesus went to visit his female friends, Martha and Mary, and their brother Lazarus. At Bethany Jesus got a nice meal, a bed for the night and, more importantly, friendship and companionship. We know from the scriptures that Mary sat at Christ's feet listening to him. Christ needed to unburden himself to Mary. Bethany symbolises Christ's need for the female dimension in his life. And Christ was God. How much more must human priests need the female? Bethany was also the place mentioned in the New Testament where, before his crucifixion, a woman came to table and anointed Christ with costly ointment. The Apostles reprimanded her. Jesus defended the woman and rebuked the Apostles, the early hierarchy. At Bethany we see Christ defending women and reprimanding the early hierarchy who tried to stop the woman ministering to him. The Church more than ever needs the full ministry of women. That must eventually express itself in women having total access to every level of ministry in the Church, including priesthood, episcopacy and papacy. If women had more power in the Church we would have a kinder and more compassionate Church. Those of us who have suffered at the hands of the patriarchy in the Church know this well. If we had women bishops and priests we would have a more human Church. If our male bishops and priests had wives we would have a more balanced and human male priesthood.

In Bethany Revisited we want to persuade the Church to take responsibility for the women involved in relationships with priests, to help with the costs of counselling them and to be responsible for those children fathered by priests. In the United States a similar group, Good Tidings, started in the 1980s with three members and now has over 1,000. Another United States group, Promises, has 42 members. At one of their centres in Chicago seven women come to their meetings accompanied by their seven priest partners. The celibacy crisis in the Catholic Church is crying out for urgent attention.

We Irish Catholics think that the Catholic world begins and ends in Ireland. We forget that we are only four million of the world's one thousand million Catholics. Ireland, like Poland, is a very conservative Catholic country. But in other, more advanced Catholic countries the practice of the faith is very different.

A few years ago I visited Holland and was invited for tea by the local parish priest where I was staying. He was a tall handsome young man in his thirties. We were sitting talking when a very beautiful young lady in her late twenties opened the door and brought in the coffee. When she left I thought that I was being smart and remarked: 'That's quite a housekeeper you have there.' The priest never smiled. 'This is not my housekeeper,' he said, 'this is my wife.' He was not joking. A few years previously he had been married by a bishop in Holland. 'What of Rome?' I asked. He answered: 'What Rome does not know does not worry it.' His parishioners knew his position and were happy. This young Dutch priest assured me that there were many married priests in Holland. He had also heard of some in Belgium and Germany.

Some time later I went back again to Holland to attend an international congress of priests who have left the active ministry to marry and of their partners. There was one very interesting couple there – a priest who was still in the official ministry and his wife or partner. The priest lives in one house. The wife lives next door. They go in and out their separate front doors but inside they have a connecting door! So where there is a will there will be a way.

In the United States some of the liberal bishops tolerate priests with partners and children and leave them as pastors of parishes. Again these bishops allow this unofficially and feel that what Rome does not know will not really worry it. If John Paul knew everything that was going on in the Catholic world he would have canaries. People are right to flout these unjust laws. We are not bound by bad laws and unjust laws.

PRIESTS IN RELATIONSHIP

I would not like the reader to think that I am without sympathy for priests who find themselves in love and in a relationship. I have great sympathy for such priests especially when they are sincerely trying to come to terms with the contradictions involved in their situation and when they are being kind and considerate to their partners. In these situations the women suffer terribly but there can be suffering of the most intense kind for the priests too.

In the very repressed and conservative Ireland from which we are thankfully emerging it was a terrible thing for a priest to be involved in a relationship and as a result many of these relationships had to be kept secret. It was also a very shameful thing for a priest to leave the priesthood. Even when a student left the seminary he was branded a 'spoiled priest' by very unkind communities. And so there were great secrets.

On a recent visit to a large Irish town I heard a most unusual and moving story in this regard. A lady stopped me on the street, asked if I was Father Buckley, and proceeded to tell me a story the likes of which I had not heard before. She had been married to a man for over thirty years. They were very happily married and had a good life together. He was a good deal older than her and a few years ago, when he was in his eighties, he was on his death bed. She sat with him every night. One night in the early hours of the morning, he opened his eyes and looked at her, and said: 'I want to say Mass.' She thought he was delirious and that the end was near. But he wasn't. He confessed to her that as a young man he had been ordained a priest but had soon left the priesthood. But he was deeply ashamed of this and could never tell anyone, not even his wife. The next morning the lady got him out of bed, drove him to a monastery where the situation had been explained to the monks. The dying man was allowed to say his Mass, his first in 35 years. He died happy. But we can only guess at how much that man must have suffered for three or four decades as he carried his terrible secret, not able to share it even with the love of his life. How many people, I wonder, has the Church condemned to live lives of quiet desperation?

In 1993 the newspapers were full of the sad case of a parish priest from Cardiff in Wales. He had fallen in love with a young Catholic teacher. He was pulled between the priesthood and his relationship. His bishop sent him to a rehabilitation centre for priests. He was not allowed to be in contact with the woman he loved. She lost her job and as a result, her home. She discovered she was pregnant. It was all too much for him – one night he threw himself in front of a train and ended his life and his suffering. His partner was left behind to cope without him. Here, in a very striking case, we see how the Church's obligatory celibacy laws are producing bad if not evil fruit. This suicide is not unique. Priests involved in relationships can suffer terribly too. They too are victims. I feel deeply sorry for them and I feel that we need optional celibacy in our Church so that these tragic situations will not be necessary.

BAD THOUGHTS

As the old joke has it, a young man once confessed to a priest that he had had bad thoughts. 'Did you entertain them?' asked the priest. 'No Father', replied the penitent, 'they entertained me.' If we had a more relaxed and humorous approach to sexuality we would be better people. What are bad thoughts anyway? They are obviously, according to our traditional Catholic thinking, thoughts of a sexual nature. But surely thoughts are neutral, at least when they first strike us. Is not our imagination a God-given gift too? If it were not for the imagination would we have artists? Without an imagination would Michelangelo have created his works in the Vatican's Sistine Chapel? And of course when Michelangelo did first paint those scenes the people in them were naked until a cardinal with 'purity' on his mind forced him to clothe his creations. The artist was surely right to include the objecting cardinal in his painting, languishing in hell. The purity pedlars have condemned so many others to a lifetime in hell – a hell of guilt.

If we get a thought flashing across our mind of a naked human body is that a bad thought? Can it be a sin to picture a naked human body? God made the human body. Can it be a sin simply to picture one of God's creations? Surely it's what we do about our thoughts that make them 'bad'. If an artist is painting a picture and imagines a naked body which he then transfers to canvas is he guilty of bad thoughts? If a Christian person, or any person, pictures or sees a naked body, inside or outside of their mind, and simply appreciates the beauty of that body or even thanks God for it, have they committed the sin of having bad thoughts? I can understand the Church teaching that thoughts of rape, child molestation or violence of some other kind might be bad thoughts. But most of us don't seriously have many of those. So are many of our thoughts not just a natural part of the human imaginative process and therefore quite 'normal' and neutral? Maybe we Christians or Catholics invest thoughts with an importance or a 'badness' by constantly harping on about such things in a negative way? Is it not the forbidden fruit syndrome? The more we ban it, the more mystique we create around it, the more compelling and attractive we make it. It's something the same with alcohol in Ireland. If our children grew up like they do in other countries having their glass of wine or beer with the family meal, would we have such a national problem with alcohol? Rather than frighten the life out of people about bad thoughts, perhaps we would be better if we encouraged people to be open and talk about things. I wonder if people brought up in naturalist or nudist communities are troubled with bad thoughts like we clothed Catholics are? Sometimes we do more harm than good. An Irish Redemptorist priest once wrote a very chilling booklet about the evils of courtship – 'company-keeping' as it was called. The Redemptorists were experts at frightening people about sexual sins during parish missions. Thirty years later, the author was giving a mission in North Antrim parish. He visited one home where there was a very elderly couple living with their daughter – an unmarried 'girl' in her fifties. During the visit the priest was reprimanding the girl about being unmarried. 'You're wasting your life, woman,' the priest boomed. 'Why didn't you marry?' 'Because,' answered the girl, 'I made the mistake of reading your bloody book!' Perhaps Oscar Wilde was right when he said that the best way to get rid of a temptation was to give in to it. Maybe bad thoughts would trouble us all a bit less if we didn't pay so much attention to them. There is not the same preoccupation in the 1990s Ireland with bad thoughts. That's a good thing. However the area which still remains a problem for many people of 40 and over is masturbation.

MASTURBATION

Pope John Paul II has said that masturbation is a serious sin and could get you to hell. If that's the case, I expect very few people to make it to heaven and hell to be bulging at the seams. Masturbation has certainly been condemned by the Christian tradition for a long time and for differing reasons. Onan, in the Old Testament, was guilty of spilling his seed on the ground and the Church often called masturbation Onanism. Some Christian thinkers believed that the whole human being was contained in the man's semen. For that reason it was believed that if a man spilt his own seed he was 'murdering' whatever number of innocent babies – mass abortions or holocausts, if you like! Obviously no sane person believes this any more. But there is this big hang-up about 'spilling the seed'. That's why, for instance, the Church condemns as sinful the withdrawal method of contraception in which the man achieves orgasm outside the woman's body.

I can't understand this preoccupation with spilling the seed. After all, if a man does not masturbate, his body will spill the seed for him during his sleep in a nocturnal emission anyway, the so-called 'wet dream'. So if nature has a built-in 'spilling of the seed' procedure, then how can spilling the seed be so sinful? God created nature. The Church would say that what the body does is natural but that people cannot use their will to bring any of these things about. So the natural wet dream does not make masturbation 'moral' any more than the natural abortion, the miscarriage, permits a procured abortion. It is all down to the will and the non-interference with nature. So nature can do what it wants with our bodies but we can't?

I think we make a mountain out of a molehill when it comes to masturbation. Many people masturbate throughout life whether they are married or unmarried. And it is more to do with habit and maybe loneliness and pleasure-seeking than it is with morality. It has no more moral meaning, in most cases, than a baby sucking its thumb or clinging to its favourite piece of blanket or its teddy-bear. Masturbation cannot make you blind. But we do know that it can sometimes interfere with the adult ability to give most generously in a two-person sexual encounter. For that reason it is important – to the mature person, to the marriage guidance counsellor or to the client/psychotherapist relationship. But it is certainly not about big sin. If it is about anything negative it is about human searching and human woundedness. It is not about hell. Nor is it something we should frighten our teenage young Catholics about. If the Church and priests want to get involved in the masturbation issue they should do so as pastors and carers who are prepared to listen and to help people towards greater self-knowledge and wholeness. In the 1980s there was at least one Irish parish priest accusing young people of committing murder by masturbating. I had to console some of his former penitents. He is still an active parish priest. I sure hope his confessional queues are mighty short or at least consist of those who are old and tired enough to have given up 'polluting' themselves ! And there's no need to worry about the seed. It's not like coal or oil. It is not about to run out on us. The good God saw to that!

PRE-MARITAL SEX

Father,' I'm often asked, 'is it a sin to sleep with someone?' I always answer: 'No, it is not. It is only a sin when you stay awake!' My experience of dealing with young people tells me that the vast majority of modern Irish young people have sex before they are married. Parents and church leaders don't like to believe this. But it is true. I'm not saying that this makes it right. I'm simply saying that it is true. Every parent thinks that their Mary or their Johnnie isn't doing it and most parents are wrong.

The Church officially teaches that sexual intercourse is morally right only within marriage. The Church is entitled to teach this and to call its adherents to live by the ethic they propose for them. I think that this definition is too narrow and I don't agree with it. I believe that sex between two consenting adults, engaged in for love's sake and not merely to use someone, is morally legitimate. It is the fact that the sexual expression takes place in the context of love that makes it most moral and good, not that there is a marriage certificate to back it up. Often sexual intercourse in marriage lacks love. Marriage does not always make it loving and moral. I recently met a man whose wife has been in hospital for years. She will never be discharged but she could live many more years. He visits her four or five times a week. He spends long hours with her and sees to all her needs. She does not reciprocate his devotion. She cannot. He would not dream of divorcing her. It would kill her. He would not do that. He has all the obligations of a husband but none of the privileges. He, too, has needs. In fact, the burden of caring for such a chronically ill wife gives him even greater needs for love and support and companionship. He needs a woman's companionship. He has found it in a female friend, herself a widow. A sexual relationship is a small part of their overall relationship. This man and this woman have a sexual relationship outside marriage. They are not committing a sin. They are in love and that love is good. The celibate Catholic hierarchy expects this man to be a life-long abstainer. He cannot be this. If he were he would be less of a person and less a child of God. His relationship is condemned by the Church as 'living in sin'. God loves him just as he is and especially as he is caring for his wife. God does not begrudge him his second happy relationship. God sent his friend his way. 'Should I go to communion?' he asked me. 'Of course you should,' I told him. 'Only serious sin can keep you from communion. You are not committing a sin. You might be if you turned your back on your sick wife who needs you. You might even sin if you turned your back on the second woman God has given you to help you carry your cross, to be your "Simon of Cyrene".' I'm reminded of that little parable of the village that was flooded. A Christian man took refuge on the roof of his house and declared that his God would rescue him. He refused to be rescued by his neighbour in a dinghy, by the police in a large boat and by an army helicopter. Only his God would rescue him. He drowned! When he arrived at the pearly gates, he complained to God for not rescuing him. 'What do you mean?' says the Lord. 'I sent a dinghy, a boat and a helicopter for you and you refused them all.' God is the God of surprises, the God who will not be confined by human beings or by our petty little moral codes and dogmas. My friend with the sick wife prayed to God for help. God sent a special friend. If the Church does not accept that, why worry? God doesn't worry. The Catholic Church thinks it owns God but it does not own Him and does not always speak for Him.

Only God can judge when sex – whether marital, extra-marital or pre-marital – is right, good or moral. We can have our guidelines. But they are not exhaustive. Sometimes love outside marriage is a love-filled and God-filled act. Sometimes within marriage it is not. In an ideal world all sex would take place in ideal conditions. We don't live in ideal world. The main responsibility for each of us is to use all our energies, including our sexual energies, in a positive and loving way. Only we ourselves and God can judge when we measure up or when we fail. Our young people may engage in pre-marital sex that is damaging for them and for others. We can advise them. When things go wrong we can help them. But we can never imprison them. Jesus never forced anyone to follow him or accept his message. He invited and he left people free. We should do the same. We should also be constantly re-examining our moral codes to see that they are in line with Christ's teachings because sometimes as a Church we are more interested in controlling people and their bodies than we are in leading people to Christ. As Christians, we have such a hang-up about sexual morality, and yet Christ Himself had so little to say about it. If our hearts are in the right place our bodies will follow. My father always quoted the two lines:

> Two men looked out from prison bars;
> One saw mud, the other stars.

Sex is either good or dirty, depending on your perspective. If you want to make it dirty you can. Too often we in the Catholic Church have opted to see it as dirty.

HOMOSEXUALITY

Archbishop Desmond Connell of Dublin is, we are led to believe, an expert in the area of the language the angels in heaven speak when they communicate with the Creator. He has also made strong statements condemning homosexuality. This led Senator David Norris, the Irish gay rights activist, to remark wittily: 'The Archbishop may know a lot about angels but seems to know nothing about fairies.' The Archbishop's ignorance is obviously shared in Rome. In the Summer of 1992, the Vatican released a document in which it was stated that in certain cases it is sometimes legitimate and, indeed, sometimes obligatory to limit the rights of homosexuals. This document was intended as a private guide-line document for the American Catholic

Bishops. The Vatican detailed those circumstances in which it would not be unjust to discriminate against homosexuals – the adoption of children, teaching, sports coaching and military service. The document states that homosexuality is 'an objective disorder' and that there is no inalienable right to homosexuality.

There was strong reaction in Ireland to this document. Senator Norris described the report as 'an incitement to discriminate'. The Roman document was also condemned by the Teacher's Union of Ireland, the Irish Council for Civil Liberties, the Green Party and the Workers' Party. The *Irish Times* reacted with an editorial headed: 'Narrow Vision'. The newspaper described the report as 'patronising, unaware and likely to reinforce prejudice against homosexuals' but says that this is hardly surprising 'given the general drift of Church teaching on matters of sexual morality under the present pontificate' (I.T. 25/7/'92). The editorial finished with the strong sentence: 'Base prejudice must not be encouraged to believe that it has a monopoly of the truth.' The *Irish Times* is the one Irish newspaper that has consistently criticised the Catholic Church when criticism was called for. In the 1950s, when Bishop Lucey of Cork declared that the Catholic hierarchy were the final arbiters, even in political matters, the *Irish Times* quite correctly declared the hierarchy to be the virtual government of the country. On 29 July, 1992, a short letter, worth quoting, appeared in the *Irish Times* from a Mr. Jerry O'Shea of Killiney, Dublin:

> 'Sir, – I note with alarm the Pope's advice on homosexuals. As a disabled person, am I next on his hit list?'

And reaction was no less muted in America where the document was meant for. The Bishop of Milwaukee, Rembert Weakland, picked up on a theme, quoted above, from Belgium's Cardinal Suenens: 'In times gone by, science was the chosen *bête noire* of the Church but today it is sexuality. Today sexuality is the modern Galileo'. The Bishop, with charitable restraint, described the Vatican document as being 'of little help'.

In 1985, the Italian Catholic bishops took a very different approach than the Vatican did in 1992. In their document the Italian bishops declared: 'A profound reflection should take place that would positively support homosexuals and also analyse the many complex aspects of their social reality, even within the ecclesiastical community

Any further marginalisation of homosexuals should be avoided'. Obviously the Italian bishops are more compassionate than their colleagues within the Vatican State. And some historians and authors point out that the Church was not always and everywhere anti-homosexual, and suggest that St. Anselm of Canterbury and St Augustine had homosexual tendencies.

It is now some years since the world psychiatric community removed homosexuality from its books as a 'disorder'. The Vatican still regards it as a disorder and is, therefore, once again in direct conflict with science and medicine. No-one knows why people are homosexual. Some claim that people are born homosexual. Others say that it is due to early environment and experiences. Some say it is a mixture of both. But no-one chooses to be a homosexual. There has never been a case where someone has riffled through a box of sexual options and said 'O, goody, I'm going to be a homosexual.' It cannot be a sin to be a homosexual. Sin always involves choice. But some in the Church will say: 'It is not a sin to be a homosexual but it is a sin to behave as one'. This is a contradiction. It is like saying that it is not a sin to be a dog but it is a sin for a dog to bark. People surely *do*, because they *are*.

If people are homosexual and remember that they have always been homosexual, then it seems most likely that they were born homosexual. If they were born homosexual then God must have made them that way. If God made them that way, then how can he, or his representatives, blame them for behaving in that way? There are many people who are homosexual who can give and receive love only through their homosexuality. The Church's answer to them is self-sacrifice and abstinence for a whole life. How cruel and unrealistic it is for the Church to suggest to a 20-year-old homosexual person that he or she must live for five or six decades and never experience the physical intimacy and love that every human being longs for. That may be the Church's expectation. I cannot believe it to be God's.

What really matters is love. I have no problem believing that sex is 'disordered' when it is abused. And all of us, heterosexual, bisexual or homosexual, can use and abuse sex. If two homosexual people have a physical relationship in the context of love, they do not sin. If two homosexual people have a physical relationship, not in love, but out of loneliness or unhappiness, they do not sin either. They bleed and they hurt. They need our love and our compassion. They do not need our condemnations or our harsh documents. I do not fully understand sexuality or homosexuality. I don't know how God really feels about it. I am conscious that the human authors of the Bible brought their own cultural baggage and prejudice to their writings. And even if people are not perfect I know that there is a world of difference between being bad and being weak. Cruel attempts in the past to use electricity and aversion therapy to turn homosexuals into heterosexuals were wrong. That was a sin. And they did it in Catholic-controlled hospitals. Sexuality is a great mystery. It is not the bad and dirty thing the Church has made it. The Italian bishops were right to call for compassion and openness. We have a lot to learn about sexuality and its place in God's plan. Our homosexual brothers and sisters must be among our teachers. In the meantime, we must leave the judging to God.

What of homosexuality within the Church today? I attended two Catholic seminaries. There were homosexual people in both. Some were practising homosexuals and others were not. Some homosexual students left the seminary of their own free will. Others were discovered and were either allowed to stay or were asked to leave. Some were ordained priests. Within a year of being ordained, I was propositioned by two priests. One suggested we go to bed. The other attempted to seduce me physically without warning. I know a number of priests who are non-practising homosexuals and a number who are active. I know of senior Church figures who are practising homosexuals. I know that homosexuality in the Vatican is not uncommon. Some years ago I met a young Irish seminarian who was shocked on his arrival in Rome by the homosexuality he found there. He asked his bishop to take him out of Rome lest he lose his faith. His bishop insisted that he stay. I find none of this shocking. The reader shouldn't either. The Catholic Church contains all of the virtues and vices that are to be found in the world at large. It has always been that way.

In my seventeen years as a priest I have listened to and counselled many homosexual people. The listening, without judgement, is a very important part. I have come to realise that homosexual relationships are more volatile and prone to insecurity than some other forms of relationship. But if two people want to live and love that way, I will have no problem accepting and supporting them. If they want to come to Mass, I will welcome them. If they want communion, I will communicate them. If they want confession, I'll not refuse them absolution. I'll not judge them. I'll let God do that. Recently two lesbian girls came to see me. I feared that they were going to ask me to celebrate a form of marriage for them. I could not regard a formal 'marriage' as such as an authentic thing to do for them. It would have been gimmicky. As it turned out they wanted me to listen to them and accept them. I did. They asked me if I would be prepared to go to their home, celebrate a Mass and bless them. I said I would. On what grounds could I refuse two sisters a visit, a Mass or a blessing? I wouldn't want to refuse them anyway. It's quite customary in Ireland for farmers to have their parish priest bless a sick cow! How could someone argue that it would be all right to bless a cow but it is not all right to bless a human being because he or she happens to be homosexual?

When it comes to homosexuality the problems are really ignorance, prejudice and fear. I'm reminded of the two Irish Catholic macho types who went to work on the building sites in London. On their first Saturday night in the big smoke they headed for a dance to view the local talent. As they stood by the door, two gorgeous blondes brushed past, nearly causing the two Paddies to faint with desire. An English bloke tapped them on the shoulder and said: 'Forget that, Paddy, they're two lesbians.' The two Irish guys stared at each other in some confusion, pulled themselves together and approached the two females. One of the Irish fellows leaned against the wall and with a feigned coolness said: 'Goodnight, girls, what part of Lesby are ye from?'

In a debate broadcast some time ago on BBC Radio Ulster – 'The Talkback Debate' – I summarised my beliefs about homosexuality from the point of view of the Bible and Christianity. My opposition included the Protestant fundamentalist, Reverend David McIlveen of the Free Presbyterian Church – Ian Paisley's church. The audience was full of fundamentalist and hostile Protestants. We lost the vote but I think we won the argument. I said:

> Explosives, in the proper hands, are most useful. They can be used to create motorways, railways and dams. They were used recently to stem the flow of an Italian volcano and to save many lives.

But explosives, in the wrong hands, the hands of terrorists, can be used for killing and maiming and for creating the chaos of Belfast, London and Manchester.

The Bible is an explosively good book. It brings healing, inspiration and growth. But put the Bible into the wrong hands and you get irrational fundamentalism, condemnation and intimidation. You get in fact, moral terrorism. We have moral terrorists here to-night. They want you to believe that the Bible condemns homosexuality. But the Bible does no such a thing.

Look through your Bible, from Genesis to Revelation, and you will see that the issue of true homosexuality, or the issue of two genuinely homosexual people living together in a long-term relationship, marked by love and commitment, is not dealt with at all. And such things are definitely not condemned.

A number of related issues are dealt with and even condemned. And this is why people get the wrong end of the stick. The issue of homosexuality is muddied by prejudice and fear, by ignorance and emotion. It is vital, therefore, to look at this issue from an informed and objective point of view.

Professor John McNeill of Fordham University has studied homosexuality and the Bible at length and has produced the Darton, Longman and Todd publication: *The Church and the Homosexual* (1977). He has brought together the views of dozens of Scripture scholars and moral theologians of all denominations. His conclusions are: That the Bible does not deal with the issue of homosexuality. The Bible was written in a time when its human authors had a primitive understanding and were culturally and historically limited. Nor does the Bible address the question of two homosexual people living in a stable relationship. Professor McNeill points out that the Bible condemns

1. Heterosexual people engaging in homosexual acts as a perversion.

2. Heterosexual men sodomising their defeated military enemies.

3. Male prostitution.

4. Homosexual acts as idolatrous worship in pagan Canaanite temples.

Those people who like to use the Bible to condemn homosexuality refer to Genesis 19: 4 - 11, the story of Lot's two male visitors at Sodom. The whole male population of Sodom, the Bible says, wanted to have sex with the two men and therefore Sodom was condemned. This is often misinterpreted as a condemnation of homosexuality. Professor McNeill says that this is wrong.

All the men of Sodom – 100 percent of them were there. The whole male population can't have been homosexual. Surveys say that between 2 percent and 20 percent are homosexual in any population. The Kinsey report said that 37 percent of males have homosexual experiences.

Rather the male population of Sodom was guilty of inhospitality, assault and intimidation. Sodom's sin was the sin of inhospitality. When Jesus is referring to the sin of Sodom in the New Testament he is referring to it in the context of inhospitality.

In Genesis we see Lot offering his daughters to the men of Sodom instead of the two male visitors. Why would Lot offer his two daughters to a crowd of rampant homosexuals ? Sodom was condemned for violence and inhospitality and not for homosexuality.

St. Paul is always used by fundamentalists. Professor McNeill says that Paul did not address homosexuality either. Paul only talked about those who turn away from women to have sex with men – heterosexual men going against their own nature to have sex with men to whom they are not naturally attracted. But Paul was very culturally limited. He didn't like women speaking in Church or men with long hair.

Professor McNeill points out other problems including the variety of translations of the Bible.

In conclusion – the Bible condemns heterosexuals performing perverse homosexual acts, the sodomy of defeated military enemies and male prostitution. But the Bible does not condemn homosexuality per se – eg: two genuine homosexuals.

Dr. Frank Lake, psychiatrist and Christian has said: 'Church people can do the Devil's work of destroying, not sins, but men and women, condemning what they do not understand.'

For many Irish Catholics homosexuals are from another planet. Those same Irish Catholics, however, should not forget that gay men and women are their brothers and sisters and will one day share the same heaven we all hope to share. At the pearly gates I would expect that homosexuals who tried to love will be treated far more kindly than 'queer-bashers', whether they wore leather and were members of the National Front, or wore episcopal purple and were members of the Catholic hierarchy!

For all Christians the most important day of their lives is the day they die because that is the day they will appear before God to be judged. There are very few exams where you receive the questions before the exam begins. However, we Christians are fortunate enough to know now the questions we will be asked at our judgement. Christ has revealed them to us in the Gospels. We are not to be asked how many Masses we attended, how many rosaries we recited, how many medals we wore or how much Lourdes water we drank. Nor are we to be asked how many orgasms we had or how often we masturbated or how many sexual partners we had. Instead we are to be asked the following questions:

> Did you feed the hungry?
> Did you give the thirsty a drink?
> Did you clothe the naked?
> Did you visit the sick?
> Did you visit prisoners?
> Did you welcome strangers into your home?

If we have done these things to others we have done them to Christ; we are 'sheep' and we will be invited into Heaven. If we have failed to do these things for others we have failed to do them for Christ; we are 'goats' and we will be sent into eternal punishment. I have often used a particular parable in my sermons. A certain good man died and appeared before St. Peter. For his goodness he was to go to heaven. But St. Peter offered him a tour of hell first so that he could see what he had avoided. When they opened the doors of hell the good man was surprised at what he saw. There was a fine table in the centre with every kind of good food and drink on it that you could imagine. But all around the table in Hell were starving people. They had to eat from the table with very long chopsticks – so long that when they tried to get the food to their mouths the food fell off and they could not eat. St. Peter closed the doors of hell and brought our good man to heaven.

Here there was the very same table, the very same fine food and drink and the very same long chopsticks. But around the heavenly table everyone was well-fed and happy. The man asked Peter to explain. 'Well,' said Peter, 'in hell everybody tries to feed themselves and they fail and therefore starve. But here in heaven everybody uses the long chopsticks to get the food to their neighbour's mouth and everybody is filled.' That's a good parable to explain heaven and hell. It's as simple as this: those who live lives of love in this world pass over to lives of eternal love. Those who live lives of selfishness here pass over to existences of eternal selfishness in the world to come. Charles de Foucauld summed it up eloquently when he declared: 'Our religion is all about love. Its emblem is a heart.'

I wish that the Catholic Church were more interested in love than in sex. I wish that, when it preached about sin, it put the sins of murder, dishonesty, unkindness etc., before the so-called 'sins of the flesh'. Murder, corruption and unkindness are often premeditated faults and sins. Sexual faults are often spontaneous and the result of loneliness, frustration and past hurt. Even God, in constructing the Old Testament commandments, put idolatry, blasphemy, non-observance of the Sabbath, disrespect for parents and murder before he mentioned adultery. And the only two sexual faults mentioned in the Christian Ten Commandments are adultery and coveting your neighbour's wife.

With the exception of things like rape and child abuse, I regard sexual sins as the least of sins. And, of course, in cases of rape and child abuse, it is the violence that is the more serious aspect, the forcing of oneself on an unwilling or under-age person. The Catholic Church has tended to over-emphasise sexual morality. We must correct that balance. We must set sexual morality in the context of total morality. I would prefer someone to have sex with a thousand people than to kill one person. I would prefer to see an employer having sex outside marriage than deprive his employees of a just wage. If there is a hierarchy in morality, I think that sexual morality is a long way down the list. If we have led overall good, loving and just lives we will not be in trouble with God for a few sexual slips. We have been and are too strict about sexual morality in Catholicism.

Father Matthew Fox, the American Dominican theologian, has written a wonderful book entitled *Original Blessing*. In this book he argues most convincingly that we should concentrate more on the

original blessings of creation than on original sin. In a thought-provoking quotation he says:

> There is no question whatsoever in my mind that among those
> who call themselves Christians, whether practising or not,
> ninety-nine per cent know about original sin; and barely one
> per cent have ever in their lives heard about original blessing.
> This is the great price we have paid in the West for following a
> one-sided, fall/redemption theology. There is a genuine scandal
> involved in this dangerous distortion of life and of biblical data.
> The scandal is one of ignoring – and then despising – creation
> and those who love creation, such as Native American peoples
> or matriarchal religions. Even if original sin is to be taken
> literally, still the facts are as follows: that, if we take the universe
> to be about twenty billion years old, as scientists are advising
> us to do, then sin of the human variety is about four million
> years old, since that is how long humans have been around.
> But creation is 19,996,000,000 years older! Fall/redemption
> theology has ignored the blessing that creation is because of its
> anthropomorphic preoccupation with sin! The result has been,
> among other things, the loss of pleasure from spirituality, and
> with this loss the increase of pain, of injustice, of sado-maso-
> chism, and of distrust. Nineteen billion years before there was
> any sin on earth, there was blessing.

Father Fox says that there was no formal theology concernin[g]
original sin until St. Augustine, that Augustine mistranslated the Bibl[e]
to justify his original sin theory. He then added his original sin theor[y]
to his 'peculiar notions about sexuality', says Father Fox. Father Fo[x]
calls for the churches to distance themselves from Augustine's 'pu[t]
down of woman and of sexuality.' 'What trust is lost in oneself,' sa[ys]
Fox, 'in one's body, in the cosmos, when children are instructed th[at]
they came into the world as blotches on God's creation?'

The reader will not be surprised to hear that Father Fox is in troub[le]
with the Vatican. I'm informed that the Vatican has instructed h[is]
religious order to discipline him. Father Fox's *Original Blessing* boo[k]
has been banned from the Veritas shops, owned and run by the Iri[sh]
Catholic bishops. I recently visited the Veritas shop in Letterkenn[y]
Donegal, and asked for *Original Blessing*. The lady assistant told m[e]

'We did have it but we don't have it now and we will not be having it again.' 'Why?' I asked. 'I don't know,' she replied. However, one is not surprised that Father Fox is being banned. Another short quotation from him shows why the Church authorities are afraid of him: 'Why has original sin played so important a role for sixteen centuries of Western Christian theology ... I believe that the basic reason is political. I believe that an exaggerated doctrine of original sin, one that is employed as a starting point for spirituality, plays kindly into the hands of empire-builders, slave-masters, and patriarchal society in general.'

One of the principal pillars on which rests the empire which is the Roman Catholic Church is the pillar made of guilt, particularly sexual guilt. Tim Pat Coogan, the Irish journalist and author, has pointed out that we had two forms of colonialism in Ireland – the British form and the Roman form. The British one has almost faded. But the Roman one is still strong. Catholic Ireland was as much a slave colony as were the cotton fields of the southern states of America. The slaves had white skins but black souls – souls blackened by 'sin', especially sexual sin. The slave-masters were the Irish Catholic bishops who were truly the 'land owners' and their parish priests, their ecclesiastical 'charge hands'. Ireland is in the process of freeing herself from this slavery. We are all at last learning to burn our ecclesiastical bras. Hallelujah!

CHAPTER 8

Marriage, Annulment, Divorce and Remarriage

Marriage is like life in this, that it is a field of battle,
and not a bed of roses.

Robert Louis Stevenson

IN THE IRISH REPUBLIC OF the 1990s there are, according to available
statistics, some 40,000 couples living in second unions. These second
unions are recognised neither by Church nor State and so the people
involved are living in both a religious and a civil limbo. Each year now
I celebrate upwards of 200 weddings. Many of the couples I marry
have previously been divorced and the greater percentage of my
marriages are of couples from the Republic. How sad it is that these
couples have to leave their own jurisdiction and join the divorce/re
marriage trail to Larne in Co. Antrim. With its peculiar and cruel
regulations, the Irish Republic is prepared to allow divorced people
with a domicile outside Ireland to remarry in Ireland but is not prepared
to offer the same facilities to its own citizens! It must be a rather rare
thing to find a country that is prepared to do something for foreigner
that it is not prepared to do for its own people. If charity begins at
home, then the Irish State has not discovered this precept in relation
to its own children who are unfortunate enough to have a marriage
breakdown and fortunate to find love again. The winds of change are
blowing in relation to divorce in Ireland but not before their time.

MARRIAGE FOR BETTER OR FOR WORSE

Most people agree that, ideally, marriage should be for life. Every sane
person entering marriage for the right reasons wants a life-long
permanent union. There is no doubt that a good and happy marriage
brings great blessings and benefits to all to partners, to their children
and to the wider community. At weddings I often tell the story of the
senior US officer taken prisoner during the Second World War. When

he was captured his wife happened to be with him. Because of his seniority she was given a choice – to go free or to go to the prison compound with her husband. She felt that life without him would not be worth living. So she opted for the prison camp. At the end of the war they were both released and returned to the US. Soon afterwards it was discovered that the wife had leprosy. She was sent by court order to a special institution. Her husband, who was free of the disease, didn't have to go. But again he felt that life without his wife would not be worthwhile. So they both went together and died there a number of years later in that sad place. That story, if made into a film, would bring tears to our eyes. But it does get across the point very strongly that love is the strongest force in the world and that, ideally, the love of a husband and wife should be one of the strongest examples of love this side of the grave. We should leave no stone unturned to help marriages to be successful. When a couple have marriage difficulties we should direct them, at first, for counselling. Some marriage problems and difficulties can be mended and healed through proper counselling. The Catholic Church's Marriage Encounter programme is a very good thing. Its aim is to make good marriages better. I'm all for that.

But while we keep life-long permanent marriage as our ideal, we must also realise that we do not live in an ideal world. There are some marriages that are doomed from the start. There are others that go irretrievably wrong. I recently described one such marriage in a letter to Patrick Walsh, the Catholic Bishop of Down and Connor:

> A young girl was married at 21 years. Three weeks after her marriage she returned home from work early one day, as she was sick. She discovered her new husband in bed with her bridesmaid who had been her best friend. The two departed together, never to return. The young wife was left alone, her world fallen around her. After some years of intense mental and emotional anguish, some of which was spent in a psychiatric unit and on a psychiatrist's couch, she regained some peace of mind. She applied for an annulment and was unsuccessful. She got a civil divorce. She met someone new and after some years decided to remarry. God was too important to her for her to even contemplate a registry office. I celebrated her marriage.

She has been happily married for five years. She has two children whom she will bring up as Catholics and who, she is determined, will attend Catholic schools. She herself teaches in a Catholic school and does voluntary secretarial work for her parish priest. She has never missed Mass in her life, not even during those times when she was in hospital or when she felt the Church was being cruel in not understanding and helping her.

I continued my letter to Bishop Walsh who was demanding that I stop celebrating these marriages:

We can't afford to alienate these people. They are looking for Jesus in us and somehow we've got to be able to reflect him for them. Jesus reconciled heaven and earth through the cross. Perhaps in the suffering there is involved for all of us, as we try to marry official Church teaching and Canon Law with where some of our poor people find themselves at, we too can somehow be instruments of salvation.

I'm afraid my appeal to Bishop Walsh fell on deaf ears. He replied that if I didn't cease to celebrate such marriages he would convene a Church court, put me on trial and sentence me to either formal suspension or excommunication!

DIVORCE AND REMARRIAGE

Some Irish Catholics simply think that God absolutely forbids divorce. They have been taught to believe this by the Catholic hierarchy. This is not God's real position at all! As Catholics we believe that God reveals himself in two ways, firstly through divine revelation in the Bible and, secondly, through the traditional teaching of the Church. It is worth taking a closer look at what Scripture and Catholic tradition have to say about divorce.

DIVORCE IN THE BIBLE

Divorce is dealt with throughout the Bible. In the book of Deuteronomy in the Old Testament (Chapter 24, verses 1 to 4) we are told that a man who divorces his wife is not to remarry the same woman. Here the biblical author does not prohibit divorce. He merely prohibit remarrying someone from whom you have been previously divorced

In verses 13 to 16 of the book of Malachi we are told that the Lord hates divorce. St. Paul, in his first letter to the Corinthians, says that if an unbelieving partner abandons a believing partner then the believing partner is 'free to act'. This scripture is used by the modern Catholic Church to dissolve the valid marriage of two non-baptised people, one of whom comes into the faith. Canon 1143 states:

> A marriage entered by two non-baptised persons is dissolved by means of the Pauline Privilege in favour of the faith of a party who has received baptism by the very fact that a new marriage is contracted by the party who has been baptised, provided the non-baptised party departs.
>
> The non-baptised party is considered to have departed if he or she does not wish to cohabit with the baptised party without insult to the Creator unless, after receiving baptism, the baptised party gave the other party a just cause for departure.

We see something strange here. The Catholic hierarchy will not allow the girl mentioned in my letter to Bishop Walsh to remarry even though she was a completely innocent victim of her young husband's unfaithfulness. And yet, under the Pauline Privilege, the Catholic Church is prepared to split up a validly-married non-Christian couple in order to gain a new member for the Catholic Church! They will then let their new Catholic member remarry. Imagine the scene. Two Jewish partners marry in Jerusalem. After ten years the couple come to live in Belfast. The wife becomes friendly with the local parish priest. The priest talks to her about Catholicism and she eventually decides to become a Catholic. Her husband, a devout Jew as once was his wife, disagrees violently. The wife becomes a Catholic against the wishes of her heart-broken husband, family, children and friends. Under the Pauline Privilege, the Catholic Church allows her to leave her husband who does not want to cohabit with a Catholic and to remarry a Belfast Catholic. This, says the Catholic Church, is in favour of the faith and to please the Creator! The bottom line is this. The Catholic Church allows divorce to gain a new member but it will not allow divorce to victims of a genuinely irretrievable marriage breakdown. The Church's position is quite simply hypocritical and totally without credibility.

In the Gospel of Mark (10:2-12) we are told that man must not separate what God has joined together and that those who divorce and remarry are guilty of adultery. We are told the same in Luke's gospel (16:18). However in two places in the Gospel of Matthew we come across Jesus saying something very interesting:

> But I now tell you, if a man divorces his wife for any cause, other than unfaithfulness, then he is guilty of making her commit adultery if she marries again and the man who marries her commits adultery also. (5:31)

> I tell you then that any man who divorces his wife for any cause other than her unfaithfulness, commits adultery if he marries some other woman. (19:9)

From all of the above scriptural references a number of things become clear.

a) That the Christian ideal is that marriage should be permanent and life-long.

b) That there are exceptions.

JESUS makes an exception in the case of unfaithfulness.

PAUL makes an exception in the case where an unbeliever leaves a newly-Christian partner.

DIFFERENCES IN INTERPRETATION

Different scripture scholars from different churches and at different times have had different interpretations of St. Matthew's passages allowing divorce in the case of unfaithfulness. They argue about such things as:

1. Was Matthew trying to tone down the moral demands of Christ which the early Christians found hard to live up to?

2. Was Matthew affected by the Rabbi Shammi's school of thought which broadened the divorce exceptions out from unfaithfulness to cover the case of a man whose wife was a very bad cook?

3. What were the original words used? Was it *porneia*, meaning prostitution, or was it *moicheia*, meaning adultery. Was something lost in the translation? Some people say that Matthew was referring only to people already living together in concubinage.

I am not going to get involved in the details of these debates here it is enough to point out that the Devil can cite scripture for his own purposes. The rows still continue. But those of us interested in people and their struggles and not in the niceties of Greek and Hebrew conclude that the ideal is life-long marriage but there are exceptions as mentioned by Jesus, St. Paul and St. Matthew.

Many of the Protestant churches interpret the scriptures on this point more liberally than does the Roman Catholic Church. In the 1990s are we still saying that the Catholic Church is absolutely right and the Protestant churches absolutely wrong? If we are, our ecumenism is rather empty.

DIVORCE AND REMARRIAGE IN CHRISTIAN TRADITION

In 1967 Monsignor Victor J. Pospishill published his book: *Divorce and Remarriage – Towards a New Catholic Teaching*. Monsignor Pospishill is a JCD (Doctor of Canon Law), a graduate of the Roman Gregorian University and the Vicar-General of the Ukrainian Catholic Archdiocese of Philadelphia. In 1979 he prepared a short summary on divorce for the *Encyclopedic Dictionary of Religion* published by the Sisters of St. Joseph in Philadelphia:

> All the Eastern Orthodox Churches without exception regard the praise of permanency in marriage expressed by Jesus (Matthew 19:3-10) as a moral ideal, but not as a legal prohibition of divorce. The Fathers, as Basil the Great, reluctantly recognised the need and the right of the Church to permit remarriage of divorced members. The original sole reason, adultery, was later extended to several other grounds on the presumption that they would anyway eventually lead to the termination of the marriage and to a relationship with another person. The only legal limitation in the Eastern Orthodox Church is the prohibition against a fourth marriage, which applies not only to divorced but also to widowed persons. The assertion of some Catholic historians that the Eastern Churches succumbed to the influence of the civil law, especially in the Byzantine Empire, is unwarranted. The early Church in the East and in the West, while always emphasising the ideal of permanency or relative indissolubility of Christian marriage, considered the legislation of Christian emperors permitting divorce as being a valid expression of the theological position of the Church. The espousal of absolute indissolubility in the Western Church goes back to the Carolingian renaissance of theology, while the Christian East retained its original practice of permitting the remarriage of divorced Christians. The Eastern Catholic Churches were

obliged to accept the teaching and practice of the Roman Church at the time of their reunions. Archbishop Elias Zoghby, Patriarchal Vicar of Egypt, proposed at Vatican Council II (29 Oct. 1965) that the Catholic Church re-examine its position with respect to prohibition of the remarriage of divorced Catholics. He was seconded by the other bishops of the Melkite Patriarchate, especially the late Patriarch Maximos IV.

The Catholic hierarchy have always reminded us that the tradition of the Church is as much God's revelation as is the Bible. We see from Monsignor Pospishill that in the united early Church of the East and West, divorce and remarriage were allowed. We see that some great Fathers of the Church, like Basil the Great who was the bishop of Caesarea, allowed divorce and remarriage.

THE PASTORAL SOLUTION

The rate of marriage breakdown is very high in the United States. The American Catholic Church has, therefore, had to take a long hard look at the questions of divorce and remarriage. The American bishops are conscious that the Vatican will not allow them to do anything 'official' for divorcees except process annulments for them. For that reason the American bishops are generally regarded as being liberal about the granting of annulments. But annulments do not solve every problem, so in the US they have developed the so-called 'pastoral solution'.

Through the pastoral solution a Catholic couple who are divorced and civilly remarried approach their local pastor or a nearby pastor if their own is not liberal. The priest will celebrate a 'private' or 'internal forum' marriage for the couple. This will not be legally registered but the couple will be allowed to receive the sacraments. In this way the American Catholic Church gets around the Roman prohibition and at the same time respects the good faith and clear conscience of the couple living in a second union.

There are a number of priests throughout the world and even in Ireland who are prepared to operate such a pastoral solution for couples. They give them a private and secret blessing and encourage them to attend Mass and communion. However, this procedure works better in America than it does in Ireland for a number of reasons.

America is a more open society and divorce and remarriage is hardly commented on. In America religion is a private thing and it is not as important, socially, to receive an official blessing to go ahead. In Ireland, things are different. Because of Catholic brain-washing and control, a couple will often feel it very important to celebrate their marriage more openly before a priest in the company of their families and friends. This makes the couple feel really married and leads to a quicker acceptance of the couple by elderly parents or devout acquaintances. And, of course, in Ireland you cannot get a state divorce and remarriage. So the couple have no way of publicly registering their new marriage. The marriages I celebrate fulfil all the couple's desires. They are married by a Catholic priest, in a Catholic marriage ceremony during a Catholic Mass. Their friends can be present. Their very Catholic parents and family attend the Mass and receive communion. Irish Catholics believe very strongly that 'Once a priest always a priest'. I explain very clearly to couples what I do. 'There is nothing I can do for you with regards to hierarchy and Canon Law,' I say. 'But I can marry you in the eyes of God, who is the most important. I can marry you legally, in the eyes of the state, which is important. And I can marry you in the eyes of the Church – which is all of us.' And I conclude by saying: 'If a man with a red hat will not accept you, what does it matter? You don't have to live with the bishop or the parish priest, do you?' This always gets a smile.

We've had very few problems. On a number of occasions elderly parish priests have called on couples married by me to congratulate them and to reassure them that their membership of their parish and their right to go to communion are not affected. Very often older priests can be more compassionate than younger and middle-aged ones.

MY MARRIAGES – CIVILLY LEGAL

The marriages I celebrate are regarded as legal Roman Catholic marriages in Scotland, Northern Ireland and the Republic of Ireland. In England and Wales the law is, at present, different, and when I travel to England to celebrate a marriage the couple generally attend the registry office beforehand to fulfil the legal requirements.

When I began celebrating marriages like this after Bishop Daly had dismissed me in 1986, I approached the Registrar General in Belfast. I wanted to be sure that I kept within the civil law for the protection of my couples. The Registrar was very helpful. His legal team studied the matter and concluded that any episcopally-ordained priest,

whether or not in good standing with the Church, could, from the civil
law point of view, validly solemnise marriages. This meant, of course,
that my marriages were regarded by the United Kingdom government
as valid Roman Catholic marriages. The Belfast Registrar General wrote:

GENERAL REGISTER OFFICE
Dept. of Health and Social Services
Oxford House
49-55 Chichester Street
Belfast BT1 4HL
12 November 1986

Dear Fr. Buckley,

I refer to your discussion with this office concerning the question of
registration of Roman Catholic marriages solemnised before you as
officiating minister, albeit you are no longer authorised by the bishop
of Down and Connor to carry out such duties.

The matter has been considered carefully and in the light of advice
taken I can now confirm that Roman Catholic marriages solemnised
before you as an episcopally ordained clergyman satisfy the common
law and may, therefore, be registered.

A book of certificates is enclosed for your use in this connection. Your
attention is drawn to the explanatory footnotes. The duly completed
certificates should be passed to the Local Registrar of Marriages.

Yours sincerely,

L.H. Anderson

I did not test the situation in the Republic until 1989. And it
happened quite simply. A young lady from the West of Ireland was
due to marry her fiancé in the local cathedral. The bishop had given
the necessary permission. It transpired that because her fiancé, a
divorced American, was previously married to another non-Catholic,
a mistake had been made by the Church and a fortnight or so before
her wedding the bishop informed her that she would have to cancel
it until she could get an annulment. The bishop suggested that might
take three years and might not be successful. The young lady was in
a dreadful state. Her marriage was days away. Her fiancé's relations
had departed their American home and would arrive for a wedding.
Other friends were invited from the Continent. The family approached

a West of Ireland priest who referred them to me. The same priest managed to get me a Republic of Ireland marriage registration form and off I went to the Beleek Castle hotel in Ballina where we had a lovely wedding. Now came the test. I quite innocently (or as innocently as my nature allows me) submitted the papers to the Mayo registrar. She nearly had a canary and sent them to Galway. Galway sent them to Dublin and Dublin referred them to the Attorney General. We all waited months. Was the couple married or not? Would my marriages be accepted in the traditionally Catholic Republic? They were. The office of the Registrar General in Dublin wrote to me to inform me that the marriage was valid and were kind enough to include a book of registration forms in case I would like to do any more:

> *OIFIG an ARD-CHLARAITHEORA*
> Joyce House
> 8-11 Lombard Street East
> Dublin 2
>
> 8 November 1989
>
> Dear Fr. Buckley,
>
> I refer to our recent telephone conversation and wish to confirm that all main Superintendent Registrars' Offices are being advised that marriages solemnised by you in the State can be registered in the normal way...
>
> ...I have sent you a book of marriage certificate forms under separate cover and would like to stress that these should be kept <u>in a very secure place</u>...
>
> Yours sincerely
> M.Mulkerrin
> Registrar-General's Office.

The couples I marry from the Republic get a United Kingdom divorce and are then remarried by me in the United Kingdom in Northern Ireland. To date none of these couples has experienced any problems. A few years ago someone told me that government departments like tax and social welfare were told to accept marriage certificates without question, even if they came on the back of cigarette packs. One man I've married is as good as a Muslim – he gets tax allowances for two wives, his present wife and his former wife! There used to be a problem about inheritance in the Republic. But this was resolved a few years ago through new legislation. So all my couples get two marriage certificates after a wedding – a church certificate from me and a state certificate from either the UK or the Irish Republic. They have everything any couple has.

THE MINE-FIELD OF ANNULMENTS

The Catholic Church grants annulments to some couples. An annulment is a very different thing from a divorce. A divorce is the government legally bringing a marriage to an end through the civil courts. An annulment is a statement by a Church court that the petitioner has succeeded in proving that there was never a proper marriage from the beginning.

Annulments are terrible, terrible things. If I loved someone I would never let them go through the humiliation and tribulation of seeking an annulment. The couples I've dealt with who have tried to get an annulment have had to pay the church between £400 and £800. Some have paid it all in one go. Others were allowed to pay by instalments. Most of the people I've dealt with have had to wait from three to six years for a decision. I've met some cases when an annulment came through in months and I met one lady who got one after 17 years! She was then too old to have children and was, understandably I think, very angry with Holy Mother Church.

In an annulment court the onus is on you to prove the marriage was invalid. The court begins from the premise that the marriage was a valid one. So you are guilty until you prove yourself innocent! You have to give a priest and the court a very detailed account of your relationship with your former partner. That has to include a detailed account of your most intimate sex life. Some women who have been put through this wringer by celibate priest Canon lawyers have told me that they felt 'verbally raped!' The former partner, the so-called respondent, has to be interviewed by a priest too. If he or she is unco-operative, even for ignoble reasons, the chance of success is reduced. A number of witnesses has to be called to support the case.

Having waited, you are either refused or granted an annulment. Either way there is an appeal. You can appeal if you have been refused.

The Church will appeal if you were successful in this first instance. And even if you are successful you cannot remarry without the permission of your local bishop. A note is put on your baptismal entry to ensure this. Getting the bishop's permission can also be very problematic. It can involve referral to a psychiatrist. One man I met was sent to three psychiatrists and, of course, had to pay the fees himself. Some years ago I married a young man. He had received an annulment and later applied to be remarried. The bishop sent him to a psychiatrist. Afterwards the bishop sent for him and told him that he had not successfully passed the psychiatric assessment. He would never be allowed to marry again! The young man asked why. The bishop told him that he could not tell him but advised him to accept it as God's will for him. The young man was very angry and threatened never to come to church again. The bishop said that he didn't care and slammed the palace door behind the young man. This case is extreme but not exceptional. A lot of couples who were unsuccessful in seeking annulments tell me of the harsh and clinical way they have been treated at marriage tribunals and by Canon lawyers. They bring their letters of refusal with them – cold, clinical letters, the kind no priest or Christian should ever write to another human being.

And, of course, even if you are successful in an Irish Church annulment court your problems are not over. The Irish State recognises Catholic marriages but it does not recognise Catholic annulments. You can marry again in church but your marriage is not legal and cannot be registered with the state. Technically if you marry again in church you are a bigamist and the priest who marries you is an accessory to bigamy. The state does, of course, turn a blind eye to this irregularity. If you want to marry legally you must go to the civil courts and seek a State annulment as well as a Church one. This costs thousands of pounds and is rarely used, probably for that reason. My advice to people is to forget the whole annulment thing, get a UK divorce and remarry again in the UK, and with someone like me if you want a religious dimension.

WHERE IS THE COMPASSION IN THE CHURCH?

From the words and actions of Christ in the Gospels we see his compassion and his regular refusal to be absolutist. We see Christ's positive attitude to sinners and strugglers and his absolute compassion.

Whenever he met anyone who had made a mess of their lives in any way, he told them they were forgiven and should go away to begin all over again. He adopted this approach with lepers, tax collectors, prostitutes, foreigners, and with people like Mary of Magdala and the woman caught in the act of adultery. What's this he said of her: 'Let him who is without sin cast the first stone!' The only people Jesus was hard on were the so-called holy people – the Pharisees, the priests, the lawyers. Had there been Canon lawyers in Jesus's day I think he would have swept the floor with them!

Why does the Catholic Church show so little compassion to the victims of marriage breakdown? In Catholic Canon Law a man can be forgiven in confession for murdering his wife and be allowed to remarry. But someone who has done far less, someone who has had a marriage breakdown is never to be forgiven and allowed remarry not even if he or she be the victim of a partner's infidelity. Imagine that monstrous contradiction. You can be forgiven for murdering your partner but they will not truly forgive you for a marriage breakdown. If it is true that the law's an ass, then Canon Law must be an ass's ass!

So if a young lady marries at 20 and her playboy husband runs away with another woman a year later, then that young lady, the victim of her husband's infidelity, must live like a nun for 60 long lonely years! How stupid can you get? That would be just like a girl being raped and the judge sentencing her, the victim, to life-long imprisonment! The Church cannot be allowed to impose life-long celibacy on people like this.

Some years ago I had a very distressed telephone call. A man was dying of cancer. He had lived in a second civil marriage with a woman for 20 years. He sent for his parish priest to request the Last Rites. The stupid priest told him that he would first have to confess his 20-years-long relationship as a sin and his four children as the result of sins. The man refused. The priest left him without the comfort of the sacraments. This is an extreme case but it shows how some priests will apply the letter of the law to the point of being UNCHRISTIAN. Soon after talking to the man, I was visited by a young lady from Belfast who went to her curate and told him she wished to marry a divorced man. The priest became very angry with her and told her that what she was proposing to do was worse than what the IRA was doing. She left him in tears and arrived on my door-step trembling. It is priests like this who should be brought before Church courts and not priests who bend the rules a little to be compassionate to others.

THE TYPES OF MARRIAGES I CELEBRATE

Some people have wrongly got the impression that I celebrate only those marriages that involve divorce. My marriage ministry is much wider than that. Since Bishop Daly dismissed me I have become the unofficial chaplain to all of Ireland's disillusioned and alienated Catholics. I am very happy in that role. When the bishop dismissed me he wrote to me telling me that if I refused to obey him I would become a 'sad, lonely and pathetic figure'. I wrote back to him saying that he was marginalising me so I would devote the rest of my priesthood, ministering to all the other people the church was marginalising. This number is so great, I told him, that I have more than a lifetime's work ahead of me. In effect, by sacking me Bishop Daly made the whole of Ireland and the whole of the world my parish.

I celebrate various types of marriage:

1. The marriage of two single Catholics who want to be married by me because they are members of my congregation, because they are liberal Catholics or because they don't want to be forced by the Catholic Church to give three months' notice or attend pre-marriage courses.

2. The marriage of couples who have been refused marriage by their own priest because he does not regard them as ready for marriage or because there is a pregnancy. I would be the first to agree that a pregnancy is not a good reason to get married. The only good reason to marry is because you have found someone you genuinely love and want to spend the rest of your life with. But we must be flexible. Some couples go together for five or six years. They plan to marry within another year or two. And then they have a 'slip'. The condom fails or the pill is forgotten. They have a pregnancy on their hands. They are committed. They want their baby to be born into a marriage rather than outside wedlock. They approach the local parish priest. He blindly applies his three or six month notice rule. Some priests are now insisting that the baby be a year old before a marriage takes place. There may be a place for this rule sometimes. But we must discriminate. I very often marry a committed couple like this who have been turned away from their own parish.

3. The marriage of 'mixed religion' couples. This is a particularly big problem in Northern Ireland. The couple are Protestant and Catholic. The Protestant will not attend the Catholic chapel. The Catholic will not go to the Protestant church. I will celebrate a joint Christian service for the couple in a hotel, a community centre or their home. I have a minister present if they wish. We can even have a joint Eucharist and communion service. This is banned by Canon Law. This service gets many a couple over a difficult day. These couples often return to me to have their babies baptised. We baptise them in a joint Christian service. We say that they are just becoming Christians and not Catholics or Protestants. We leave the decision of the denomination to the family. I advise such couples to send their children to a mixed school.

4. The marriage of divorced people who wish to remarry in a Christian or Catholic ceremony. I don't marry only Catholics to Catholics. I have married Protestants to Protestants. I have married Protestants to Muslims because their own ministers would not marry them to a 'pagan'! It is not only the Catholic church and clergy who give 'different' couples hassle.

SOME INTERESTING MARRIAGES I'VE DONE

Every priest or person working with the public can tell you funny or hair-raising stories of things that have happened to them. I'm not without my sticky moments!

One day I was due to marry a couple at 12 noon. At 11, I had a telephone call from the groom to tell me the bride had just had a baby. Taken aback, I extended my hearty congratulations and told the groom to contact me after the bride had recovered in order to fix a new date. 'I think you've got the wrong idea, Father,' the groom said. 'We're still coming. We're going ahead with the wedding.' At noon, I told the unsuspecting guests that we had a slight delay. At 1 o'clock the bride arrived from the hospital in a wheelchair escorted by a maternity nurse. She was married and wheeled to the wedding reception. From there she was returned to the hospital to feed her new-born baby. I called my organist aside: 'That was a near thing,' I told him. 'From now on want you to have a basin, a towel and some hot water to hand.' The baby could have been born during the wedding Mass.

Another couple asked me if I could do an 'Earth Wedding'. I agreed I like to say yes. But I had my fears. Would it be a wedding in the nude? If so I was hoping to be allowed to wear some type of ecclesiastical fig-leaf. The wedding was to be at a waterfall in a country park. Clothes were allowed. It was a lovely occasion. I married another 'green' couple in a nursery among the plants and flowers. I enjoyed that too. 'You're nearer to God in a garden than anywhere else on earth!' as the saying goes.

A Presbyterian bride who was approaching her 50th year asked me if I would be prepared to marry her to her 24-year-old groom who was Muslim. Her two grown-up sons had sent her on a Nile cruise and she had fallen in love with the cruise barman, a handsome Egyptian. To allow for his sensitivities we went first of all to the Belfast mosque for the Muslim religious marriage, which has no standing in civil law. The women, including the bride, had to stay at the back. The bride's son went up and held the groom's hand, to represent his mother, as the Muslim priest performed the wedding. The joke at the reception was that the handsome Egyptian had actually married the son and not the mother! Before the reception I married the couple in a Christian and civil ceremony in the hotel.

I've celebrated a number of weddings for North Americans who wanted to marry in an Irish castle. The nicest of those was when I celebrated the marriage of a Canadian clown in Waterford Castle.

Recently I had a wedding in The Oratory in Larne where the guests were from both Ireland and England. Many people are slow to agree to read the lesson at a wedding ceremony. At this particular wedding, a gentleman was willing. He didn't seem nervous but he was. The first reading was the Book of Genesis. He should have read: 'And God made the man fall into a deep sleep'. Instead he read: 'And God made the man fall into a sheep dip'. The congregation fell around the place laughing. The poor reader was very embarrassed and didn't realise his mistake until he returned to his seat and was put in the picture by his much-amused wife.

Today, very many people in our Catholic Church, in Ireland and elsewhere, are suffering through marriage breakdown. When a marriage goes on the rocks everyone hurts – the husband and wife, the children, the wider family, the community and the church. Marriage breakdown is a tragedy. When it happens marriage counselling should be the first option. A breakdown can be of two kinds – one that can be repaired or one which is irretrievable. If a couple can get their relationship back on the road they have a huge responsibility to do so. You can't lightly walk out of a commitment as important as marriage. There are two types of counselling available. There is Catholic Church marriage counselling and secular marriage counselling. I always recommend the secular counselling, even to Catholics. If you go to the Catholic marriage counselling service you are going to meet Catholic priests and dedicated lay Catholics. In my opinion they will be prejudiced in favour of saving the marriage, almost at all costs. This is not helpful. The best counselling is always neutral. Sometimes, the counsellor will have to help a partner to see that it is all over. But I have seen marriage counselling really help in what appeared to be rather hopeless cases. In Northern Ireland and the rest of the UK we are fortunate to have the marriage counselling charity RELATE, which is non-denominational.

But some relationships come to an end. This is the case with the 40,000 couples who are living in second unions in the Irish Republic. Their previous relationships are gone, a thing of the past. They are now in a new relationship, have set up a new home and have a new family. Some of the couples I've married had been living together for 10 or 20 years. Their children didn't even know that they were not married. I married one couple who were living together for 60 years. They have children, grandchildren and great-grandchildren. Their secret will not emerge until they die and a relatively new marriage certificate is found.

The State has a responsibility to help people in this position. They should be allowed to divorce, make a settlement with the departing partner, see to the needs of children and marry again if they wish. The British State lives up to its responsibilities in this area. The Irish State does not but, hopefully, will do so soon.

The Church has a huge responsibility in this area too. The Church can maintain the Christian and Scriptural ideal of life-long permanent marriage. But when people fail to reach the ideal, as we all do in some way, the Church must have a way, in compassion, of picking these people up and letting them make a fresh start. And this approach can't be wrong. All Catholicism did this in the past. The Eastern Catholic Churches, with whom we shared the first 1,000 years of Christianity still do it. Some of the Protestant Churches do it. And in parts of the Roman Catholic world bishops and priests apply the pastoral solution

The Catholic Church must come to terms with the divorce/remarriage issue and come to terms with it in a way that is pastorally helpful to people who find themselves in tight corners. We Catholics can be so very cruel on this issue. Let me illustrate what I mean.

A number of years ago I met a couple who wanted me to celebrate their marriage. The girl was unmarried and from a very traditional conservative Irish rural family. The young man was divorced and the girl's father hated him for three reasons – he was English, he was a Protestant and he was divorced. The father forbade the girl to see her boyfriend. The girl disobeyed. She was then locked in an upstairs room over the family shop and pub. She was beaten by her father and older brother. She helped herself to the spirit store and to drugs. Eventually the family had her taken to a private psychiatric unit. She was rescued from here by her fiancé. They eventually married and moved to a different county. They are happily married. Forgiving that she is, the young wife still visits home. But she must leave her wedding ring in her car. These things did not happen in the Ireland of the 1930s. They happened in the Ireland of the late 1980s. Perhaps you see now why things must change. Perhaps you also see why I am becoming more and more committed to my ministry to these people. I could not see Christ turning these people away. The official Church, in the name of Christ, does turn these people away. I'm afraid I can't be part of that.

CHAPTER 9

Northern Ireland –
Religion, Politics, Bigotry

When men quarrel, even God's anger does not frighten them.

Zohar

NORTHERN IRELAND IS A 'CHRISTIAN' society in which some Protestants and Catholics seem to think that it's permissible to hate, kill and maim each other! We all know that the war in Northern Ireland is not, strictly speaking, a religious war. But it cannot be denied that it is a political conflict with a religious dimension. Most paramilitaries in Northern Ireland, whether Republican or Loyalist, do not go to church at all. If you like, these people are political Protestants and Catholics. But if you asked them what religion they were they would without hesitation answer either 'Protestant' or 'Catholic'. The two titles, Protestant and Catholic, are more about tribal identification than they are about religious conviction. There is the story of the American Jew who got lost on the Falls Road in Belfast and was stopped by the 'terrorists'. They asked if he was a Catholic or a Protestant. He puzzled his attackers by announcing that he was a Jew. After a silence he was asked: 'Well, are you a Catholic Jew or a Protestant Jew?'

Having said that, however, there is a sense in which Republican paramilitaries (they are the ones I know best) are, at heart, superstitious Catholics. Like the Italian mafia, these people turn out to church for christenings, first communions, confirmations, weddings and funerals. They also carry strange things in their pockets. In many an IRA man's jacket you will find a Rosary beads and a little plastic wallet with the Prayer to St. Joseph in it – the prayer asking for protection from sudden death! I suppose such a prayer is useful if you are out at night with an armalite trying to shoot policemen and soldiers. Some prominent IRA men do attend daily Mass and communion. They see no contradiction. They quote the traditional Catholic teaching about a 'just war'. To them, the Northern Ireland war is a just war and traditional Catholic teaching allows them to kill the enemy, in this case the British Army and the RUC. During the beginning of the 'Troubles' there was a Citizens' Defence Centre on the Falls Road. One of their most colourful volunteers was a very republican old man who used to sit saying his Rosary there all day. When the news would come on, this was Billy's tack: 'Hail Mary, full of grace, the Lord is with thee...how many Brits killed? Seven. Thank God...Blessed are thou among women...' Billy saw nothing wrong with breaking his prayers to rejoice that seven more people had been killed.

THE NORTHERN IRELAND CATHOLIC

I have described how I first came to live in Belfast in 1978 and was sent by the Bishop of Down and Connor to live in Divis Flats on the Falls Road among thousands of Catholics where I immediately noticed two things. First of all, the Northern Ireland people are very straight and blunt. If they have something to say to you they give it to you straight between the eyes. I admire that honesty. In the Republic people are what you call more 'diplomatic'. At times that could be called insincerity. On the negative side, your Northern Ireland Catholic in inclined to be more bigoted than the average Catholic from the Republic. This, I think, is explained by the fact that Northern Catholics have been treated as second-class citizens for so long and quite naturally resent it. Their Church and their faith was the one open and legitimate way in which they could assert themselves.

I was brought up in Dublin in a street of twenty-four houses. Twenty-three of the homes were Catholic and one was Protestant – Church of Ireland. But that never impinged on me. When I was being ordained a priest it was the Protestant family I invited to my ordination. They were the ones we were friendliest with. I was struck by the 'Catholic bigotry' I saw in Northern Ireland. For instance, I found some of the Northern Ireland priests I knew strongly anti-Protestant and anti-British, with little or no interest in such things as ecumenism. I have often heard Northern priests refer to Protestants as 'heretics'. This was, to say the least, slightly out-of-date in the late 1970s – 12 or 13 years after the ending of the Second Vatican Council. I was once reprimanded by a Belfast priest for allowing a Protestant minister, a relation of the groom, to read one of the lessons at the wedding ceremony.

Northern Ireland Catholics have suffered terribly since the foundation of the Protestant and unionist statelet in 1922. Protestants had better job prospects than Catholics. Catholics were discriminated against in both employment and housing. Northern Ireland was a 'Protestant state for a Protestant people'. The police force – the RUC – was a Protestant police force for a Protestant people. There were very few Catholic policemen. And the infamous B Specials were the worst of all. In many cases the police were just Protestant and loyalist citizens who were uniformed and armed to keep the Catholic population in check.

In my 16 years in Northern Ireland I have seen much security force misbehaviour. On one occasion, I was called to the RUC interrogation centre at Castlereagh to collect a young man who had been detained by the police for questioning. I had to help him to the car. He couldn't walk. He told me that the detectives had put the leg of a wooden chair up his back passage to torture him! Is it any wonder that such young men, filled with hatred and bitterness, want to join the IRA to shoot the people who tortured them in such a fashion? I cannot agree with someone joining the IRA to sort a problem out. But I can certainly understand it. One of the painful things I have to admit is that if it were not for the IRA we would still have corrupt Stormont running Northern Ireland!

On one occasion when I was in Divis Flats an unarmed member of the IRA was shot in the back by a British soldier. I was in the area at the time of the shooting and administered the Last Rites. The ambulance came and I travelled in it to the Royal Victoria Hospital. On the way, we were stopped by the British Army, taken out and held at gunpoint. I could hear the wounded man choking in his own blood. I said to the soldier in charge: 'That man is dying.' He smiled and answered: 'That's the idea, mate.' The patient did die. Those extra minutes might have saved his life. I complained about the incident to the Chief Constable of the RUC and to the Chief of Staff of the army. I was told that there was no case to answer!

There has been a long history of the police and the army harassing people in nationalist areas of Northern Ireland. They seem to pick especially on young men. This in turn makes the young men hate the security forces. In that way, the security forces act as recruiting officers for the IRA.

The UDR – the Ulster Defence Regiment, now part of the Royal Irish Regiment – were the worst I saw. There were many good UDR men,

Catholics and Protestants. Some of them were parishioners and friends of mine. But the UDR had more than its share of bad apples. It's a good thing that the regiment was disbanded. There was a very bad element in the regiment – particularly among the part-time members.

In Kilkeel in Co. Down, where I was a curate from 1983 to 1984, I saw members of the UDR behave like thugs, as I have described in an earlier chapter. I complained about them to their senior office in Ballykinler Camp, a man from East Africa. He had to admit to me that some of them were out of control! The UDR, in many instances, were the B Specials and the B Specials' sons in a new uniform.

One parishioner in Kilkeel heard a noise in his garage in the middle of the night. He got his shotgun down, told his wife to telephone the police and went to the garage to confront the intruder. He found two UDR men with the bonnet of his car open, tampering with his engine. He quite rightly suspected that they were placing a device. The man was a well-known nationalist in the area. He held the UDR men at gunpoint until the police came. The police freed the two UDR men and told the house-owner that it was a civil matter and there was nothing that they could do. They advised the man to go to a solicitor and take a case for trespassing! Had the tables been turned and the nationalist been found messing with a car in the house of a policeman or UDR man he would have been shot dead on the spot or sent to prison for 25 years. There have been two laws in Northern Ireland – one for Catholics and nationalists and another for Protestants, security forces and loyalists. In Kilkeel there was one policeman who, I learned, was strongly Protestant and Orange and virulently anti-Catholic. I was out walking one night and happened to be carrying an ornamental sword-stick which a parishioner had presented me with during my walk. The policeman stopped the police car beside me and said: 'That's a very dangerous-looking weapon you have, Mr. Buckley.' He stressed the 'Mister', of course. I replied: 'Wouldn't I need it with fellas like you cruising around.' He scowled and drove off at high speed.

One night in Kilkeel I was parking my car in the presbytery garage behind the house. I heard a couple of UDR jeeps stop out on the road. One of them fired a shot over my head and sped off laughing and cheering. I informed the police. They called up an hour later. They did not seem too interested.

In March 1986 the unionists of Northern Ireland held a day of protest to oppose the Anglo-Irish Agreement. Many loyalists stayed off work for the day and proceeded to block roads everywhere. Larne, being 80 percent Protestant, was well blocked off. I had to go to Belfast that day on business. But I only got to the edge of the town where I was stopped by a crowd of 100 fist-waving loyalists. They were being led by a Protestant minister. He came towards my car, his fist waving and his camera at the ready, and bellowed: 'You're not in the Free State now, MISTER Buckley.' I calmly answered, 'It looks as if I'm not in the FREE anywhere.' At this, the Reverend became terribly excited and shouted at me: 'I'm standing here today as Moses stood in front of Pharaoh.' A man dressed up as King Billy came up alongside me and tried to punch me through the open window. The crowd surrounded my car and began to rock it from side to side. They stuck 'ULSTER SAYS NO' posters all over my car and I had to turn back as the crowd was getting murderous. Three policemen stood twenty yards from this scene, smiling. They made no effort to see that I was safe. As I turned back towards Larne, the crowd cheered. It was another great victory to add to the Battle of the Boyne. When I got home I telephoned the police inspector, who said there was nothing he could do to get me to Belfast. Larne's loyalists were telling the police what to do that day. During that day of protest many off-duty UDR men were manning the illegal road-blocks, dressed in paramilitary uniforms and balaclavas.

This is the kind of treatment that Northern Ireland Catholics have had to live with for 70 years. It makes their anti-Britishness and anti-police and loyalist positions very understandable. Northern Ireland Catholics have been treated like the blacks in South Africa.

But things have been gradually getting better for Catholics. The Government's fair employment legislation and the Fair Employment Commission under Mr. Bob Cooper have certainly improved things in the area of discrimination in employment. However, there are two-and-a-half times as many Catholics as Protestants unemployed. Some people and groups, like Mr. Oliver Kearney and the Fair Employment Trust, are working for the MacBride Principles – they are trying to get Protestant employers to take a fair proportion of Catholics on their staff. These principles say that the situation in Northern Ireland requires positive discrimination in favour of Catholics. The arguments are very convincing. But there are also very strong social and political forces opposed to these principles.

The housing situation for Catholics has greatly improved. The Northern Ireland Housing Executive has been building lovely new houses all over the area for their tenants. The old tenements of the '60s and '70s, like Divis Flats, are disappearing and are being replaced with beautiful new red-brick homes. The rents are expensive. But many Catholics are unemployed and so the social services are picking up the rent tab.

There has been a huge improvement in the behaviour of the police and security forces in the past ten years. The merger of the UDR has brought many regular soldiers from Britain and Ireland into the combined Royal Irish Regiment and that takes away the narrow Northern Ireland perspective. All members of the regiment can be posted throughout the world. That will take away the home soldiering element. There seems to be a trend towards the phasing out of the part-time soldiers, who were the most dangerous section. They were mostly bigoted Protestants and loyalists, in the UDR for the money, the thrill of having a uniform and a gun and for the thrill of hassling Catholics.

The RUC is much more balanced than ever in their outlook, though there are still far too few Catholics in the force. Since the signing of the Anglo-Irish Agreement, the Protestant community has turned somewhat against the police, who have had to keep the loyalists in order on the protest marches against the Anglo-Irish Agreement. Policemen and their homes were attacked and more and more of the RUC have moved to the middle between the two communities. The RUC also became involved in policing and re-routing the provocative Orange July marches. This led to further confrontations and to loyalist antagonism towards the police. All of this helped to shift the RUC from being a Protestant force for a Protestant people to being a police force for the whole community.

Of course, it will take time for the RUC to be accepted in Catholic and nationalist areas. We still have the memories of the beatings in the interrogation centres and the harassment on the streets. The police problem in Northern Ireland will be fully solved only when the major political question is settled. I have met very good RUC men in my years in Northern Ireland. It would be helpful if more Catholics joined the force. But Catholics take their lives in their hands by doing so. If you're from a Catholic area and join you can never go home in comfort again. All RUC men and women are under great pressure. There is a high incidence of suicide, mental problems, alcohol abuse and marital breakdown and in recent years the RUC has had set up a special unit to deal with such cases.

Many of the RUC personnel I met, even during my time on the Falls Road, were quite realistic about the position they were in and were sometimes prepared to break and bend the rules. On one occasion, I was sent for by a prominent police officer who told me that the INLA (Irish National Liberation Army) had placed a large bomb under the new motorway going through Belfast because the contractor had refused to pay thousands of pounds protection money. The policeman said: 'If I cordon off the area and the bomb goes off, people will be killed and great damage caused. Could you contact the Provos for us and get them to tell the INLA to shift their bomb.' This was done without anyone getting hurt. That same senior police officer was overheard disciplining a policeman who tried to stop an old lady whisper an Act of Contrition into the ear of a joyrider who had killed himself in a crashed car. 'Constable,' he had said, 'you should learn to respect the religious sensitivities of the people you are called to serve.' One time when we had an eight-day festival in Divis Flats, the police and army kept soldiers and policemen out of the area in order to avoid trouble. We were allowed to do our own policing that week. We had very few incidents. On the last night of the festival, rival Provo and INLA gunmen fought and waved their guns about. But we solved the trouble ourselves.

Northern Ireland Catholics, particularly in big population centres like Belfast and Derry, have grown up as members of the minority community, second-class citizens. Many of them didn't mix with Protestants. They lived in Catholic ghetto areas and went to schools that were exclusively Catholic. This left them, from childhood, with a suspicion of Protestants. On one occasion, I was showing 15 Methodist ministers around Divis Flats. One of the ministers was wearing a clerical collar. A young girl stopped us and asked the minister: 'Are you a priest?' 'No, love,' he answered warmly, 'I'm a Protestant. What do you think of Protestants?' 'I hate yez,' replied the child. 'Why do you hate us?' asked Reverend. 'Because,' said the wee one, 'yez don't believe in Jesus.' 'Well,' said the minister, 'I believe in Jesus.' The little girl studied the minister in disbelief. After a moment she said: 'You're a quare Protestant then.' Catholics in Northern Ireland very often do not know Protestants well. It is easy to hate or suspect what you don't know or understand.

What kind of Catholics are Northern Ireland Catholics? There is a variety of Catholics north of the border. You have your middle- and upper-class Catholics who live in places like the Malone Road or Derriaghy in Belfast. Most of these were born in poorer circumstances and have climbed up the social ladder, maybe by starting small businesses that did well. Or they are members of the medical and legal professions. These Catholics are establishment types. They go to church every Sunday and send their children to the good grammar schools run by the Catholic Church. They behave obsequiously in front of the bishop and the priests. The middle- and upper-class Catholics of Northern Ireland will not generally rock the boat anyway. They are upwardly mobile!

What about working – and unemployed – Catholics? If you challenge any of these they will tell you that they are Catholic. But many of them don't go to Mass regularly. In Belfast now the Catholic churches are attended by the women, the children and the older men. The young and middle-aged men are missing. In some nationalist areas many people have stopped going to Mass because of the church's anti-Sinn Féin stand. In Belfast, as elsewhere, the Catholics do not accept or practise Papal teaching on birth control. The numbers attending confession are dwindling. Many Northern Catholics are superstitious or political Catholics. They are Catholics *rather than* Protestants, and they are Catholics at times of baptism, confirmation, marriage and death and, as the old catechism said: 'in times of dangers, temptations and afflictions'.

There is a growing number of Catholics in Northern Ireland who are breaking away from the tribal ethos and thinking for themselves. One indication of this is the number of Catholics disobeying the Church and opting for integrated education rather than for Catholic schools.

But the Church still has a hold on Catholics in general – a hold that is based on brain-washing and guilt. The Church has publicly admitted in recent years that it is engaged in the 'battle for the minds and hearts'. In general, I think that Catholics from the Republic, particularly Dublin, are more liberated, liberal and radical. Dublin strikes me as the centre from which radical and liberal Irish Catholicism is emanating. Great stuff! It's badly needed.

THE CATHOLIC CHURCH AS BRITISH AGENT

When Cahal Daly came as bishop to Belfast in 1982 he asked for suggestions as to how he could improve the Church's standing and reputation. As I mentioned before, I invited him to abandon his palace on the leafy Somerton Road and come to live with us at his cathedral – St. Peter's in the middle of Divis Flats on the Falls Road. Bishop (now Cardinal) Daly was visibly shocked at my suggestion. He said that he could not do that. My facial expression must have demanded an explanation. 'If I came to live at Divis important people like British politicians and senior security force people could not visit me.'

He was excusing his reluctance to live among his people by saying that his political visitors would not be safe. I felt that if people were not prepared to visit him in Divis at his cathedral then he should not worry about them anyway. He obviously saw things differently and not only lived at the palace but renovated, decorated and extended it.

Cardinal Daly is 'well got' at Stormont and in London. The British did not like his predecessor, Cardinal O Fiaich. He was too nationalist for the Brits. But Daly is conservative. He condemns the IRA, which is most important to the British. When I learned that Cahal Daly's sermons were being photocopied in the British embassy in Washington and distributed around America to influential people I understood very fully how important Cahal Daly was to the British.

Cardinal Daly has travelled to America to preach against the MacBride Principles. He has condemned the IRA. He has publicly praised John Hume and the SDLP. He has refused to have talks with Sinn Féin and the IRA even though he is supposed to be responsible for their souls and eternal salvation.

What have the Brits done for Cardinal Daly and the Catholic Church in return? Well, they have continued to fund the segregated Catholic teacher training colleges, schools, hospitals and institutions. This is worth millions of pounds to the Catholic Church each year. The schools are particularly important. Through their school empire the Catholic clergy control teachers, school staff, children and parents.

But more strikingly still the Northern Ireland Office has channelled grants for training schemes for the unemployed through the Catholic Church. This is worth millions more every year. The British Government feels that this money is in safe hands. The bishops and the priests get money for training schemes. The places on these schemes are advertised in Church on Sunday. So if you want to hear about the vacancies you must be a Church-goer. The Catholic Church benefits by enticing people go to Mass in this way. When you are on the schemes you are under the control of the church and the priest. You must continue going to Mass and not rock the boat.

THE NORTHERN IRELAND PROTESTANT

The Labour movement has never done well in Northern Ireland. That's rather bewildering and rather sad. Both the Protestant and Catholic working and unemployed classes have much in common. They must both battle against joblessness, homelessness and poverty, although things are a bit better for the Protestant. You would think that the Labour and trade union movements could mobilise the Protestant and Catholic working-classes on issues they have in common. But no, that has failed. The two communities are kept separated by the 'national' question.

They say that the Northern Ireland Protestant is more loyal to the half-crown than to the Crown! This is particularly true of the middle- and upper-class Protestants who do not become involved in the political hassle. They leave this to their working-class friends and the political leaders. When you meet them they will be quick to point out: 'But we have many good Roman Catholic friends.' If there were a British withdrawal in the morning the upper-and middle-class Protestant would not resist as long as their money, privilege and property were left intact. They would fit into a united Ireland as well as their co-religionists have fitted into the Republic. At present only 3 percent of the Republic's population is Protestant. But they control 27 percent of the country's wealth!

So your Northern Ireland middle-and upper-class Protestant is not a rampant roaring Orangeman at all. In fact he will look down his nose on such types. But yet come election time that same person will vote for politicians like the Reverend Ian Paisley! Paisley is almost like their barking guard-dog. They don't openly associate with him but in the privacy of the ballot box they vote him in for security's sake.

But the working-class Northern Ireland Protestant is a horse of a different colour. He is often a rampant raging Orangeman. In a blind way he is interested in protecting his so-called 'culture' and 'heritage'. Most Protestants from the working-class do not go to Church. They are Protestants in name only – political Protestants. They are very blinded by a religious and political hatred and bigotry. The best way I can convey this is to share my experiences on Larne Borough Council as a councillor.

LARNE BOROUGH COUNCIL

Larne is an 80 percent Protestant town. The 20 percent of Catholics have survived because they have kept a low profile. They've had to do this to survive. In the 1970s a loyalist gang shot Catholics in Larne because their heads were not quite so low.

When the Local Government election came around in 1989, I had been living in Larne for five years. During that time I had commented on discrimination against Catholics in Larne and as a result I was verbally abused and attacked. Protestant youths spat at me on the street. In 1989 many people suggested to me that I should stand as a non-party political community candidate in the council elections. I thought about it and eventually decided to stand. I was elected on the first count with more than 300 first-preference votes to spare. I attracted, it appeared, a mixture of Protestant and Catholic votes.

During the election campaign my harmless election posters had been removed by unionists. On the day of the vote, the Larne branch of Mr. Paisley's party – the DUP – had a van going around Larne broadcasting messages like 'KEEP THE LARNE CHAMBER PURE...KEEP ROME OUT...KEEP THE DUBLIN PRIEST OUT.' Those attacks may very well have helped me to be elected. The DUP leader in the town, watching the people going into the polling booths shaking hands with me, predicted half-way through the day: 'You're definitely in.'

At the count, the DUP leader's vote was down 600 votes. When the count was completed he refused to stand with me. He said: 'I will not stand with Rome.' It never even occurred to him that Rome might have even less time for me than he would!

The council which eventually emerged was 15 members strong – 7 Ulster Unionists, 3 DUP, 2 Alliance Party, 1 British Conservative, 1 Independent nationalist and myself. They elected an Ulster Unionist member, Mrs Rosalie Armstrong, as Mayor.

The unionists, at our first annual general meeting, appointed themselves to all the 50 or so committee and board appointments. Councils in Northern Ireland send members to health, education committees and so on. We were four Catholics. We were excluded by the unionist majority. I complained about this and the DUP leader told me that I was a 'new boy' and that I would have to 'earn my spurs'.

For a number of months I decided to try to work with the unionists. I was naive. I went with them all on a trip to Sellafield nuclear plant in Cumbria. We had good banter in the minibus. We had meals, drinks and walks together. It was a pleasant few days. When we were sailing back on the Larne-Stranraer ferry, a delegation of the Larne DUP approached me. They announced: 'The truce is over, Mr. Buckley.' As soon as we had come in sight of Northern Ireland their old bitter defences went up again. Working with them achieved absolutely nothing. They simply saw it as a sign of weakness and walked all over us.

I began to challenge them at council meetings about discrimination against Catholics, about the wisdom of spending tax-payers' money on stained glass windows of King Billy and about Larne Council's exclusion of us four Catholic councillors and the council's poor record in the employing of Catholics. I also disagreed with their opposition to the Anglo-Irish Agreement. All hell broke loose. One DUP man, waving his bible at me, announced: 'I'm a bigot and proud of it!', explaining that the word bigot came from the Protestant refusal to bend the knee to Rome: 'By God, I'll not,' he declared. There were certain accusations of fraud and misbehaviour. There was an allegation that our country park was being used for immoral activity and the making of blue movies and that some senior people of our community were involved. The councillors went bananas. The council staff, blinded by their Protestantism and unionism, refused to facilitate our meetings. There were weeks of disruption. Much to my horror, the two Alliance party members, two Catholic women, Mrs Amelia Kelly and Mrs Pat Gay, sided and voted with the unionists who gave them absolutely nothing in return.

The RUC had to protect me going to and coming from meetings. When I would arrive there would be an angry mob armed with guns, iron bars and sticks, singing: 'Go back to the bog, Paddy.' Eventually this unionist mob was allowed up into the council chamber. When I tried to speak they shouted me down. They stood behind my chair nudging me with their iron bars and sticks. I was waiting to have one of those iron bars crash down on my head at any minute. The unionist councillors encouraged the mob and laughed with glee when I was threatened or prevented from speaking.

One night at a meeting, the Mayor, Mrs Armstrong, slandered me. The slander was printed in the council minutes and that became libel. I immediately issued writs against the Mayor and the Council. I won my case. The matter was settled out of court. I got an apology and damages. It was a condition of the settlement that I would not reveal the amount of the settlement.

I found that having to attend Larne Borough Council meetings seemed to exacerbate my Crohn's disease. I was only elected in May of 1989 and by September I needed major surgery. I was horrified by the bigotry and hatred and discrimination of the unionists. They are a hopeless case. They will only change when they are forced to, when they are dispossessed and disempowered as they soon will be. The famous poem *Desiderata* tells us to avoid troublesome and quarrelsome people. For the last couple of years of my term on the Council I deliberately attended the bare minimum of meetings. I went for five minutes once every three months to keep up my membership. The Gospel tells us that if we go into a town where they do not make us welcome that we are to go out into the street and shake the dust of that town from our feet. I have shaken the dust of Larne Borough Council and its bigoted unionists from my feet and, by Christ, it feels good!

I discovered that the Larne unionists had little sense of humour either, especially when it came to themselves, their politics or their religion. One night at a council meeting the DUP presented me with a brown package. Inside was a little teddy bear – red, white and blue the British colours. The teddy was carrying a banner which read: ' love Ireland' and was wearing a badge which read: 'No pope here'. enjoyed the joke. And I was going to get my own back.

A week or two later I was in Dublin and parked illegally outside Bewley's café. The Gardaí gave me a parking ticket. I brought the ticket home to Larne with me. I removed my own name and registration number from the ticket and put the DUP leader's name and registration number on it. I placed it on his van outside a council meeting. When he came out of the meeting he saw the ticket, presumed it was from the RUC, ripped it off his windscreen in anger and went towards a RUC man waving the ticket and demanding: 'What's this for?' The policeman took the ticket and examined it and replied: 'But Alderman this is not from us. It's from the Garda.' McKee was furious. He went straight to the police station and handed the ticket in and complained

He told the RUC that it was a message from the IRA to say: 'If we can put a ticket on your windscreen, then we can put a bomb under your van.'

I had a telephone call from the police. They wished to interview me. When I went to the police station I was brought into a room with an inspector and another police officer. I was cautioned that anything I might say would be taken down and used in evidence against me! The interview went like this:

Inspector: 'Father Buckley, have you any knowledge of the Garda traffic ticket placed on Alderman McKee's vehicle?' (The RUC had checked with the Gardaí to see who the ticket had been issued to.)

Fr. Pat: 'Yes, Inspector, I have knowledge of the ticket.'

Inspector: 'Were you responsible for placing the ticket on the vehicle?'

Fr. Pat: 'No, I was not really responsible. But I know who was.'

Inspector: 'Are you prepared to tell us the name of who was responsible?'

Fr. Pat: 'Better than that, Inspector, I have the responsible person with me and in the interests of justice I'm prepared to hand him over to you for questioning and for punishment.'

I put my hand in my pocket and took out the little red, white and blue teddy bear and placed him on the desk in front of the two policemen. 'That's who is responsible,' I declared. The two policemen looked at the teddy, looked at each other and burst out laughing. The Inspector closed his file and said: 'I think the matter ends here.' It was a funny incident. But it showed me just how bereft of humour the extreme Northern Ireland Protestant and unionist really is. I had taken the teddy presentation with humour. But when I returned the joke the DUP had to involve the police and claim that they were the victims of an IRA threat. The Northern Ireland problem will not be solved until people like the DUP can laugh at themselves.

PROTESTANT HATRED AND BIGOTRY

Ian Paisley is often regarded as the worst face of Northern Ireland Protestant hatred and bigotry. But I don't believe that Ian Paisley is the worst. At least you know where you stand with him because he shoots off his mouth about his views all the time. The private Paisley is a different person from the public one, especially when he is standing before a crowd of his DUP Free Presbyterian supporters.

Paisley says that he does not hate or detest Roman Catholics but just the Roman Catholic system. But that's like saying to someone: 'I don't hate you, I only hate your family.' However, Paisley is more than willing to help Catholics with their difficulties. After my 'divorce' from Cardinal Daly I was barred by the Catholic prison chaplains and therefore by the Northern Ireland Office from having pastoral visits to the various prisons I had visited for years. I tried in vain to get the Northern Ireland Office (NIO) to let me in. One evening at tea time, I telephoned the home of the Reverend Ian Paisley, my Euro MP, about the problem. He told me straight that he had no time for my religion but felt I was being unfairly treated. Within days I heard from the NIO to say that the problem was solved. Since then I have been admitted for my pastoral visits and I have been able to by-pass the Catholic chaplains altogether.

Protestant hatred for Catholicism does interfere with ordinary everyday life in Northern Ireland. If you are in the Orange Order you are not really allowed to associate with Catholics. If you court or marry one they will expel you. You are not even supposed to frequent a Catholic pub. Both in Kilkeel and Larne, where I have lived, the Orange Order and their associated bands like to march right through the Summer. This means that your town is blocked off weekly for hours. Often you cannot drive to your home or to the shops. And if you are on the way home and run into the bands you will often be treated to abuse, to bad language and to verbal threats. Many of these bands are now followed by beer-drinking louts who really turn on the abuse. When these bands are marching, the Catholics must hide indoors.

But you do not have to look to the Orange Order for bigotry and hatred. In Larne I have visited most of the churches in the town. But I have never once had a minister from the town return my visit. One time I asked one of the Presbyterian ministers, Dr. Lynas, a former Moderator, to come to The Oratory and to talk to the people about what Presbyterians believed. He told me that he couldn't come as his congregation would not tolerate such a visit! Dr. Lynas had been in trouble some years before for inviting the parish priest of Larne to a service in his church. And Dr. Lynas was the minister, not of a working-class church but of a church, Gardenmore, attended by the fur-coat brigade.

When I first came to Larne I visited a different Protestant church every Sunday evening. I would announce at Sunday morning Mass which church I was going to and I was always joined by 20 or so Catholics from Larne. One minister wrote to me to say that he had heard I was coming around the churches and that he would ask me not to come to his church. His notice board outside the church said: 'All welcome'. I wrote to him to ask him why he did not want us. He replied that he was in the light and that I as a Catholic was in the dark. He did not want me to bring darkness into his light!

We even visited Paisley's Free Presbyterian church in Larne. Out of courtesy, we rang the minister the week before we went. The Reverend Gordon said: 'My church is the house of God. It is open to all sinners on the Lord's Day. In that context, Pat Buckley will be more than welcome.' I was happy that being a sinner qualified me for a seat at the Free Presbyterian service.

But a lot of the Protestant bigotry in Northern Ireland is quite subtle and comes from so-called respectable and middle-class Protestants. Recently a young Catholic girl from Larne was planning to get married to a Protestant young man. The Catholic priests gave them such a difficult time about what religion any children might be that the couple decided to get married in the Methodist church in the town. The bride's father, a devout Catholic, was upset about this. I talked to him and to the couple. We all agreed that the marriage should be in the Methodist church and that I would go and take part in the service, particularly to keep the father happy. I turned up and was waiting in the sacristy for the service to begin. The groom came and told me that I could not take part in the service!

INTEGRATED EDUCATION IN NORTHERN IRELAND

Traditionally in Northern Ireland we have had two education systems – one run by the Catholic Church for Catholics, and the state schools, which are really run by the Protestant community. Northern Ireland's state schools generally have Protestant clergymen on their boards, and there are many clergymen on the North's Education and Library Boards.

The Catholic schools promote Catholicism. They are part of the problem of Northern Ireland. Northern Ireland Catholic children are often born into areas that are totally Catholic ghettos. They never meet a Protestant in school. So Catholic children are often 16-18 years old before they are exposed to a Protestant. Such separation and ignorance feeds the misunderstandings that exist in Northern Ireland. In turn, this fuels the violence. In Northern Ireland, Catholicism and nationalism and republicanism have all become interlocked. Catholic schools are also nationalist schools. A Protestant or unionist might not always feel at home there.

The state schools in Northern Ireland are not, in practice, secular state schools. They are really the Protestants' schools. Ministers, as I say, act on boards and ministers also come to these schools to take assemblies and classes. When you pass these schools you find the Union Jack flying in the grounds or over the building. Catholics and nationalists would not necessarily want to walk under the Union Jack to get into school. Many of the Protestant pupils at these schools are members of the Orange Order, Orange bands and other groups associated with the Protestant and unionist tradition. Catholics are not always comfortable with these activities. I know of many cases where Catholic children were made very uncomfortable in these state schools and had to be removed.

For a number of years now we have had an integrated education movement in Northern Ireland. This movement sets up schools (now with full government funding) which attract Catholic and Protestant children and others. The teachers are both Catholic and Protestant. The mix of pupils is not allowed to fall below the 40/60 percent religious divide one way or the other. There is an attempt to give a more enlightened approach to history. Religion is taught in a more comprehensive way but there is provision made for denominational religious instruction – particularly for Catholics preparing for First Holy Communion and Confirmation. Many of these schools promote both British and Irish sports and the Irish language and other cultural things. As well as the pupils having the opportunity to attend school with members of the opposite community there is a fair interchange at the level of parents.

Those Catholic clerics who are at present opposing integrated education in Northern Ireland, people like Bishop Cahal Daly and Father Denis Faul of Dungannon, do so, I believe, for the wrong reasons. They say it is important that children attend Catholic schools in order to benefit from the 'Catholic ethos' pervading the whole curriculum and day. This is a view with which I totally disagree and find even irrational. Surely there is not a 'Catholic' way of teaching geography, mathematics, accountancy. Is the biology of the Catholic different from that of a Protestant or the atheist? I think that if you saw a Catholic and a Protestant in the bath together, you would be hard-pushed to tell them apart!

Anyway, if we are to go on present evidence, the Catholic school with its Catholic ethos has been a great failure. One of the basic teachings of the Catholic Church is observance of the obligation of attendance at Sunday Mass under pain of 'mortal sin'. In parts of Dublin now, up to 80 percent of Catholics do not attend Sunday Mass; in Belfast the figure is up to 60 percent. Very often in the inner city you find that Mass-goers are mainly female or elderly. The men and the young are missing. All of them are products of our Catholic schools with their Catholic ethos. What, then, has gone wrong?

Nowadays, between four and five thousand young Irishwomen head over to England for abortions, which are outlawed in the Republic. Most of these girls are Catholics, educated in Catholic convent schools. From the Catholic Church's point of view, what has happened here? The schools had ten to fourteen years to instruct these girls in the intricacies of Catholic morals. And yet the Catholic school system and the ethos of the convent did not so impress these girls with Catholic teaching as to prevent them having abortions and thereby sinning in a most serious way against Catholic morality.

The IRA and other nationalist paramilitary organisations have wreaked havoc in Northern Ireland these past twenty or more years. Most of their members have passed through the Catholic schools with the famous Catholic ethos. How then, if such a school and such an ethos form such good people, such good citizens and such good Catholics did these young men graduate to maim and kill? Were these young potential paramilitaries all out with the 'flu the day the Christian Brothers taught God's fifth commandment, 'Thou shalt not kill'? I accept that in the national context that Mass-missers, abortion-seekers and paramilitaries are in the minority. However, they constitute sizable minorities. The Catholic school and the Catholic ethos cannot be all that good or all-powerful if, in spite of the schools and their teaching, such minorities emerge. I cannot see that state or integrated schools could do worse. In fact, the decade or so of mixing with people of other political and religious persuasions would more probably lessen the tendency to prejudice and bigotry. While that might not rid us of

Mass-missers and abortion-seekers – and let me say that I am not judging these folk in any way – it would, I think, lessen the number of paramilitaries and their supporters.

All this said, I must emphasise here that, in the past year or so, I have changed my mind considerably about the advantages of integrated education. I used to be whole-heartedly in favour. Now I see a number of problems concerning it. First of all, integrated schools are for the middle and upper classes. Someone has called them 'schools for little toffs'. They are being set up in rather posh areas and there is very little attempt to establish them where it really matters – in the divided ghetto areas of Belfast and Derry. Some of those involved are pseudo-liberals. In some of the integrated schools I have visited I'm not sure that the working- or unemployed-class persons from the Falls or Shankill would feel at home.

Because the people setting up these schools are middle-class and snobbish types, they are terribly worried about the Establishment and its values. And so the Catholics in these projects are concerned about what the Catholic hierarchy think of them. They try very hard not to rock the boat so that eventually the Catholic hierarchy will accept them and give them the stamp of approval. At meetings, integrated education Catholics sit around lamenting the attitude of the Catholic clergy to them. I don't know what's wrong with them. Do they not realise that officially the Catholic Church regards them as big sinners for not sending their children to Catholic schools? Why do they want to break the rules on one hand and then lament the fact that the hierarchy does not love them on the other? There is hypocrisy here.

I believe that something far more radical is needed in education in Northern Ireland. If people, whether the Catholic or Protestant churches or NICIE, want to set up schools then, of course, they should be allowed to do so. But they should get absolutely no government or tax-payers' money to set up religious schools.

I believe that the British Government in Northern Ireland should set up schools that are absolutely secular schools. In those schools I believe that God or religion should never be mentioned except in a comparative or sociological way. I think that there should be no political or religious emblems on display.

For me religion is a private thing. Its place is the family home and the church and Sunday School. I believe that the integrated school are defeating their purpose when Roman Catholic pupils are taken off for their separate religious education. Integrated education in Northern Ireland is a false notion now. It is for the middle- and upper-classes who have little trouble with each other in the first place.

ECUMENISM

Unfortunately ecumenism in Ireland and Northern Ireland has not come to very much. It generally consists of meeting once or twice a year for a harmless joint prayer service followed by tea and cucumber sandwiches. Those attending these services are clergy and the more middle- and upper-class Catholics and Protestants. Irish ecumenism is all talk. Very few concessions are made to the other side.

One big stumbling-block is the area of mixed marriage. The Catholic Church will generally insist that the marriage take place in the Catholic church building. Here, the Protestant, if the Catholic Church gets its way, is the loser. Then the Catholic partner will have to promise to do all in his or her power to see that the children of the marriage are brought up Roman Catholics. Again the Protestant is the loser. If the Catholic Church were really interested in ecumenism then it would have a more relaxed attitude to mixed marriages. It would recognise marriages that take place in Protestant churches and it would be satisfied if the children were to be brought up as Christians. This issue is very important for some Protestants in the Irish Republic. In 1922, the Protestant population of the Republic stood at 12 percent. In the 1990s it is at 3 percent. The Catholic Church's behaviour on the mixed religion marriage issue and the religion of the children is greatly contributing to the annihilation of the Protestant community in the Republic. This issue causes even greater problems in Northern Ireland where feelings are so much stronger. If the Catholic Church were truly ecumenical it would be more flexible on the mixed marriage and religion of children issues. It would also be more open on inter-denominational or non-denominational schooling.

The Protestant churches are not without fault in this area either. I have often suggested that Protestant churches and cathedrals should be stripped of British Government and British Army flags, emblems and paraphernalia. These trappings of earthly empires really have no place in the house of God. I also think that Protestant ministers should not belong, as they do, to anti-Catholic organisations like the Orange

Order, nor encourage them by granting them church parades, etc. In Northern Ireland the Protestant churches are often seen to behave like branches of the civil service. They are very slow to criticise the injustices of the state and the security forces. The Republic has been and, to some extent, is still a confessional Catholic country. Northern Ireland is a confessional Protestant statelet.

A SOLUTION FOR NORTHERN IRELAND

The Irish and the British have been trying to solve the national question for 800 years and have failed most miserably to do so. I have a poster which says: 'If you are part of the problem, you cannot be part of the solution.' The Irish and the British on their own will never be able to solve the Northern Ireland conflict. It will take more than that.

The Northern Ireland problem will never be solved by the two old models of Irish nationalism or Ulster unionism. These models are part of the problem and both models exclude one community or the other. Irish nationalists will never settle for a unionist-run Northern Ireland. During their 50-year misrule at Stormont, the unionists forfeited their right to govern Northern Ireland. Northern Ireland is a failed entity. It can never be a successful one.

Nor indeed is there any future in Sinn Féin's 32-county socialist republic. Apart from all else, this excludes the Northern Ireland unionist population. You cannot totally ignore the wishes and aspirations of one million people. There is also the very grave question of the Catholicity of the Irish Republic, its laws and Constitution.

Something new is needed. I have a notion of what might work in Ireland. But it is very idealistic. But, as I always say, my dream is surely better than the present nightmare. I believe that the British should declare their intention to withdraw totally from Ireland on a set date not too far in the future. At the same time, the Irish Government should announce that it is holding a referendum to scrap the present Constitution and to replace it with a totally secular and pluralist one. Both governments should then invite a body like the United Nations or the European Union to send a peace-keeping force to Northern Ireland while a negotiated way forward is worked out. That new structure could be most imaginative. I see it as being like this:

Ireland should have four new provincial parliaments – Ulster, based in Belfast, Connaught, based in Galway, Munster, based in Cork and

Leinster, based in Dublin. A decision would have to be made as to whether to include Donegal, Cavan and Monaghan in the Ulster region. The views of the Northern Ireland unionists would be important on this point. If they did not want to be swamped in a Catholic province, then Cavan, Monaghan and Donegal could be incorporated into the Leinster and Connaught regions.

Above the four regional parliaments (which should have as much power as possible) there should be a national assembly. This should be based neither in Belfast or Dublin but perhaps at a venue straddling the present border. As well as a new Constitution there could be a bill of rights to safeguard the Protestant 'minority' on the island. There could also be a Council of the British Isles and some structure at European level to supervise the whole new arrangement, which would need to be generously underpinned by money from Britain, Ireland, the EU and the United States.

I believe that an imaginative and adventurous move like I'm suggesting is the way forward. It would be opposed by reactionary and conservative elements both north and south. But we cannot allow those elements, who have dictated the past, to dominate the future.

CHAPTER 10

The Republic – a Catholic State

'We have two forms of colonialism in Ireland – an overt form we see in the north and the more spiritual, mental colonialism we see in the Roman Catholic Church.'

Tim Pat Coogan

THAT THERE HAVE BEEN AND STILL ARE reactionary and conservative Catholic elements in the Republic of Ireland hardly needs elaboration. It is true that there has been some movement towards a greater pluralism and even secularisation in recent years and no Catholic bishop would say now, as a former Bishop of Cork, Dr. Cornelius Lucey, did in 1955, that the bishops were 'the final arbiters of right and wrong, even in political matters'. But, by and large, the Irish Republic is still a confessional Roman Catholic state. To me that is a bad thing. There will never be any peace on the island of Ireland until such time as all the people on it can live together in some mutually-accepted arrangement. One of the major things blocking progress on that front is that the unionists of Northern Ireland see the Republic as a Catholic Church-dominated state. As Protestants, they feel they could not live in such a state. They are right. They should not be expected to accept the degree of control which the Catholic Church wields over many areas of activity in the Republic. I don't accept it and I am some kind of Catholic and some kind of Catholic priest. I have lived a lot of my life in Northern Ireland and I feel far happier, far freer in the North than I could in the South as things stand there at present. Here in the North, despite all our 'troubles', we still have more civil liberty than the people of the Republic.

From the very beginnings of the modern Irish state in 1922, the bishops, sensing the developments in post-World War I society, set their faces against any change in their traditional power over the ordinary people. Any diminution in that power, which might express itself in changing religious practices, was condemned. In 1924, Cardinal

Logue of Armagh could warn student priests at Maynooth that the Irish people 'had lost much of their reverence for religion and the Church'. The Bishop of Ardagh and Clonmacnoise spoke of 'the very low level of degeneracy' reached in Ireland. Down the years, the bishops' Lenten pastoral letters condemned intemperance, gambling, perjury and violence. Concern was expressed that the Irish Catholic people were being tempted by the mass media – cinema, radio and, worst of all, the English newspapers. 'Company-keeping' and immoral dancing were condemned. Archbishop Gilmartin of Tuam lamented that the rosary had been replaced by 'debasing pleasure'. Archbishop Byrne of Dublin was worried about parents sending their children to non-Catholic schools. Conor Cruise O'Brien wrote that the 1920s were the time when 'the specific influence of the Catholic Church in politics was growing palpable again.' Sean O'Faolain said this was a time when 'the Catholic Church was felt, feared and courted on all sides as the dominant power.'

Traditionally, the Irish Catholic Church has been quite happy to 'legislate' its adherents into being 'good moral Catholics'. As the political scientist, Dr. J.H. Whyte, says: 'From its early days, the government proved willing to use the power of the state to protect Catholic moral values.' He goes on to give examples. In 1923, the government introduced the Censorship of Films Act which gave the censor power to cut or refuse a licence to films he regarded as 'subversive to public morality.' Two Intoxicating Liquor Acts were introduced, one in 1924 and another in 1927, to reduce the number of licensed premises in Ireland and their hours of opening. At the time of the establishment of the Irish Free State there were no divorce courts in Ireland and an Irish resident could be divorced only by introducing a private bill in the Westminster House of Commons. The government brought in a bill to make it impossible for this course to be taken again. The Prime Minister of the day, Mr. Liam Cosgrave, introduced it saying: 'I have no doubt but that I am right in saying that the majority of the people of this country regard the bond of marriage as a sacramental bond which is incapable of being dissolved. I personally hold this view. I consider that the whole fabric of our social organisation is based upon the sanctity of the marriage bond.' Here was a Prime Minister, speaking in the civic parliament, preaching Catholic Church doctrine and using such words as 'sacrament' and 'sanctity', the words of theology, not of politics.

In 1929, the Censorship of Publications Act was introduced. The Board appointed under it had a Catholic priest as chairman and three Catholic laymen and one Protestant as members. In 1930, the Vocational Education Act was passed. While, theoretically, the Catholic clergy did not get control of this sector of Irish education, in practice local authorities consistently elected priests as Board members and very often as chairmen. In 1930 the Legitimacy Act was introduced, making 'illegitimate' children legitimate if their parents later married. The Deputy who introduced the private member's bill which later led to this Act pointed out that the proposal simply followed Canon Law.

The stranglehold of the Catholic Church and its clerics over legislative and administrative processes in former years in Ireland was well-illustrated by the case of Miss Letitia Dunbar-Harrison, a Protestant and graduate of TCD, who was appointed by the Local Appointments Commission in 1931 as county librarian for Mayo. A meeting of Mayo Library Committee, consisting of the Bishop, five Catholics priests, a Christian Brother, a Protestant rector and four laymen, refused to ratify the appointment, offering as a reason that she could not speak Irish, but clearly because she was not a Catholic. The Dean of Tuam, Dr. E.A. D'Alton, was more open about the reason: 'Supposing there were books attacking these fundamental truths of Catholicity [he referred to birth control and divorce], is it safe to entrust a girl who is not a Catholic and is not in sympathy with Catholic views with their handling?' Even Eamon de Valera, who had not yet come to power, backed the Committee's decision. The County Council followed suit. The government initially stood up against the Committee's decision. The Council refused to submit and was dissolved and the Commissioner imposed in its place appointed Miss Dunbar-Harrison. The Church then organised a boycott of all library services in the county. The Government had to give in and transfer her to another appointment. The County Council was restored and bigotry had won another victory.

The deference of the state to the Church continued. When new factories or housing estates were opened, the local bishop was always invited to bless the premises. In recent and more ecumenical years the local Protestant Rector is often invited as well. Irish politicians are assigned prominent places at church ceremonies at home and abroad and usually manage to get included in the television pictures of the event. When the de Valera government took office in 1932, it sent message of 'respectful homage and good wishes' to the Pope. In the following year, a tax was placed on imported newspapers, pleasing the Catholic Church which was critical of the immoral foreign press. In 1935 the Criminal Law Amendment Act prohibited the importation and sale of contraceptives, a law which stood until recently. In the same year, the Public Dance Halls Act attempted to enforce Catholic teaching on this long-talked about 'evil'. Legislation was consistently introduced that accorded with Catholic teaching and enforced it.

It was when Eamon de Valera came to write the new Constitution for Ireland, passed by a narrow majority in the 1937 referendum, that the Catholic bishops found an opportunity of flexing their muscles. The 1922 Constitution, which de Valera had opposed, was, according to Dr. Whyte, 'a liberal democratic document which would have suited a country of any religious complexion. The only article on religion was one which briefly guaranteed religious freedom and equality.' Dr. Whyte points out, however, that the corresponding articles in the 1937 Constitution 'were obviously marked by Catholic thought.' He noted four articles which bear particularly the 'stamp of Catholic teaching.' Article 41 recognises the family as the natural primary and fundamental unit of society; guarantees to protect the family as the necessary basis of social order; recognises that by her life in the home woman gives a support to the state without which the common good cannot be achieved; will endeavour to ensure that mothers shall not be obliged by economic necessity to neglect their duties in the home, and that no law shall be enacted providing for the grant of a dissolution of marriage. 'In other words', according to Dr. Whyte, 'Mr. de Valera had set up a new hurdle against the introduction of divorce in Ireland.'

Article 42 of the Constitution limits the state's role and rights in education, guaranteeing to respect the inalienable right and duty of parents for the education of their children. This obviously has facilitated the Catholic Church's near-monopoly in the provision of education throughout the state.

Article 43 echoes Catholic teaching on ownership of property. Article 44, while reflecting the sentiments of the old 1922 Constitution on religious freedom, went on to add: 'The State recognises the special position of the Holy Catholic Apostolic and Roman Church as the guardian of the Faith professed by the great majority of the citizens' (it was later removed from the Constitution in a referendum). This was, in fact, a weaker statement than the bishops wanted – they had sought the official establishment of the Catholic Church in Ireland.

The Irish Labour Party went along with the two larger parties in the Dáil (lower House) in accepting the Catholic ethos of the new Constitution. Dr. Whyte points out that even Protestant opposition to it was only 'half-hearted'. The only opposition came from such literary figures as W.B. Yeats, Oliver St. John Gogarty, Sean O'Faolain, Lennox Robinson and George Russell through the weekly *Irish Statesman*. Yeats wanted to provide 'a solid body of informed opinion that might encourage young writers and discourage the Catholic Church from oppressing them'. On 11 June, 1925, Yeats spoke in the Seanad (upper House) on the right to divorce. Dr. Whyte says of this period: 'The years 1923-1937 reveal, so far as religious values are concerned, a remarkable consensus in Irish society. There was overwhelming agreement that traditional Catholic values should be maintained, if necessary by legislation.'

Why was the Catholic Church so successful in ensuring that Ireland should be a Catholic country with a Catholic Constitution? Of course, it helped that the majority of politicians were Catholics themselves and dependent on their Catholic voters for their seats. The French sociologist, Dr. Michel Peillon, now teaching in Maynooth, suggests in his work *Contemporary Irish Society* that as well as being a moral force it is also a social force. He says the Irish Catholic Church has always been flexible and 'never loses sight of its ultimate essential goals – its own survival and expansion.' In order to achieve this, he adds, the Church must constantly reaffirm itself.

One of the most blatant instances of the degree of episcopal control of Irish political affairs was provided by the controversy over the Mother and Child scheme which preoccupied Irish people, north and south, in the late 1940s and early 1950s. Dr. Noel Browne, Minister for Health in the 1948 Fine Gael-Clann na Poblachta coalition government in Dublin, set about reforming health care for women and children. At that time, the Catholic Church ran most of the hospitals and had a quasi-monopoly on health care in the Republic. The bishops believed that health and family matters were the concern of the Church and they voiced their disapproval of the scheme in a letter, dated 10 October, 1950, to the then Taoiseach (Prime Minister). It said:

The Archbishops and Bishops of Ireland...had under consideration the proposals for a Mother and Child health service and
other kindred medical services. They (the bishops) feel bound
by their office to consider whether the proposals are in accord-
ance with Catholic moral teaching...Experience has shown that
physical or health education is closely interwoven with important moral questions on which the Catholic Church has definite
teaching...We have no guarantee that State officials will respect
Catholic principles...The Bishops desire that your Government
should give careful consideration to the dangers inherent in the
present proposals.

A nod was a good as a wink. The Minister for Health was summoned
before three bishops at Archbishop's House, Dublin. Dr. Browne tells
the story in his autobiography, *Against the Tide*. The outcome was that
he was sacked from his office and the coalition government fell. During
the Cabinet debate leading to the Minister's removal, the leader of his
own party summed up the Government's attitude: 'You cannot afford
to fight the Church.' Another Minister blustered: 'How dare you invite
me to disobey my Church...I don't want to get a belt of a crozier.' Later,
the Taoiseach himself, John A. Costello, was to say: 'As a Catholic, I
obey my authorities.' In his letter to the Archbishop of Dublin to
announce abandonment of the scheme, the Taoiseach stated: 'That
decision expresses the complete willingness of the government to defer
to the judgement...given by the hierarchy.' The *Irish Times* declared,
with justification: 'The Catholic hierarchy is the virtual government of
the country.'

Apologists for the Church and hierarchy might argue that one cannot
judge their present-day attitude and activities by reference to happenings in the 1950s. True, but things have not changed all that much. In
the 1980s, the then Fine Gael Taoiseach, Garret FitzGerald, set about
'liberalising' and 'pluralising' the Irish state. He campaigned for social
and Constitutional reform. His government initiated a Constitutional
referendum which would have had the effect of permitting divorce. A
month before the referendum, opinion polls indicated that some 70
percent of the people favoured the move. The Catholic bishops, as a
body, signalled their intention of leaving politicians and citizens to
make up their own minds on the matter. Then, in a pastoral letter, they

said they were 'convinced that the proposed amendments would weaken rather than strengthen marriage and the family.' The letter was distributed to one million Irish homes. Two prominent bishops – the late Archbishop McNamara of Dublin and Bishop Jeremiah Newman of Limerick – made public statements condemning divorce. Pressure was brought to bear on priest-journalists and broadcasters to take the anti-divorce line. Two other priests who spoke on a television programme in favour of the introduction of divorce were quietly reprimanded by their Archbishop during a later priests' retreat and given 'a second chance' and 'forgiveness'. However, two West of Ireland priests took the bishops at their word that the issue was a matter of conscience. Fathers Pat O'Brien and Padraig Standún spoke out publicly in favour of removing the ban on divorce legislation from the Constitution. They were soon reprimanded, the general belief being that it was not particularly because of the displeasure of their own Archbishop but because of the attitude of the then papal Nuncio, Archbishop Gaetano Alibrandi.

However, the Church's greatest push against civil divorce came from rural clergy in the weeks leading to the referendum. In many places, priests used their pulpits to tell people how to vote. In one County Monaghan parish, the priest pointed to two large 'ballot boxes' on the altar, one marked 'yes' the other 'no'. He explained: 'Those who vote "yes" to divorce are voting themselves into the eternal fires of hell. Those who vote "no" to divorce are voting themselves into the everlasting happiness of heaven, with God and his angels and saints.' Other factors, particularly a strong campaign by ultra-Catholic lay organisation and fears among farmers that divorce would mean the splitting of their lands between two wives, combined with the clerical opposition to defeat of the referendum. Had FitzGerald's reforms succeeded, the Republic would have been a more democratic country and one where everyone would have greater civil liberties. It would also have become a more attractive potential partner for a new arrangement with Northern Ireland, where for many decades now the Unionists have protested that 'Home Rule means Rome Rule'.

But the Catholic bishops and their unthinking followers beat FitzGerald and his reforms failed. When Archbishop Alibrandi was leaving the country, *Irish Times* journalist Joe Carroll quoted him as boasting that he had 'crushed Garret FitzGerald'. Dr. Tom Inglis, in his book *Moral Monopoly: The Catholic Church in Modern Irish Society*, summed up: 'The referendum demonstrated the continuing ability of the hierarchy to set limits to the political sphere of Irish society.' At the time of writing, the Republic still denies its citizens the civil right of divorce, though a new referendum on the issue is expected.

I deal at present with a great number of couples who live in both a legal and a religious limbo in the Republic of Ireland. These couples are living in 'second unions', one or both of them being separated from previous partners. I notice all the time that those from rural areas of Ireland are much more afraid and 'priest-ridden' than those from Dublin. How often a young man or woman from the country has said to me, when I am trying to sort out their situation: 'What do you think the Canon at home will think? Will I have to go to him for a "letter of freedom"?' Thankfully, I am now able to help these people without referring to the Canon at all and indeed the whole problem is solved before the Canon ever gets to hear about it. Having said that, I must add, for truth's sake, that not all priests give these 'second union' couples a hard time. Some are very sympathetic. They visit these couples and, against Canon Law, encourage them to attend the Sacraments.

Generally, however, the Catholic Church in Ireland has traditionally been quite happy and anxious to 'legislate' their people into being 'good moral Catholics'. This does not augur well for the quality of the faith of the average Irish Catholic. The Christian faith is an invitation to think, speak, live and act in a certain way. For that faith to be truly authentic, it needs to be embraced freely. Most Irish Catholics have never really been given the freedom to accept or reject their faith. They have been born into it and live in a Catholic social ethos where the very laws of the country impose Catholicism on them. The Irish legal framework is Catholic. The laws forbid divorce and abortion. They set limits to contraception. They allow for Catholic schools, colleges and institutions. The fact that this system and these laws deny certain civil rights to others does not seem to disturb the conscience of Catholic bishops or people in the Republic. This is not true democracy. It is unjust to nominal or non-convinced Catholics and members of other faiths. It amounts to majority domination. We condemn that sort of thing elsewhere and yet are prepared to tolerate it at home. Apart from everything else, this sort of uncaring and uncritical attitude leads to a very negative and grudging attitude on the part of many Catholics themselves.

'Home Rule' may or may not still mean 'Rome Rule' in the Republic. But it is an undisputed fact, denied only by those who wish to conceal the wheeling and dealing, that the Catholic hierarchy still wield huge power south of the border. The Irish hierarchy meets secretly, without any laity present, thrice yearly at the national seminary at Maynooth. They have been nicknamed 'the Purple Parliament'. Many people still see them as the virtual government of the country.

It is small wonder, then, that Irish politicians generally will not take the Church on. Rather, they will mumble and grumble in private about change and reform. The President and Government Ministers will turn out faithfully at Church functions – funerals of bishops, etc. Not to be there would be a black mark. State visits are regularly paid to the Vatican. Being photographed with the Pope during his 1979 visit to the Republic was important. The Papal Nuncio in Ireland is not only the Vatican's ambassador but, however recent his arrival, is automatically the *doyen* of the diplomatic corps. Politicians and their parties are careful not to introduce legislation that will displease the 'Purple Parliament' at Maynooth.

The Catholic Church has strong influence in the Republic's media. The hierarchy is conscious nowadays of the power of the press, radio and television. It has its own Catholic Press and Information Office. At the Catholic Communications Centre in Booterstown, bishops, priests, religious brothers and nuns are trained in the use of the media. Religious affairs correspondents are expected to toe the establishment line. Some time ago, Fr. Michael Keane of Dublin, the founder of the Knock Marriage Bureau, and myself picketed the hierarchy's meeting at Maynooth. We were protesting about the lack of justice within the Church itself, within its structures and within Canon Law. To be fair, the media carried news of our protest. One religious affairs correspondent, from a large daily paper, was criticised at the press conference after the meeting for associating with the enemy. It was indicated to him that he might not get co-operation in the future from the Church, something that would make his work difficult, to say the least.

The Roman Catholic call to prayer, the Angelus bell, which is offensive to the faith of some and the secularism of others in Ireland, is belted out twice daily on national radio and television. Why should the principal broadcasting organisation in the state allow itself to be used by one denomination, albeit the largest, to call its members to prayer? I personally find this repulsive and switch the radio or television off while it is being broadcast. I resent being made to pray at a particular time. From the Church's point of view, the broadcasting of *The Angelus* is important. It is a symbol of the dominance of the Catholic Church in the state.

The Catholic Church in Ireland has been described as 'the conscience of the nation.' That term is far too kind. The Church thinks for the nation and the nation is not allowed to think for itself. The Church controls most of the educational establishments in the country or has a major input into them. From the day the three-year-old attends nursery until the day the 21-year-old graduate from university, Mother Church has been exerting her influence. Having control of education, especially at the primary and secondary levels, gives the Church immense power. It gets large Government grants to run its schools. This leaves the Church a wealthy organisation with huge financial and property resources. The Church employs the teachers and the school staff. You must keep in touch with the Church and the clergy to be employed and to stay in employment. The church, therefore, controls the livelihood and the very daily lives of thousands and thousands of people who depend on the education field for their existence.

A few years ago I had a conversation with a Catholic curate in a Dublin parish. We talked a long time about issues affecting religion and the Catholic Church. After a while, the priest said to me: 'What I'm going to say to you now may shock you. I'm an atheist. I don't believe in God. The only reason I stay in the priesthood and continue to say Mass and preach is that I feel this whole religion and Catholic thing helps people, I mean psychologically. I'm too settled to leave and change my way of life. I have a comfortable existence and I do a certain amount of good.' That priest had no real faith. However, he believed in the Catholic system. For him, as for so many other Catholics in the Republic, it's the system that counts.

CHAPTER 11

Is Our Catholic Church
Losing Credibility?

'Anyone who wants to achieve something depicts the
inadequacy of what has gone before.'

Mario von Galli SJ

ON ONE OCCASION THE EMPEROR NAPOLEON met a Cardinal and said to
him: 'Your Eminence, I am going to destroy the Church of Rome.' The
Cardinal replied: 'You have no chance of success; we priests have been
trying to do just that for hundreds of years.' The story may be amusing
but, sadly enough, what the Cardinal said contains large grains of truth.
I am very proud and happy to be a Catholic and a priest but I am very
unhappy about many of the directions in which our Church is heading.
I am especially concerned about the lack of courageous leadership at
the present time.

I feel that one could say at least the same about the other Christian
Churches but for now I am staying at home and confining myself to
my own Church.

The following are four important areas about which I am unhappy:

1. In the context of Northern Ireland and what we call 'the
troubles', I believe our Church to be lacking in direction and
courage.
2. I believe that our Church has not taken up the challenge of
this modern age and even the challenge of the Second Vatican
Council. We have not allowed the group we call the 'laity' to
take its just and rightful place in our Church affairs.
3. The Catholic Church in Ireland has in too many cases become
dictatorial and dismissive of people, even loyal Catholics who
are constantly being abused by their priests.
4. The organised and structured Church is not giving authentic
witness. It is not practising what it preaches.

I have been arguing throughout this book against the way the Irish bishops abuse their authority, lord it over their priests and the laity, interfere with all our lives and adopt a disproportionately strict attitude to matters of sex when there are so many other things wrong with our society. At other times, in my opinion, they do nothing when they should act. Take the matter of politics. Most Catholics would say, and rightly, that the bishops should keep their noses out of politics altogether. In most cases, they are right. Certainly, the Church, as an institution, should never mix itself in party politics or in telling people how to vote. But many political questions have moral and social implications. In such cases, morality and the well-being of the community are very much the business of the Church. Divorce, contraception and abortion are political issues. People are asked to vote about these matters or to decide on their place in a country's Constitution. But they are also very involved moral questions and, apart from their political aspects, the Church has the right and the duty to become involved in the debate and to teach, to make statements and, indeed, to take positive stands on these issues. What it cannot do is to coerce its followers to follow its lead.

Silence and evasion from the bishops can sometimes be as dangerous as over-interference. In Ireland today, we have a major political problem which has grave implications for the lives of the people who live on this island. I'm speaking of the division of our country into north and south and its consequences, the worst being the present violence and disruption which on this occasion has continued for 25 years. It's a political problem; it's a social problem; it's a geographical problem; it's an economic problem, and, like it or not, it is very much a moral problem and a religious problem.

Is it not a moral problem for men to be hating, hurting and killing each other? Is it not a moral problem for men to be destroying property with explosives, injuring innocent people, and placing the security and economy of the country at risk? Is it not a moral problem when Christians of different denominations talk about each other in terms of hate, fear, suspicion and gross misunderstanding? Is it not a moral problem when policemen torture people in places like Castlereagh and Gough Barracks, Armagh? Is it not a moral problem when special units of a police force or an army are secretly encouraged to 'shoot to kill' suspects whom the ordinary processes of the law cannot deal with?

Have we not got serious moral and ethical problems when people are tried without juries and convicted on the evidence of paid 'super-grasses'?

These are all questions that anyone is entitled to ask from the moral point of view. They are questions that many are asking, questions that need to be answered, and answered from the place we as Catholics expect guidance from on moral issues – the bishops of Ireland. But these questions have not been seriously studied. In an evasive way, they have been touched on in bishops' pastoral letters or in their submission to the New Ireland Forum. But much, much more is needed.

Some time ago, Sinn Féin challenged the Church to make a statement on the morality of the British presence in Ireland. That challenge has not been acknowledged or taken up and no promise has been given that it will be. There are people who say that Sinn Féin are trying to set the bishops up to make a statement for their own purposes. But that argument does not hold water. The truth is always the truth and the Irish bishops must not be afraid to speak it, no matter how much danger there may be of that truth being afterwards abused or misused. In fact, too many people would see the bishops' silence as their reluctance to embarrass or hurt the feelings of the British Government, the establishment in Northern Ireland or even the Protestant community. Cardinal Cahal Daly has been very outspoken but he is consistently tougher on the Republican camp and their misdeeds than he is on the 'Establishment' camp and its misdeeds. Many of Cardinal Daly's own priests and people feel that he is being strong with the weak and weak with the strong.

Why can there not be inter-Church discussions on all these questions, discussions that get down to the very roots, based not on prejudice, but on an agreed objective theological process? At the end of that let there be a gospel-based, objective Christian answer to these questions which would not take into account whose sensitive political feelings their findings might hurt. We have had agreed statements from the Churches on issues like Eucharist and ministry. Why then can we not have an agreed statement on this other issue where there is such a need for an authentic, Christian approach by all the people of Ireland? What has our Church done about this so far? Not too much, I'm afraid. Some individuals have spoken out. One or two bishops have made very careful statements. One or two priests have been much more courageous. But so often they are voices crying in the wilderness and when they do speak they meet with disapproval, especially from fellow-clergy. More is needed. Guarded statements are not enough. We need a courageous, well-thought-out, objective, Christian statement on the whole situation, beginning with a moral examination of the British presence on this island. Until that happens, Irish Catholics will be confused; they will be ambivalent about violence and they will have less and less regard for and loyalty to a Church which out of fear or awkwardness fails to give them the moral leadership to which they are entitled.

There are similar but greater problems of this nature in South America and some years ago the South American bishops were challenged by their own priests and people to 'go beyond statements about situations, to concentrate on concrete events and to take positions regarding them.'

One of the greatest challenges before the Church in Ireland today is to grasp this very difficult moral nettle, to go beyond statements and to take up positions which all of us as Catholics can be proud to fall in behind voluntarily and to follow. Will we get this leadership or will it be, as the author in the old testament said: 'At this time, there is no priest or prophet to ply his trade in the lands.' If that situation is allowed to continue, the future of Irish Catholicism looks very bleak indeed.

THE CHURCH AND ITS LAITY

Many messages and trends came from the Second Vatical Council which opened 32 years ago. Its purpose was to renew the Church. It had a lot to say about the place of lay people in the Church. The Council in one place quotes St. Augustine, the Bishop of Hippo, talking to his lay people: 'When I am frightened by what I am to you, I am consoled by what I am with you. To you I am a Bishop; with you I am a Christian. The first is an office, the second is a grace. The first is a danger, the second, salvation.'

A very strong message from that Council called for the involvement of the laity in every level of Church life. Obviously, from the theological and pastoral points of view, there are certain distinctions to be made between the roles of laity, religious and clergy. But it is stressed time and time again in the Council documents that the laity have their vital place in the operations of the Church.

Our Catholic Church in Ireland has tended to be very clerical. Many Irish Catholics saw, and still see, the Church as consisting of the bishops, priests, brothers and nuns. They regard themselves as spectators. That model is totally out of keeping with the Council's vision of the Church. It sees the Church as all the people of God and the bishops, priests and religious are supposed to be like Christ who said of himself: 'I come among you as one who serves.'

In far too many Irish parishes the parish priest still rules supreme and runs the parish as a one-man band. He dictates and no-one, be it the curates or the people of the parish, is allowed any say. In fact, very often the curates and the parishioners are the last to know what is in the parish priest's mind, even when it comes to issues that affect all of them very deeply.

A more serious problem, too, is that conservative clergy are holding up the proper application of the teachings of the Vatican Council. If the parish priest does not fancy lay-people reading at Mass, then they do not read. If he does not like folk-music, the youth of the parish are not allowed liturgies that help them to praise God better. If he does not fancy the option of open confession or ministers of the Eucharist, then they do not happen. If the parish priest does not appreciate programmes like Marriage or Engaged Encounter or Parish Renewal, they are not allowed.

In many cases other priests in the parish and the parishioners have no-one to appeal to. They do not always like to go to the bishop about the parish priest. When they do they don't often get too far. It has been traditional for the bishop to support the parish priest, not because he is right, but because he is the parish priest. There is no structure in our Irish Church to which people can appeal individual cases and get justice. This is very serious in a Church which often preaches and publishes on questions of justice.

It is time for the laity to be given their rightful place in our Irish Catholic Church. Each diocese should have a commission of lay people, independent and representative of the diocese, to advise the bishop and help him in his policy and decision-making. That commission should not be without teeth. It should not only be a talking-shop. It should have a real say in the running of the Church in that diocese.

Each parish should have a properly-constructed parish council and finance committee, which again should have a real say in the running of the parish. It would not need to be dictated to by any individual, clerical or lay. It should be involved in all matters affecting the parish liturgy, schools, social matters, pastoral care, finances, buildings, etc.

The new Code of Canon Law is strong on this way of running the Church. 'If, after consulting the Council of Priests, the diocesan Bishop considers it opportune, a Pastoral Council is to be established in each parish. In this Council, which is presided over by the parish priest, Christ's faithful, together with those who by virtue of their office are engaged in pastoral care in the parish, give their help in fostering pastoral action.' (Canon 536)

'In each parish there is to be a Finance Committee to help the parish priest in the administration of the goods of the parish.' (Canon 537)

'In each diocese, in so far as pastoral circumstances suggest, a Pastoral Council is to be established. Its function, under the authority of the Bishop, is to study and weigh those matters which concern the pastoral works in the diocese.' (Canon 511-Canon 514)

How often we hear parish priests telling the people, especially during sermons looking for money: 'This is your parish, your church, your parish hall, your schools.' And yet the people, having paid for these facilities, have no real say in how they are run. Indeed, it is a common enough experience for a group of parishioners requesting the use of a parish hall to be refused by the parish priest because he does not like the particular activity or for some other petty reason.

If we do not involve our people in the running of our Church they will become more and more disinterested and discouraged. People today do not want to be pawns in the hands of autocratic clerics. They want to play a full and real role in the running of THEIR Church. St. Paul warned the first bishops and priests: 'Do not be a dictator over any group.' We clerics need to take those words to heart and indeed learn a lesson from our brothers and sisters in the Protestant Churches who for so long now have had their lay ministers, vestry councils and elders.

It is a grave mistake for any bishop or priest to think that the grace and inspiration of God comes only through clerics. God works through all. Granted, he works in a very special way through the teaching Church, but his grace also comes strongly through our married couples, our young people, our old and our sick. These people, in their unique Christian vocations, teach lessons that we priests do not teach.

PRIESTS ABUSING PEOPLE

In the Gospel of St. Matthew, Jesus issues a very serious warning: 'If anyone would cause one of these little ones to lose his faith in me it would be better for that person to have a large millstone tied around his neck and he be drowned in the deep sea.' How terrible for them that make people lose their faith. Such things will always happen. But how terrible for the one who causes them.

People lose their faith for all kinds of reasons and I suppose that in a world full of limitations that's not surprising. But I have met so many people in the last eighteen years, since I became a priest, who have been caused to lose their faith by the unkindness of priests that it makes me worried and sad. You meet so many people who have been away from the sacraments for years because of a hurt inflicted by some priest in the past. Now, you may say that is only an excuse. But surely we priests should never give anyone such an excuse, if that is what it is. I've met many who were hurt by a priest on the occasion of the last illness or death of a close relative or friend. I've met others who were distressed at the time of their wedding. You constantly meet people who have been abused at presbytery doors because they called at an inconvenient time for the priest or simply because the priest was in bad form. You meet people who have been abused at the altar rails during Mass because they put out their hand instead of their tongue for Holy Communion. You meet young parents who have been abused during Mass by priests because their babies cried. You meet people who have been dealt with far too harshly in confession. You meet altar boys who have been abused or even physically beaten by priests before, during or after Mass. Archbishop Fulton Sheen, the great American Bishop and preacher, used to tell a story of a little boy in part of former Yugoslavia who broke the glass wine cruet by mistake while serving Mass. The priest hit him and ordered him out of the church, never to return again. The little boy never did return but went on instead to become the Communist leader of the country. He was called Tito.

It's not as uncommon as people think for priests to strike people – children and adults. One hears stories, and not from the other side of the world, of people being abused during sermons, having the contents of collection plates flung down the church at them or their weekly envelopes being torn open during Mass and derogatory comments being made about their contents. You hear of people being the victims of bad language from priests.

It is a wonderful thing when people love and respect their priests. In our humanity we need the love of our people. It helps us to be faithful even in our celibacy. But priests need to realise that people need love and respect from them too. We must treat them like brothers and sisters whom we really love. We are challenged by our vocation to treat every person we meet like we would treat Christ if we met him. Every funeral we celebrate should be as if it were the funeral of a close relative of our own; every wedding as if our own brother or sister were marrying. In every confession we hear, we should remember the words of Christ: 'If you show mercy, mercy will be shown you.'

We should practise hospitality. Every caller at our door, day or night, should be received as Christ would receive him or her. Our priests' houses should be famous for their warmth, their hospitality and welcome. Our sermons should not be abusive but gently challenging and uplifting. People should be able to say of us priests what the crowd said of Jesus as he stood crying at the graveside of his friend Lazarus: 'See how much he loved him.' It is far too common for our Catholic people to find their priests cold, rigid, autocratic and lacking in real brotherly warmth. Of course, there are many exceptions to this and that is why people feel so close to those priests who prove themselves to be such exceptions.

THE CHURCH AND AUTHENTIC WITNESS

St. Anthony of Padua, a great favourite of many Irish Catholics, said the following in a sermon: 'Actions speak louder than words. Let your words teach and your actions speak. We are full of words and empty of actions and therefore we are cursed by the Lord, since he himself cursed the fig-tree when he found no fruit but only leaves.' St. Gregory says: 'A law is laid upon the preachers to practise what they preach.'

Today, in the world, people look for authenticity. If a message does not ring true then people ignore it. This is especially so in the case of young people. Many people in Ireland, especially young people who have to live on one side of the border with materialism and on the other side with violence, hatred and injustice, are looking at the Church and asking themselves if it is putting its money where its mouth is.

People hear us speak of justice but feel we are one-sided on the

Northern Ireland problem or that in the Church structure itself we do not always offer justice and a fair hearing. They point to Fr. Des Wilson in Belfast or Fr. Keane in Dublin as true prophets.

They hear priests speak of poverty, unemployment and deprivation and at the same time witness a Church in which bishops still live in palaces and the priests themselves are wealthy. When will bishops and priests be prepared to let go of their worldly goods to help the poor and the needy? Until they do, their words will ring very hollow to the 'have-nots' among us. Catholics are told in church that parochial property is their property and yet they have no say in its administration and no real right to its use. They approach priests' houses and feel more like someone going to an appointment with a dentist rather than visiting a friend and helper.

They are told that as lay-people, God's people, they are the Church and yet at every level of Church structure they are more like an audience looking on at a play being acted out before them and are just expected to listen, to clap and to spend their money at the 'interval'.

When I saw the people of Eastern Europe casting off the chains of extreme communism and socialism, I wondered to myself if the Irish people would ever follow their example and cast off the fetters of extreme Roman Catholicism. I have a feeling that some day they will. But it will not be easy. After all, the communist dictators could threaten only with Siberia; the ecclesiastical dictators can threaten excommunication in this life and eternal punishment in the next! The risks are great!

The structures of the Church so often obscure the reality behind the structures. It is a bit like a house on which ivy was sown and has now obscured the building itself. Our Catholic people, although they do not put it in these terms, are calling us back to authenticity. They want us clerics to be 'simple' and 'straight' and 'poor'. We need to get rid of our episcopal palaces and have our bishops live where the people live. We need, at least, to open up our presbyteries and convents and share all that we are and all that we have with our people. These are not days for investing. Our spare pounds and even the ones we cannot spare need to be dedicated to the relief of the poor, the homeless and the jobless. How can a Church be saving for the rainy day when its members are already experiencing the rainy day. Why does the Church have to be so preoccupied with planning for the future when the present is so hard on so many? When Christ does come and calls us to account for our stewardship, will he find us like the man from the gospel who buried his talent to secure his future with his master? We must be like the other two men in the parable. We must take risks with our talents, speculate, be bold. We must 'squander' what we are and what we have on those in need and then, indeed, in the true sense we will be a wealthy Church.

The Catholic Church in Ireland is far too institutionalised, far too settled, complacent and dead. As was pointed out recently, we are in danger of becoming the 'Church of the middle-classes and the middle-aged'. To do something about all this is going to take a new vision. It's going to take courage. I think heads may have to roll. But it's got to be done, because Christ wants it done. He wants his Church renewed.

All that I have said in this book I believe with all my heart. I do not wish to offend even one person by what I've written. Many, I know will disagree with me. Others will accuse me of disloyalty. Others again will say: 'Who does he think he is? What right has he to speak out?' I believe that Christ wants these things said. So, like St. Paul, I can at least say: 'I believe, and so I speak.'

I do not wish to take away one little bit from the great good that exists in the Church, or from all the excellent bishops, priests and religious in the world. But ground is being lost, precious ground in the minds and hearts of people and that loss must be stopped. It's not that our Church is no good. The problem is that its proper potential is not being realised. Archbishop Sheen, whom I mentioned earlier, liked to quote the following verse.

> I think my soul is a lame old duck,
> Dabbling around in farmyard muck,
> Fat and lazy with useless wings,
> But sometimes when the north wind sings,
> And the wild ones hurtle overhead,
> It remembers something lost and dead,
> And cocks a weary, bewildered eye
> And makes a feeble attempt to fly,
> It's fairly content with the state it's in,
> But it's not the duck it might have been.

There are an awful lot of people in our Church like that duck – they are fairly content with the state it's in. But it's not the Church it might have been. However, with a real effort at renewal it can become the Church it was meant to be.

Today, at the time of writing, it is over twenty-three years since I entered Clonliffe College, Dublin, and over seventeen years since 'Morris Minor' ordained me in the cathedral in Waterford. I have no big regrets. I am, of course, sorry for any mistakes I've made or for any innocent people I may have hurt. But I wouldn't change the main pattern at all. I love being alive. I love being a Catholic and a priest. I am happy using my conscience and my brain. I don't want to be a simple Catholic. I want to be a thinking free Catholic. Jesus came to give us the freedom of the sons of God. I jealously guard that freedom. I'll not surrender that freedom to any pope, bishop, priest or lay person. Nobody can put me out of the Church. The Church is God's family. Only God can put you out of it and God does not do that. God is the prodigal's father always welcoming his wandering sons and daughters home. Jesus told us in the gospels that his kingdom is like a net that brings in fish of every kind. There should be room for a great variety of fish, even the odd ones. The Church will be truly Catholic only if it tolerates within itself a great variety of members. The Church will not be truly Catholic if it cannot tolerate and even cherish its dissidents. The hierarchy and the clergy have hurt me more in my life than all the other people I've ever met put together. But the Church is not merely the hierarchy and the clergy. They are just part of the Church. Often they are the ugly and uncaring part. We are only showing our ignorance if we say: 'My mother right or wrong.' Some of us oppose because we love. I don't always love the Catholic Church as she is. But I love her for all that I know she can become. The Church will be perfect only in Heaven. But until then all of us who belong to the Church have the solemn obligation to work for her perfection just as we struggle daily for our own personal perfection. We can only do our best. The all-powerful God will do the rest. But he does help those who help themselves.